LABORATORY Manual

SCIENCE

CBSE Class X

Authors
Priyasha Gupta (Physics)
Abhishek Gupta (Chemistry)
Richa Raj (Biology)

Name..

Class......................... Section........................ Roll No.......................

School...

Arihant Prakashan (School Division Series)

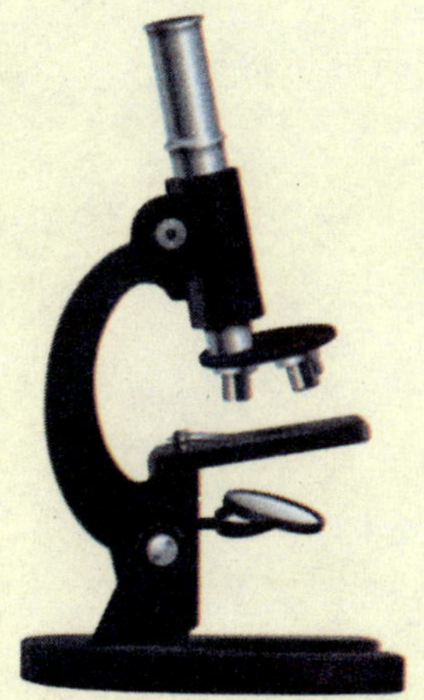

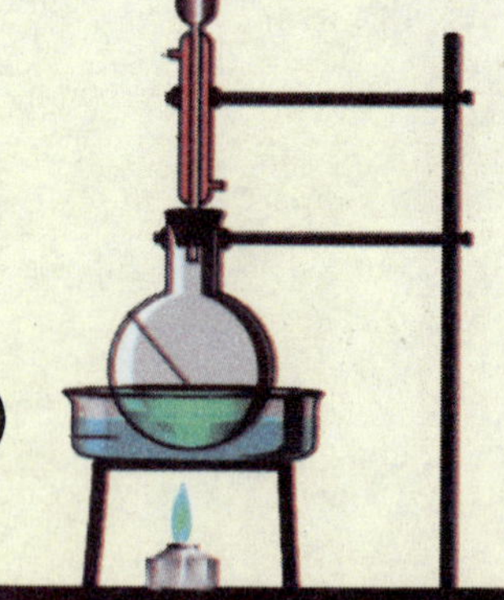

Arihant Prakashan (School Division Series)

卐 **Administrative & Production Offices**

Regd. Office
'Ramchhaya' 4577/15, Agarwal Road, Darya Ganj, New Delhi -110002
Tele: 011- 47630600, 43518550; Fax: 011- 23280316

Head Office
Kalindi, TP Nagar, Meerut (UP) - 250002, Tel: 0121-7156203, 7156204

卐 **Sales & Support Offices**
Agra, Ahmedabad, Bengaluru, Bareilly, Chennai, Delhi, Guwahati, Hyderabad, Jaipur, Jhansi, Kolkata, Lucknow, Nagpur & Pune

卐 **Price :** ₹375.00

卐 PO No. : TXT-29-T071082-5-26

Published by Arihant Publications (India) Ltd.

For further information about the books from Arihant, log on to www.arihantbooks.com or email to info@arihantbooks.com

Follow us on

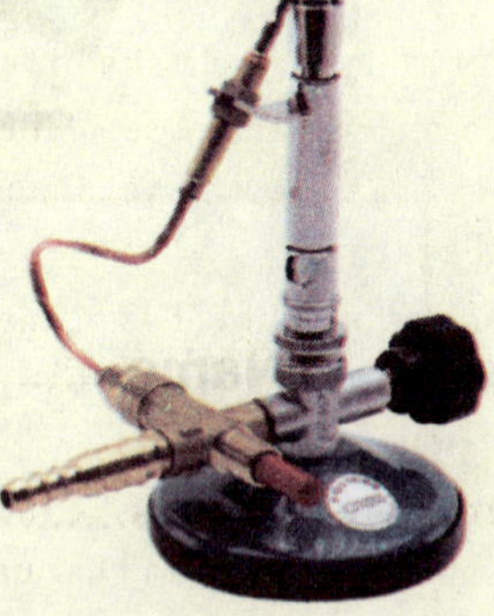

Contents

LIST OF EXPERIMENTS

Syllabus

PRACTICAL

1. A. Finding the pH of the following samples by using pH paper / universal indicator **Unit-I**
(a) Dilute Hydrochloric Acid
(b) Dilute NaOH solution
(c) Dilute Ethanoic Acid Solution
(d) Lemon juice
(e) Water
(f) Dilute Hydrogen Carbonate solution

B. Studying the properties of acids and bases (HCl and NaOH) on the basis of their reaction with **Unit-I**
(a) Litmus solution (Blue/Red)
(b) Zinc metal
(c) Solid sodium carbonate

2. Performing and observing the following reactions and classifying them into **Unit-I**
(a) Combination reaction
(b) Decomposition reaction
(c) Displacement reaction
(d) Double displacement reaction
(i) Action of water on quicklime
(ii) Action of heat on ferrous sulphate crystals
(iii) Iron nails kept in copper sulphate solution
(iv) Reaction between sodium sulphate and barium chloride solutions

3. Observing the action of Zn, Fe, Cu and Al metals on the following salt solutions: **Unit-I**
(a) $ZnSO_4\ (aq)$
(b) $FeSO_4\ (aq)$
(c) $CuSO_4\ (aq)$
(d) $Al_2\ (SO_4)_3\ (aq)$
Arranging Zn, Fe, Cu and Al (metals) in the decreasing order of reactivity based on the above result.

4. Studying the dependence of potential difference (*V*) across a resistor on the current (*I*) passing through it and determine its resistance. Also plotting a graph between *V* and *I*. **Unit-IV**

5. Determination of the equivalent resistance of two resistors when connected in series and parallel. **Unit-IV**

6. Preparing a temporary mount of a leaf peel to show stomata. **Unit-II**

7. Experimentally show that carbon dioxide is given out during respiration. **Unit-II**

8. Study of the following properties of acetic acid (ethanoic acid) **Unit-I**
(i) odour
(ii) solubility in water
(iii) effect on litmus
(iv) reaction with sodium hydrogen carbonate

9. Study of the comparative cleaning capacity of a sample of soap in soft and hard water. **Unit-I**

10. Determination of the focal length of : **Unit-III**
(i) Concave mirror
(ii) Convex lens
by obtaining the image of a distant object.

11. Tracing the path of a ray of light passing through a rectangular glass slab for different angles of incidence. Measure the angle of incidence, angle of refraction, angle of emergence and interpret the result. **Unit-III**

12. Studying (a) binary fission in *Amoeba* and (b) budding in yeast and *Hydra* with the help of prepared slides. **Unit-II**

13. Tracing the path of the rays of light through a glass prism. **Unit-III**

14. Identification of the different parts of an embryo of a dicot seed (Pea, gram or red kidney bean). **Unit-II**

INDEX

S.No.	Name of the Experiment	Page No.	Date	Remarks

INDEX

S.No.	Name of the Experiment	Page No.	Date	Remarks

LABORATORY Manual

SCIENCE

CERTIFICATE

This is to certify that Experiments recorded in this Practical Notebook have been performed by ______________________________
(Student's name)

of __________ of ______________________________
(class/section) (school name)

during academic session ____________________

....
Examiner Signature

....
Principal Signature
(with school stamp)

....
Teacher Signature

General Introduction of Laboratory Work

Introduction

Experiments play an important role in the progress of science, as a large number of inventions and path breaking discoveries have been possible through investigations that are usually carried out in laboratories. A school science laboratory is a place, where basic experimental skills are learnt by performing a set of prescribed experiments.

Seeing experiments being performed (demonstration experiments) is quite important for the understanding of the principles of science, but performing experiments by one's own hands is not only a thrilling experience but is also important because it entails "learning by doing". It also helps in understanding the concepts of science.

The experiments prescribed in the syllabus intend to develop basic skills of measurement, handling of some common measuring instruments, equipment and chemicals, setting simple apparatus, handling microscope and preparing slides, making observations, collecting data and presenting it in appropriate format, interpreting and drawing their conclusions and result.

General Laboratory Facilities

A science laboratory is fully equipped with working tables, items of common utility and space for storing equipments, chemicals and glassware.

1. The working tables in science laboratory are provided with
   - **Sinks with Water Taps** For washing purposes and liquid waste disposal are provided on working table. Never throw any insoluble solid material like filter papers, broken glass apparatus into the sink as these can block the drain. Students should use taps only when required and should not waste any water. It is essential to clean the sinks regularly.
   - **Reagent Shelves** Reagents or chemicals to be used very frequently are kept on these shelves. Reagent bottles are arranged in a definite order on these shelves.
   - **Gas Taps** These are fitted on the working table for supply of LPG to the burners for heating purposes. A gas tap should be opened only when the gas is required for lighting the burner. Any leakage should be immediately brought to the notice of the teacher or other laboratory staff. Every laboratory is equipped with a few fire extinguishers fixed at convenient places.
2. The equipment and glassware of common use are stored separately in an almirah. These are generally issued to the students at the time of performing experiments.
3. The equipments like balances and microscopes are used less frequently, therefore, these are placed permanently at a fixed place. A physical balance (Fig. 1) is used for weighing

powdered or solid materials (One must use weighing tubes or butter paper depending upon the nature of the material). The pan of the balance must be kept cleaned. The microscope (Fig. 2) must be placed near the window to ensure the availability of sufficient light needed.

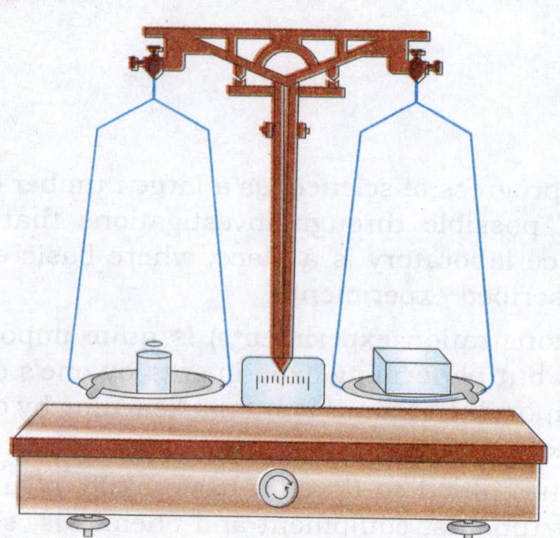

Fig. 1 A physical balance

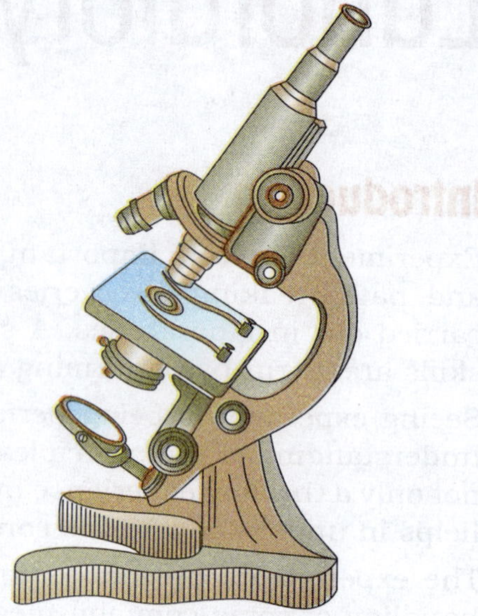

Fig. 2 A compound microscope

4. Electrical connections are provided with all working tables for performing electricity and magnetism experiments.
5. A demonstration table is placed for teacher demonstration.
6. For the disposal of solid wastes, a dustbin may be provided either near each working table or at a common place in the laboratory.

Utility items like soldering rod, hammer, drill machine, pliers, hacksaw, cutter, screw drivers, etc. must be placed at a convenient place inside the laboratory.

Safety Requirements in a Science Laboratory

A science laboratory should be equipped with the following safety requirements :

Exhaust Fans	The laboratory should be well-ventilated and for this, exhaust fans must be fitted near the ceiling of laboratory for speedy removal of the waste gases to keep the laboratory free from polluted air.
First Aid Box	A first-aid must be readily available in science laboratory for use during accidents and emergencies. It is equipped with tincture of iodine, ferric chloride (alcoholic), burnol, savlon, cotton, sodium bicarbonate solution, adhesive plaster, bandages and scissors.
Fire Extinguishers	Every laboratory should be equipped with two or more fire extinguishers fixed at convenient places and science teacher/lab assistant should be well versed with its use. Sand or dry mud should also be available in laboratory.
Eye Wash Fountain	An eye wash fountain should be available in the laboratory. It is used in the case of irritation of eyes caused by chemicals and fumes.

Different apparatus are required for performing different experiments of physics, chemistry and biology. In this section, we will discuss the apparatus that are commonly used in the laboratories.

Commonly Used Apparatus

Different apparatus are required for performing different experiments of physics, chemistry and biology. In this section, we will discuss the apparatus that are commonly used in the laboratories.

PHYSICS LABORATORY

Experiments performed in a physics laboratory are of a wide range. Different sets of apparatus are used for performing different experiments. Apparatus need to be handled carefully to retain their sensitivity. It is very essential to understand the sources of error for obtaining accurate results.

Some of the commonly used apparatus in physics laboratory are

Name of the Apparatus	Use	Figures
Spring Balance It is a type of weighing scale. It has a hook on one end from where the object is suspended by a string. Reading is taken from the graduated brass plate present on the metallic case.	It is used to weigh various objects.	
Meter Scale It is a straight strip made up of wood, metal or other material having a straight edge. It is graduated in centimetres and inches.	It is used to measure the length.	
Stopclock It is a timing device similar to stop watch and often designed for measuring very brief time intervals.	It is used as a timer to measure the time of oscillations of pendulum.	
Galvanometer It is an instrument for detecting the existence of small currents and determining their strength.	It is a sensitive instrument used to detect the direct electric current.	

Name of the Apparatus	Use	Figures
Ammeter A meter designed to measure the electric current is called ammeter. It is always connected in series within the circuit.	It is used to measure the current flowing in a circuit.	
Voltmeter A voltmeter is an instrument for measuring electrical potential difference between two points in an electric circuit.	It is used to measure the potential difference and is always connected in parallel within the circuit.	
Rheostat It is an adjustable resistor whose resistance may be changed without opening the circuit in which it is connected, thereby controlling the current in circuit.	It is used to vary current in the circuit.	
Concave Mirror A spherical mirror which is silvered from the outer curved side such that its reflecting surface is towards the inner side of the hollow sphere is called a concave mirror.	It is capable of reflecting all the parallel beams to the focus.	
Prism It is a block of glass or other transparent material enclosed by two inclined plane refracting surfaces at some fixed angle called "angle of prism". It has two triangular bases and three rectangular lateral surfaces which are inclined to one another.	It is capable of splitting the light into band of seven colours.	
Convex Lens It is a converging lens with both surfaces convex in nature. It is thicker in middle and thinner at edges.	It is capable of converging all the light rays to the focus.	

CHEMISTRY LABORATORY

Commonly used apparatus in a chemistry laboratory are

Name of the Apparatus	Use	Figures
Test Tubes These are the hollow glass tubes closed at one end and have a circular rim at the other. These are available in different diameter and lengths or different volumes.	These are used to carry out the chemical reactions.	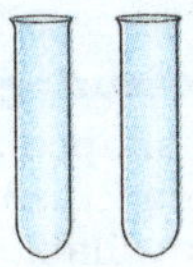
Boiling Tube It is similar to the test tube but it is of larger diameter.	It is used for boiling or heating large volume of solution.	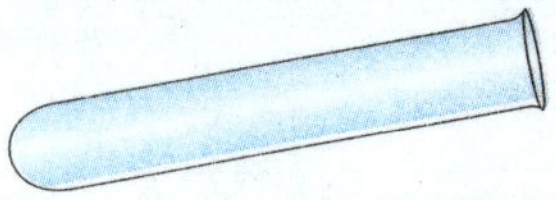
Test Tube Holder It contains an iron strip fitted in cylindrical wooden base.	It is used to hold the test tube containing liquids or solids during heating.	
Test Tube Stand It is made up of plastic polypropylene. The holes in the top plate can hold the test tubes and its vertical pins for drying the tubes.	It is used for keeping the test tubes vertically. The cleaned test tubes are kept upside down to drain out water.	
Test Tube Brush It is made up of thick hard iron wire with soft plastic bristles.	It is used for cleaning the test tube.	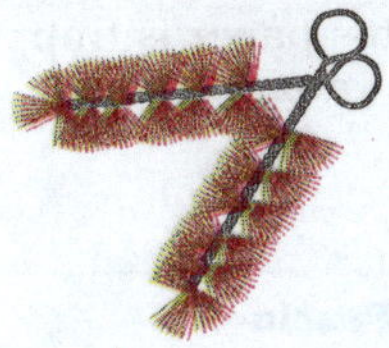
Beakers These are the cylindrical vessels with a large diameter and are usually made up of pyrex or corning glass. These are available in various sizes ranging from 5 mL to 2000 mL.	These are used for keeping the liquid solution during experimental work and to pour solution from one beaker to another.	
Flasks These are of three types: (a) **Round Bottom Flask** It is round glass bottle flask and cannot be placed on the table directly due to its round bottom.	These are used for heating the contents.	
(b) **Flat Bottom Flask** It is a glass bottle having a flat bottom with a long narrow neck. It can be kept on the table without falling.	These are used for carrying out the chemical reactions and in distillation process.	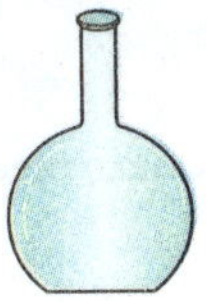
(c) **Conical Flask** It is a hollow glass vessel which is of conical shape and are available in various sizes ranging from 5 mL to 2000 mL, also referred as Erlen Meyer Flasks.	These are used for carrying out volumetric titrations.	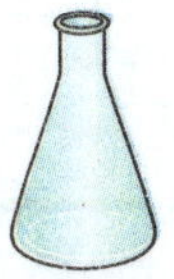

Name of the Apparatus	Use	Figures
Funnel It is cone shaped hollow glass apparatus with a narrow long stem. These are available in various sizes.	It is used for filtration and transfer of liquids from one vessel to the other. They have diameter from 5-7 cm and may be made of plastic or glass.	
Graduated or Measuring Cylinders It is a cylindrical shaped apparatus with graduated marking. It is made up of glass or plastic and is available in various volumes.	These are used for measuring volume of liquids and may be made of glass or plastic. These are available in sizes 10,25,50,100 and 250 mL.	
Iron Stand It is made of heavy cast iron base and a thick iron rod fitted on one side of the base.	Clamps and rings are fitted on the rod which is used to hold and separate the apparatus.	
Wire Gauze A flat square piece of iron wire mesh in which asbestos paper is trapped at the centre of the gauze.	It is kept on the tripod stand to heat the beakers and flasks.	
Mortar and Pestle It is a thick walled vessel with a hemispherical shape with a base. It is made up of porcelain.	It is used for grinding compounds and solid substances into fine powder with the help of pestle.	
Water Bath It is a vessel made up of brass having oval shape.	It is filled with water and used for controlled heating or when direct heating of the flame is to be avoided.	
China Dish or Evaporating Dish It is a hollow hemispherical shaped apparatus usually made up of porcelain.	It is used for evaporation and crystallisation purposes.	
Watch Glass It is a small, circular piece of glassware.	It is used to dry and weigh the substances.	
Glass Rod It is a thick cylindrical stick of glass which is not hollow and available in various thickness.	It is used for stirring and mixing of substances.	

Name of the Apparatus	Use	Figures
Spatula It is made up of horn or plastic with a spoon like shape.	It is used like a spoon for handling small quantities of substances.	
Tripod Stand It is made up of cast iron and possesses a triangular shape fitted with three rods acting as legs.	It is used to support the vessel to be heated.	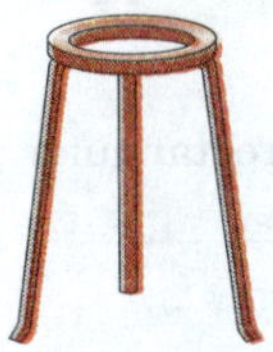
Crucible Tongs It is made up of steel or iron.	It is used to hold hot beaker, China dish.	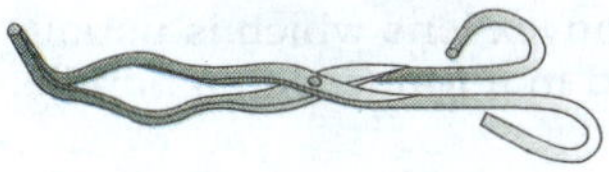
Bunsen Burner It is the most commonly used gas burner in school laboratories.	This apparatus is widely used in experiments that require heating.	
Spirit Lamp A spirit lamp is like an ordinary lamp but this lamp uses spirit as a fuel.	In case Bunsen burner is not available in the laboratory, then spirit lamp can be used for heating.	
Wash Bottle It is made up of plastic, polythene containing a thin tube.	It is used for washing and rinsing glass apparatus.	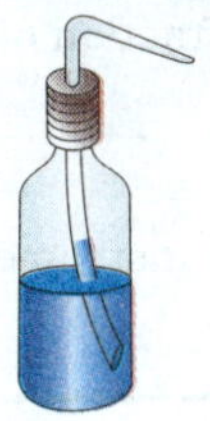

BIOLOGY LABORATORY

The commonly used apparatus in biology laboratory are

Name of the Apparatus	Use	Figures
Glass Slide It is a thin flat rectangular piece of glass.	A specimen is placed on the glass slide and seen under a microscope.	
Magnifying Glass (Hand Lens) It is a convex lens which is usually mounted in a frame with a handle.	It is used to produce a magnified image of an object.	
Dropper It is usually a glass or soft plastic tubes tapered to a narrow point and fitted with a rubber bulb at the top. It is of various sizes.	It is used to add solutions in small quantities.	
Petri Dish It is a shallow glass or plastic cylindrical shaped dish.	It is used for keeping small specimens.	
Cover Slip It is a thin, flat piece of transparent material usually made of glass. It is typically square or rectangular, about 20 mm (4/5) wide and only a fraction of a millimetre thick.	It is placed over the specimen for viewing with a microscope.	
Forceps These are hinged instrument.	These are used for grasping and holding objects.	

CLEANING OF GLASSWARE APPARATUS

For obtaining accurate and appropriate results, the glass and porcelain apparatus should be thoroughly cleaned before starting of an experiment.

- If the apparatus is very dirty and contaminated with dust and impurities like grease, then concentrated acids like HNO_3, HCl or chromic acid is used for cleaning. The apparatus is dipped in chromic acid solution for some time and then washed with excess of water.
- Sodium carbonate is used to clean beakers, flasks and China dish.
- Employ a suitable brush to clean the inner surface of burettes, test tubes, flask. Place the washed apparatus in an inverted position so that the water is drained off.

How to Record an Experiment?

A neat and systematic recording of experiment in the laboratory notebook is very important for keeping an upto date record of the work which has been done in the laboratory. Infact, a proper record of the experimental results and conclusions is an indispensable part of scientific work. The laboratory notebook must be well maintained and protected from mechanical and chemical damage. It should be made checked regularly by the teacher.

Sample Format to Record the Experiment

The experiment should be recorded in the laboratory notebook under the following heads as:

Date......	Experiment No.	Page No. ......

Aim It should clearly state the objective of the experiment.

Material Required List all equipments, measuring devices and other items or materials to be used for performing the experiment.

Theory It must explain the basic principle(s), laws or theories on which the experiment is based. Wherever necessary, the mathematical law involved in the experiment should be supplemented with mathematical equations.

Procedure All the steps followed while carrying out the experiment should be mentioned in a proper sequence. Labelled diagrams, if any, should be drawn to present a pictorial view of the experimental set-up.

Calculations/Observations In case, calculations based on the observations are required to obtain the result of an experiment, correct formulae and units must be used while substituting the data. All calculations must be carried out carefully. The answer should be stated with proper SI units.

Result Clearly state the conclusions drawn from the experimental observations. If result depends upon the conditions of temperature and pressure, mention these conditions along with the result.

Precautions All the precautions taken while performing the experiment should be clearly mentioned. Although, some of the precautions taken during some experiments may be common, these usually change from one experiment to another depending on the nature of the experiment.

Sources of Error The possible sources of error that arise because of limitation of equipment, due to change in atmospheric conditions or any other reason, should also be stated.

These may include points for making the experiment more accurate and for better understanding of the basic principle involved.

Lab Instructions

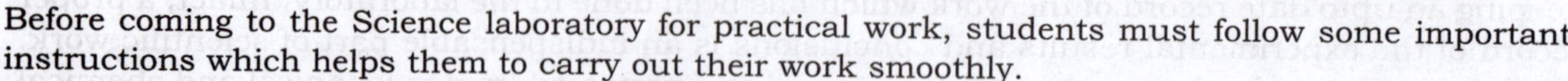

Before coming to the Science laboratory for practical work, students must follow some important instructions which helps them to carry out their work smoothly.

Instructions to Perform Physics Experiments

To work efficiently in Physics laboratory, a student must follow the following instructions :

1. Before performing an experiment, the student should first thoroughly understand the theory of the experiment the objective of the experiment, the kind of apparatus needed and the procedure to be followed. The difficulties and doubts, if any, should be discussed with the teacher before hand.
2. The student should check up whether the right type of apparatus for the experiment to be performed is given to him or not.
3. Repeat every observation a number of times even though their values may be exactly the same each time. The student must bear in mind the proper plan for recording the observations. Recording in tabular form is essential in most of the experiments.
4. Wherever possible, the observations should be represented with the help of a graph.
5. Always mention the proper unit (if any) with the result.
6. **Accuracy** of a measuring instrument is considered as half of its least count. **Least count** is the smallest distance that any measuring instruments are able to measure. Measuring instruments that are used commonly in laboratory are scales, vernier callipers, screw gauge, spring balance, thermometer, analytical balance.
7. **Zero error** arises in a measuring instrument when its pointer, at its resting point, does not coincide with the zero mark on the scale. To obtain the accurate value, the zero error has to be added or subtracted from the reading taken after measurement.
8. **Error due to friction** may arise if movement of an object over another surface is involved. Hence, error due to friction should be minimised.
   For example, in a spring balance, the strip carrying the pointer should be lubricated and tapped gently before the use otherwise errors due to friction arises which would affect the result.
9. **Error due to suspension** can arise if the support from which an object is suspended moves during the oscillation of the suspended object i.e. in the case of a simple pendulum. To avoid this error, the support should be rigid, so that time period can be measured accurately.
10. **Error due to spilling** arises when a solid or liquid is added to another liquid readily in a hurry. To avoid this type of error carefully and gently transfer the liquids (or solid).
11. **Error of parallax** should be avoided by placing your eye at right angle to the plane of the scale and vertically above the point to be read.
12. **Percentage error** between 5% to 10% for recording observations and calculation of result is allowed.
13. The degree of accuracy of measurement of each quantity should always be kept in mind so that the final result does not show any fictious accuracy. The result obtained should be suitably rounded off.

Instructions to Perform Chemistry Experiments

To work efficiently in Chemistry laboratory, a student must follow the following instructions :

1. After the instructions given by the teacher, collect the apparatus from the laboratory assistant in queue.
2. Before starting an experiment, check all your apparatus carefully to make sure that they are in good condition. Do not use any cracked apparatus.
3. Thoroughly clean the apparatus to be used.
4. Do only the experiments assigned, unallotted experiments should not be done.
5. All the experiments must be conducted under the supervision of qualified teachers only.
6. Do your experiment honestly without caring for the final result. Record the observations on a rough note-book instead of writing on the pieces of paper.
7. Plan your work, so that it is finished in the stipulated time.
8. Keep your seat clean. If an acid or other corrosive chemical is spilled, wash it off with water.
9. Always wear goggles to protect your eyes.
10. Wear closed-toe shoes to protect the feet from chemical spills and sharp objects.
11. Do not eat or drink in the laboratory.
12. Wash your hands thoroughly with soap after performing the experiment.
13. Switch off gas burners when they are not in use.
14. Solid waste materials like filter paper and test tube should be thrown only in the dustbin and not in the sink.
15. After the experiment, clean all the apparatus and return it to the laboratory assistant.
16. Dispose all waste liquids in the sink and allow water to run for some time by opening the water tap.
17. Never dilute an acid by adding water to the concentrated acids because it is an exothermic reaction and the liquid may bump out. Always dilute the acid by slowly adding acid to water with stirring.

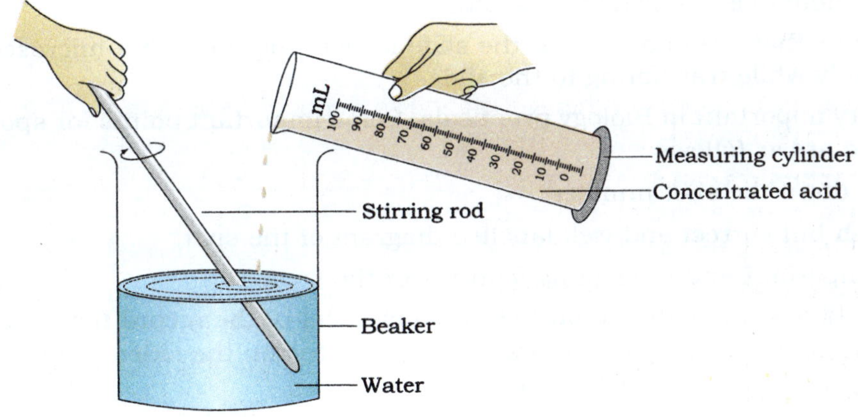

Fig. 3 Correct way of adding acid to water for dilution

Instructions to Perform Biology Experiments

Before coming to the Biology laboratory for practical work, students must be acquainted with certain basic rules of the laboratory. This enables them to do their practicals smoothly, effectively and efficiently.

Some important instructions for the students are discussed below :

1. A student must carry the following things to the laboratory for every practical session to perform various type of experiments.
   - Laboratory notebook
   - Laboratory manual
   - Auxillary (or rough) notebook
   - A pencil
   - Eraser
   - Scale
   - Dissection box

Note Dissection box should contain a pair of small forceps, a pair of large forceps, a pair of small and large scissors, a fine blade or razor for section cutting, needles (two), brush (No. 00) and a magnifying glass.

2. Handle the microscope carefully. It should always be placed on a stable table.
3. Always keep the microscope in upright position by holding it with both the hands. Do not swing the microscope with one hand while carrying it as the loosely fixed lens may fall.
4. Always clean the lens mirror and stage of the microscope properly before use.
5. Do not touch the lens or mirror as fingerprints may spoil the image.
6. Do not lower the lens too much, as it may touch the specimen or water.
7. While **studying slides** under the microscope, do not disturb the slide focussed by the teacher. In case you face any difficulty, seek the help of your teacher. You can move the fine adjustment screw to bring the slide in sharp focus.
8. For **studying the museum specimens**, the following steps need to be followed :
   - Carefully study the characteristics of the specimen from the book.
   - Try to find out these characteristics in the specimen.
   - Draw a line diagram of the specimen. If needed, draw more than one view of the specimen.
   - Always write classification for the entire specimen.
   - Specimens should be handled very carefully.
   - The specimens that are to placed on the slide for viewing through a microscope should be handled gently while transfering to the slide.
9. **Spotting** is very important in Biology practicals. Some important points for spotting that should be remembered are as follows :
   - Always note down the spot number.
   - Draw a rough but correct and well labelled diagram of the spot.
   - Write only important and interesting features of the spot.
10. Diagrams should always be drawn on the drawing sheet of the record file. Draw large and neat diagrams in the centre of the page so that enough spaces on the sides is available for labelling. While labelling lines should not cross each other.

General Lab Instruction

1. Always carry practical record book, laboratory manual, notebook (to record observations), pen, pencil, scale, eraser, sharpener, scissors, forceps, scalpel, dissecting needle, brush, blades, etc. to the laboratory.
2. Maintain discipline and silence in the lab.
3. Replace all laboratory equipment to its assigned place in the laboratory once the practical work is over.
4. Follow the instructions given by the teacher attentively.
5. Perform the experiment carefully and note down the observations.
6. Do not manipulate your results in any circumstances.
7. Use newspaper or blotting paper while using stains so as not to spoil the table.
8. Draw the diagrams neatly and label them correctly. Use fine HB pencil while drawing.
9. Do not play, whistle or stoop into your partner's set-up.
10. Be familiar with the handling of first aid kit and fire extinguisher. In case of any accident or injury or breakage of apparatus, report to the teacher immediately.
11. Students must prepare in advance for the experiment, they will perform in the laboratory.
12. Students must be punctual and should not be absent from their practical class and should reach the laboratory as soon as the period starts. This will enable to keep their practical work upto date.
13. All equipments such as microscope, physical balance, measuring items and glassware must be handled with care. Carelessness will not only damage the instrument or apparatus but may also cause injury to the students.

Safety Precautions

To avoid unnecessary risk or injury during laboratory work, the students are advised to observe some general and safety precautions. Here, we will discuss all the precautions that are need to be observe in Physics, Chemistry and Biology laboratory.

Physics Laboratory

Although in Physics laboratory many chemicals are not used still there are chances for accidents to occur. In order to avoid such accidents, we need to follows some safety precautions :

1. Handle the objects carefully and cautiously especially those made of glass to avoid any damage.
2. Use gloves while handling hot objects and always test the temperature of an object before picking it up.
3. Always pay proper attention while loosening or tightening screws and bolts as some of them may break easily.

Precautions while Performing Experiments with Electricity

While performing the experiments with electricity some safety precautions should be observed :

1. Do not touch the live wire directly.
2. While making connections, the circuit diagram should be followed carefully. Take the polarity of the terminals of the battery, ammeter, voltmeter into consideration while making the connections.
3. The power switch should be turned off and the connections should be removed on finishing an experiment involving electricity.

Chemistry Laboratory

The following safety precautions will enable us to perform experiments in a more secure way.

1. **Handling of Glass Apparatus**
   (i) Hot apparatus should not be placed on working table directly because it may spoil the working table. Place it on a glazed tile or a wire gauze.
   (ii) Be careful with glass equipment, while inserting a glass rod or tube or thermometer through a rubber cork, lubricate the glass and protect your hands with a cloth towel and use a gentle twisting motion.

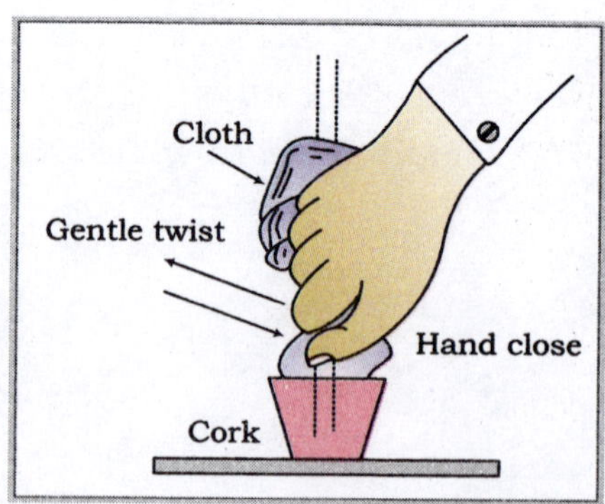

Fig. 4 Correct way of inserting a glass tube in a cork

2. **Handling Chemicals**

(i) Do not touch or taste or smell any chemical with your bare hands as it may be corrosive and poisonous.

(ii) Before using a reagent bottle, read the label very carefully to be sure that you are using the correct reagent.

(iii) Always keep reagent bottles securely closed and labelled.

(iv) Replace reagents to their original positions after use.

(v) Never pour partially used reagents back into the reagent bottle.

(vi) Be economical with reagents and chemicals, only small quantities need to be used.

3. **While Heating the Apparatus**

(i) Take proper care while heating the test tube. Never heat the contents of test tube by pointing towards your face. Hold it at an angle of 45° away from your face.

(ii) For smelling the vapours, fan the vapours gently with your hands towards the nose. Avoid direct smelling of vapours.

(iii) Heat the test tube gently and uniformly. Move the test tube in and out of the flame to allow time for heat transfer.

(iv) Heat the area near the surface of the test tube slightly more than the base of the tube. This concentrates boiling near the surface of the liquid and reduces the potential for bumping and boil over.

(v) Do not heat any flammable liquids like alcohol directly on flame.

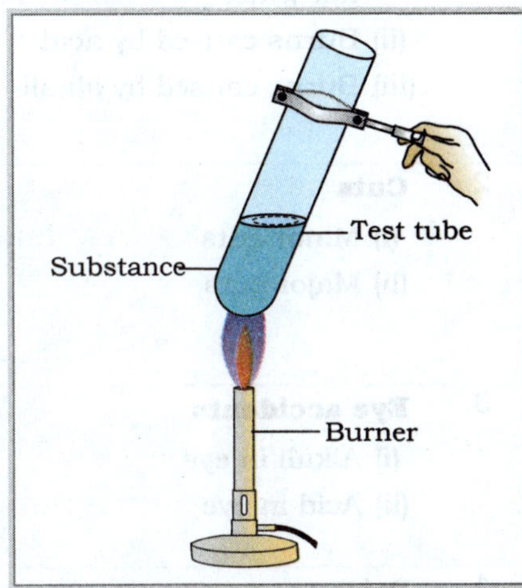

Fig. 5 Proper heating

Biology Laboratory

In Biology laboratory, following safety precautions are need to be observed :

1. Care should be taken while handling of all dissection instruments like razor, blade etc.
2. Do not use excessive force when working with sharp instruments.
3. All needles and syringes, razor blades and other sharp items need to be disposed of in a sharp container.
4. Do not touch broken glass with bare hands.
5. Never use fingers to hold a part of the specimen while cutting.
6. Gloves should be worn while handling the stains.

FIRST AID TREATMENT

A first aid kit is an important part of a science laboratory which is placed at an easily accessible place. Accidents in the laboratory are often occur due to the carelessness or lack of attention. Most of the accidents take place due to improper handling of chemicals and apparatus.

In case, if it happens, first aid treatment must be provided immediately. The victim should be taken to the doctor, if required. The probable accidents, injuries and their first aid emergency treatments are listed below :

	Type of accident	First aid treatment
1.	**Burns**	
	(i) Burns caused by steam or hot water	• Wash the affected part with cold water, cool and dry it with clean cloth and apply burnol.
	(ii) Burns caused by acid	• Wash the wounded part with water and apply a dilute solution of sodium hydrogen carbonate.
	(iii) Burns caused by alkali	• Wash with ample of water to remove alkali and then wash with dilute acetic acid.
2.	**Cuts**	
	(i) Minor cuts	• Allow to bleed for a few seconds. Remove the glass piece if any. Apply methylated spirit and cover it with a piece of cotton or you can apply $FeCl_3$ solution to stop bleeding.
	(ii) Major cuts	• Apply pressure above the cut to stop bleeding. Call the doctor immediately.
3.	**Eye accidents**	
	(i) Alkali in eye	• Wash thoroughly with water and then with 1% boric acid solution.
	(ii) Acid in eye	• Wash thoroughly with water, afterwards with 1% sodium bicarbonate solution and then with water again.
4.	**Poisons**	
	(i) Poisons not swallowed	• Spit out immediately. Wash mouth with plenty of water.
	(ii) Inhalation of gases like Cl_2, SO_2, Br_2, etc., causing suffocation	• Loosen the clothes at the neck. At once go in the open air. Inhale dilute vapours of ammonia or gargle with sodium bicarbonate solution.
	(iii) Acid swallowed	• Drink lot of water. Drink lime water. No emetic should be taken.
	(iv) Caustic alkalies swallowed	• Drink plenty of water. Drink a glass of lemon or orange juice. No emetic should be taken.
5.	**Fire**	
	(i) Beaker containing inflammable liquid catches fire	• Immediately cover the beaker with duster or damp cloth.
	(ii) Clothes catch fire	• Do not run in haste. Wrap with a blanket, then lie down on the floor and roll.

Go to the doctor after getting first aid.

Experiment 1 (a)

AIM

To find the pH of the following samples by using pH paper/universal indicator.

(a) Dilute hydrochloric acid (HCl)

(b) Dilute sodium hydroxide (NaOH) solution

(c) Dilute ethanoic acid (CH_3COOH) solution

(d) Lemon juice

(e) Water (H_2O)

(f) Dilute hydrogen carbonate solution

Materials Required

Six test tubes, test tube stand, test tube holder, glass rod, pH paper, dropper, measuring cylinder, standard pH colour chart, universal indicator, sample of solution—dil. HCl, dilute NaOH, dilute CH_3COOH, water, lemon juice and dil. H_2CO_3.

Theory/Principle

The pH Scale

It is a scale used for measuring hydrogen ion concentration. The pH describes the acidic or basic power of the solution. Here, **p** stands for potenz, meaning power or potential and **H** stands for hydrogen. To measure the acidic or basic strength more conveniently, a Danish biochemist Sorensen defined a new scale called **pH scale**, which could measure hydrogen ion concentration in the solution.

Higher the hydronium ion concentration present in the solution, lower is its pH value. [pH means power of hydrogen ions] [see Fig. 1]

- If pH > 7, solution is basic.
- If pH < 7, solution is acidic.
- If pH = 7, solution is neutral.

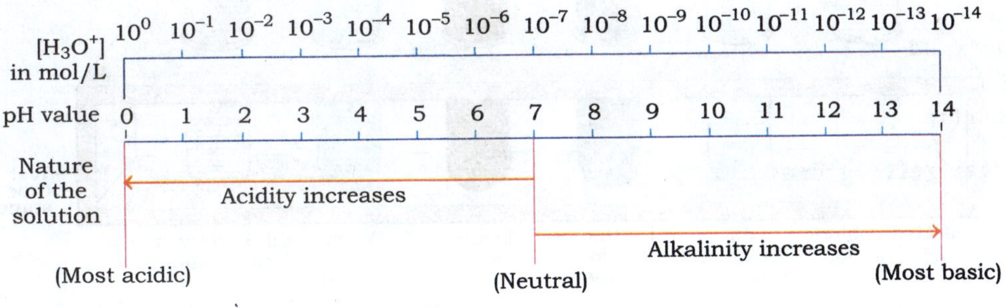

Fig. 1 pH scale

pH Paper

pH of a solution can be determined by using pH paper. When the pH paper is dipped in the solution whose pH is to be find out, a colour is developed on the pH paper. The colour is matched with the standard colour chart (as shown in Fig. 2).

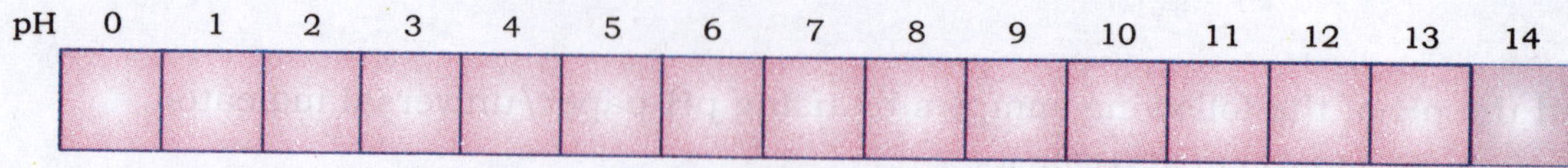

Fig. 2 pH colour chart

In the place of pH paper, we can use universal indicator solution or universal indicator paper to measure the pH. A **universal indicator** is a liquid/solution substance that is dropped into a sample and changes the colour of substance according to the pH. The colour is then matched against a colour chart showing the pH value for different colours.

The colours produced by universal indicator at different pH values are given in table below.

pH	Colours	pH	Colours	pH	Colours
0	Dark red	5	Orange-yellow	10	Dark blue
1	Red	6	Green-yellow	11	Purple
2	Light red	7	Green	12	Dark purple
3	Orange-red	8	Green-blue	13	Light violet
4	Orange	9	Blue	14	Violet

Note Violet/blue colour indicates alkaline solution, red/pink colour indicates acidic solution and green colour indicates neutral solution.

Procedure

(i) Take six clean test tubes and place them one by one in a test tube stand. Now, put each sample solution in a separate test tubes and label them as *A*, *B*, *C*, *D*, *E* and *F* (as shown in Fig. 3).

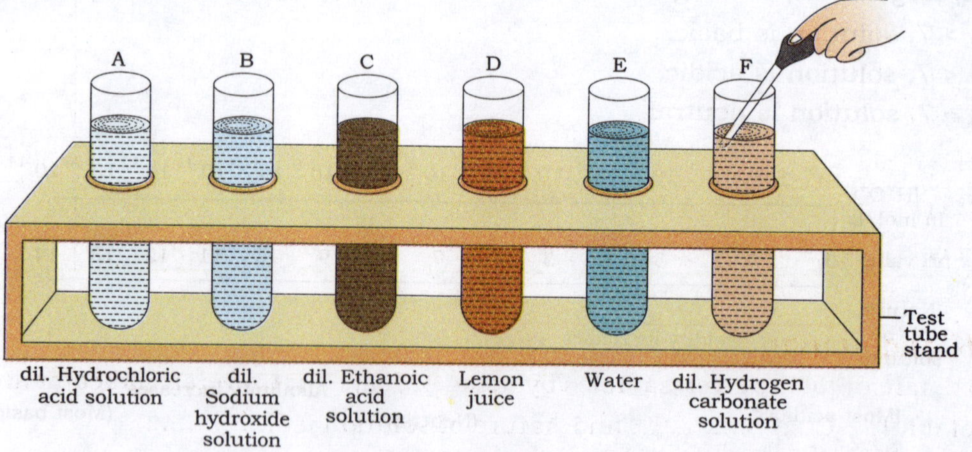

Fig. 3 Test tubes containing given samples of solutions

- **With pH paper**

(ii) Take a strip of pH paper and place it on cleaned and dry white surface.

(iii) Put one or two drops of each sample solution on different strips of pH papers using a glass rod as shown in Fig. 4.
Note that glass rod used for one sample must be washed with water before using for the other sample.

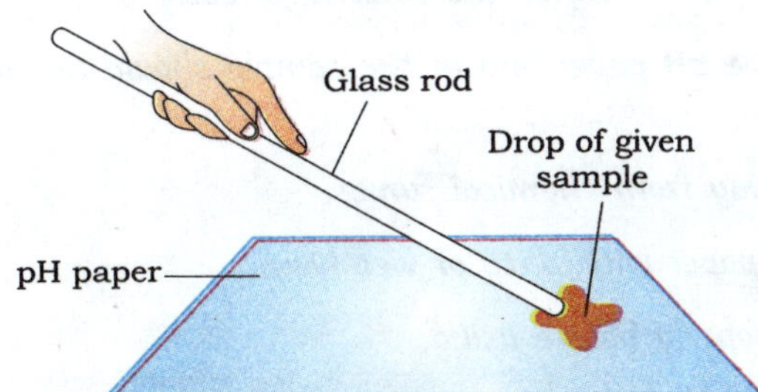

Fig. 4 Testing the pH of a sample by putting a drop on pH paper using a glass rod

(iv) Observe and note the colour produced on pH paper and compare it with the different colour shades given in the standard pH colour chart.

(v) Note down the pH value of the sample in the observation table.

- **With universal indicator**

(vi) Add few drops of universal indicator in all the six sample solutions separately.

(vii) Observe and note down the colour change and compare it with standard pH value colour chart.

(viii) Clean the glass rod properly, before taking another sample solution.

(ix) Observe the colour change in each sample and record pH in observation table.

(x) Decide nature of solutions of each sample, i.e. acidic, basic or neutral with the help of respective pH value.

Observations and Inferences

S.No.	Sample solution	Observations (Colour produced on pH paper)	Inferences (Approximate pH)	Observations (Colour developed in the sample using universal indicator)	Inferences (Approximate pH)
1.	Dilute HCl				
2.	Dilute NaOH				
3.	Dilute CH_3COOH				
4.	Lemon juice				
5.	Water				
6.	Dilute H_2CO_3				

Results/Conclusions

The approximate pH of the given samples by using pH paper or universal indicator are as follows:

1. pH of dilute HCl is .... and nature of solution is ....
2. pH of dilute NaOH is .... and nature of solution is ....
3. pH of dilute CH_3COOH is .... and nature of solution is ....
4. pH of lemon juice is .... and nature of lemon juice is ....
5. pH of water is .... and it is ....
6. pH of dil. H_2CO_3 is .... and nature of its solution is ....

1. Use the dilute solution of all samples and label the test tube carefully.
2. Do not touch, smell or taste any of the solution directly.
3. Colour developed on the pH paper and in the sample should be compared carefully with that of the chart.
4. Keep the pH strips away from chemical fumes.
5. Do not touch the pH paper with dirty or wet hand.
6. Clean the glass rod properly before using.
7. The test sample solutions should be freshly prepared and the lemon juice samples should also be fresh.
8. Glass rod used for one sample should be used for the other sample only after washing it with water.

Suggested Experiments

1. Take a solid chemical oxalic acid and prepare a solution of this chemical and determine its pH.
2. Find the pH values of juices of unripe and ripe fruits and compare the pH values and note the change in pH during ripening.

Viva-Voce

Q. 1 How is the concentration of hydronium ions (H_3O^+) affected, when a solution of an acid is diluted?

Ans. On dilution of an acid, the concentration of hydronium ions (H_3O^+) per unit volume decreases.

Q. 2 Solid sodium bicarbonate was placed on a strip of pH paper. What colour would you observe on a strip of pH paper?

Ans. The colour on a strip of pH paper would not change. (Since, an acid or base shows their nature in aqueous state only and not in solid or pure state, hence solid sodium bicarbonate does not affect the colour of pH paper).

Q. 3 What effect does the concentration of $H^+(aq)$ have on the acidic nature of the solution?

Ans. Higher the concentration of H^+ ions in a solution, more acidic is the solution.

Q. 4 A student was given four unknown colourless samples labelled *A*, *B*, *C* and *D* and asked to test their pH using pH paper. He observed that the colour of pH paper turned to light green, dark red, light orange and dark blue with samples *A*, *B*, *C* and *D* respectively. Which sample is most acidic?

Ans. Dark red has least pH, followed by light orange, light green and dark blue. Thus, sample *B* is most acidic.

Q. 5 **A student observed that the colour of pH paper changes to green when she dipped it in water. She added a few drops of concentrated hydrochloric acid to the water.**

What change in colour she would observe on pH paper?

Ans. The colour of pH paper would turn to red.

(**Reason** The colour of pH paper is green in neutral medium while it is red in acidic medium).

Q. 6 **Four students *A, B, C* and *D* measured the pH values of water, lemon juice and sodium bicarbonate solution. What is the correct decreasing order of the pH values?**

Ans. The correct decreasing order of pH values is : sodium bicarbonate > water > lemon juice.

Q. 7 **A student test a sample of drinking water and reports its pH as 6 at room temperature, which kind of compound do you think may have been added to water?**

Ans. Acidic compound like bleaching powder in drinking water reacts to form hypochlorous acid (HOCl), a weak acid which makes its pH value 6 (i.e., the solution becomes acidic).

Q. 8. **Which will be more acidic and why?**

(i) A solution with pH value of 6.0

(ii) A solution with pH value of 5.0

Ans. A solution with pH value of 5 will be more acidic as the lower a substance's pH, the more acidic it is.

Q. 9 **Choose strong acid and strong base from the following:**

CH_3COOH, NH_4OH, KOH, HCl

Ans. Strong acid—HCl, Strong base—KOH

Q.10 **Two solutions *A* and *B* were found to have pH values of 6 and 8 respectively. What inference can be drawn from this?**

Ans. pH value of solution *A* is 6, it means solution is an acid. On the other hand, pH value of solution *B* is 8, it means solution is a base.

Q.11 **During an experiment a student accidently spilled hydrochloric acid on his hand. His teacher applied dilute solution of another chemical substance which relieved him from the burning sensation. What could possibly that dilute solution?**

Ans. The applied solution could be a basic solution like $Mg(OH)_2$. It reacts with acid to form neutral salt.

Q.12 **Reena place one drop of each of hydrochloric acid, sodium hydroxide and lemon juice on a strip of red litmus paper one by one, in which case would you observe change of colour of litmus paper?**

Ans. Among the substances, NaOH (sodium hydroxide) would change the colour of red litmus paper as it is basic and thus, it can change the red litmus blue while acids has no affect on red litmus.

Questions From NCERT Lab Manual

Q. 1 **What do you mean by pH?**

Ans. The pH is the measure of the acidic (or basic) power of a solution. It is used for measuring hydrogen ion concentration in a solution. Higher the hydronium ion concentration in the solution, lower is their pH values.

Q. 2 **What is the pH of pure water at 25° C (298 K)?**

Ans. The pH of pure water at 25°C is equal to 7.

Q. 3 What according to you should be the pH of dil. HCl and dil. NaOH solution? Observe and explain your findings.

Ans. pH of dilute HCl is found to be in range of 1 to 3 and pH of dilute NaOH is between 12 to 14. Solutions with pH = 0 to 3 are strongly acidic, so dilute HCl is a strong acid. Whereas, the solution with pH = 12 to 14 are strongly basic, so dilute NaOH solution is a strong base.

Q. 4 On opening the soda water bottle the dissolved CO_2 comes out, would the pH of the solution increase or decrease as the gas comes out? Explain your answer either way.

Ans. As a liquid with a high amount of CO_2 is acidic while a liquid with less amount of CO_2 is basic. When a soda bottle is opened, the dissolve CO_2 escapes, decreasing the acidity of the solution and increasing the pH.

Practical Based MCQs

Q 1 A student adds few drops of the universal indicator to a solution of dilute hydrochloric acid in the way shown here.

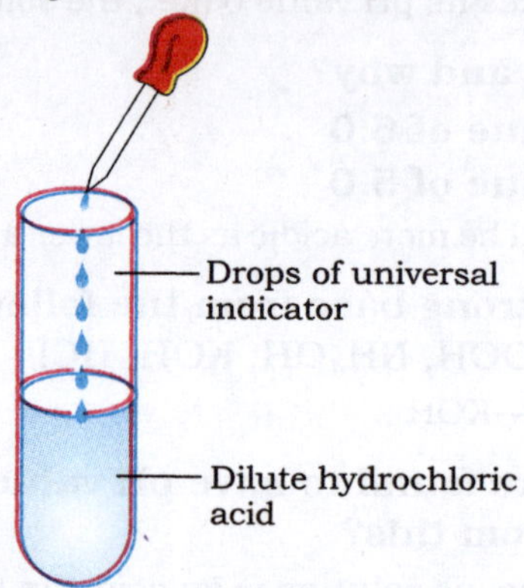

The colour observed is

(a) red (b) green (c) blue (d) violet

Q 2 In an experiment to test the pH of a given samples using pH paper, four students recorded the following observations :

Samples taken	pH paper colour turned to
(a) Water	Blue
(b) Dil. HCl	Red
(c) Dil. NaOH	Blue
(d) Dil. ethanoic acid	Orange

Which one of the above observations is incorrect?

Q 3 A student observed that the colour of pH paper changes to green, when she dipped it in water. She added a few drops of concentrated hydrochloric acid to the water. The change in colour she would observe on the pH paper is

(a) blue (b) red

(c) violet (d) green

Q 4 **Which is the correct method to find the pH of solution?**

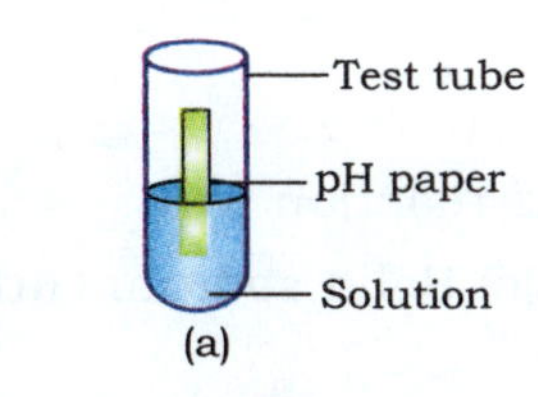

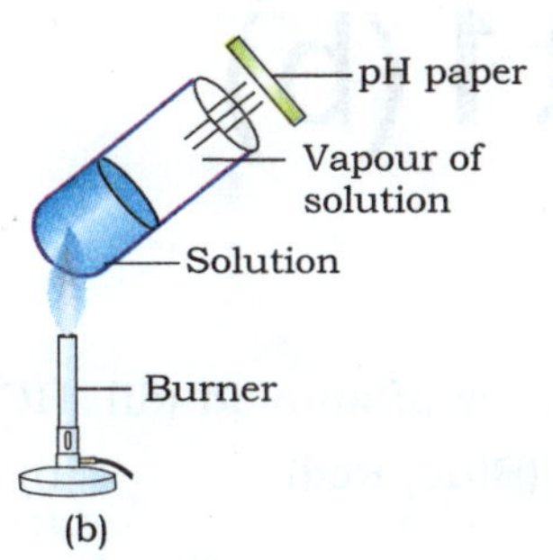

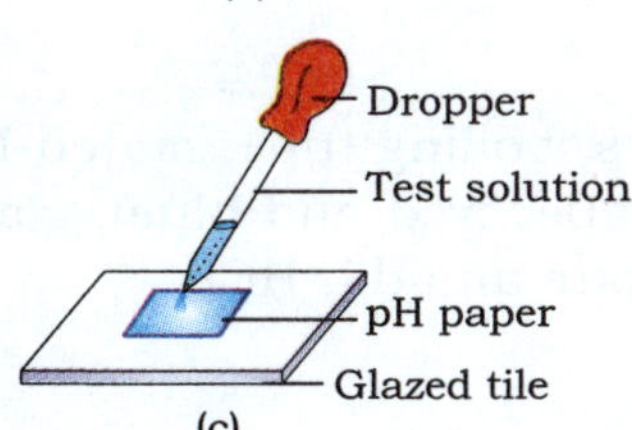

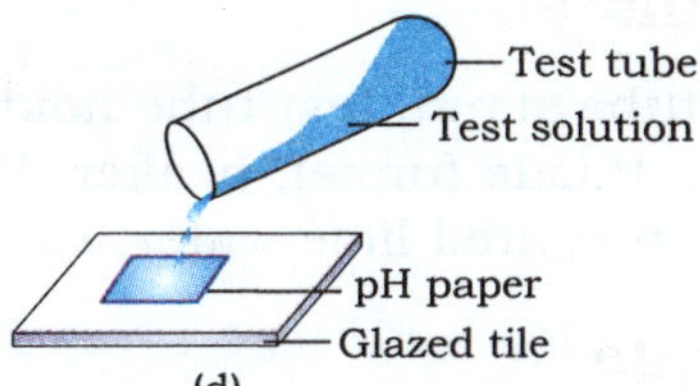

Q 5 **On adding a few drops of universal indicator to three unknown colourless solutions *P, Q* and *R* taken separately in three test tubes shown in the following diagrams, a student observed the changes in colour as green in *P* red in *Q* and violet in *R*.**

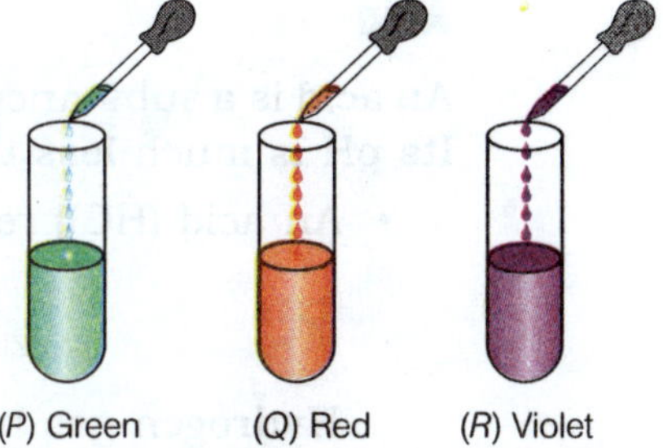

The decreasing order of pH of the solution is

(a) $P > Q > R$ (b) $P > R > Q$

(c) $Q > P > R$ (d) $R > P > Q$

Q 6 **2 mL of ethanoic acid was taken in test tube I and test tube II. A red litmus paper was introduced in test tube I and a pH paper was introduced in test tube II. The experiment was performed by four students *A, B, C* and *D;* and they reported their observations as given in the table.**

Students	Action on red litmus	Action on pH paper
A	Turned blue	Turned pink
B	Remains unchanged	Turned green
C	Turned blue	Turned blue
D	Remains unchanged	Turned pink

Student, who has given correct set of observations is

(a) *A* (b) *B* (c) *C* (d) *D*

Q 7 **Test tube I contains sodium bicarbonate solution while test tube II contains lemon juice. On introducing pH paper strips in both of them, it is observed that the pH paper turns**

(a) red in test tube I and blue in test tube II

(b) blue in both test tubes I and II

(c) blue in test tube I and red in test tube II

(d) red in test tube I and pink in test tube II

Answers

1. (a)	**2.** (a)	**3.** (b)	**4.** (c)	**5.** (d)	**6.** (d)	**7.** (c)

Experiment 1 (b)

AIM

To study the properties of an acid (dil. HCl) on the basis of its reaction with

(a) Litmus solution (Blue/Red) (b) Zinc metal (c) Solid sodium carbonate

Materials Required

Test tubes, test tube stand, test tube holder, cork, droppers, boiling tube, match-box, burner, flat bottom flask, thistle funnel, beaker, litmus solution/paper (red and blue), glass rod, zinc granules, freshly prepared lime water, solid sodium carbonate and dil. HCl.

Theory/Principle

Acid

An acid is a substance which furnishes H^+ ions when it is dissolved in water. HCl is a strong acid. Its pH is much less than 7.

- An acid (HCl) reacts with metals like zinc to produce a salt and hydrogen gas.

$$\underset{\text{Zinc metal}}{Zn(s)} + \underset{\text{Hydrochloric acid}}{2HCl(aq)} \longrightarrow \underset{\text{Zinc chloride}}{ZnCl_2(aq)} + \underset{\text{Hydrogen gas}}{H_2(g)}$$

Hydrogen gas burns in air with a blue flame and produces a pop sound.

$$\underset{\text{Hydrogen gas}}{2H_2(g)} + \underset{\text{(From air)}}{O_2(g)} \longrightarrow \underset{\text{Water}}{2H_2O(l)}$$

- An acid (HCl) reacts with **sodium carbonate** (aqueous/solid) and **sodium hydrogen carbonate** to liberate carbon dioxide (CO_2) which turns lime water milky due to the formation of calcium carbonate. When excess of CO_2 is passed through the solution, the milkiness disappears.

$$\underset{\text{Sodium carbonate}}{Na_2CO_3(s/aq)} + \underset{\text{Hydrochlaric acid}}{2HCl(aq)} \longrightarrow \underset{\text{Sodium chloride}}{2NaCl(aq)} + \underset{\text{Water}}{H_2O(l)} + \underset{\text{Carbon dioxide}}{CO_2(g)}$$

$$\underset{\text{Calcium hydroxide}}{Ca(OH)_2(aq)} + \underset{\text{Carbon dioxide}}{CO_2(g)} \longrightarrow \underset{\text{Calcium carbonate white ppt (milky)}}{CaCO_3(s)} + \underset{\text{Water}}{H_2O(l)}$$

- An acid (HCl) reacts with NaOH (base) to neutralise and to produce sodium chloride (salt) and water.

$$\underset{\text{Hydrochloric acid}}{HCl(aq)} + \underset{\text{Sodium hydroxide}}{NaOH(aq)} \longrightarrow \underset{\text{Sodium chloride}}{NaCl(aq)} + \underset{\text{Water}}{H_2O(l)}$$

- Acid turns blue litmus to red while it has no effect on red litmus.

Procedure

1. Litmus Test

(i) Take two test tubes and mark them *A* and *B* and put them in a test tube stand. In test tube *A*, take 5 mL of dil. HCl solution and in *B*, take 5 mL of dil. HCl solution (as shown in Fig. 1).

(ii) Using a dropper, add few drops of blue litmus solution in test tube A and red litmus solution in test tube *B*, respectively. Stir each tube with separate glass rods. Note, if there is any colour change occurs in the solutions.

Observation In test tube *A*, blue litmus solution turns red and nothing happens to red litmus solution in test tube *B*. Hence, it can be concluded that acids (like HCl) turns blue litmus to red.

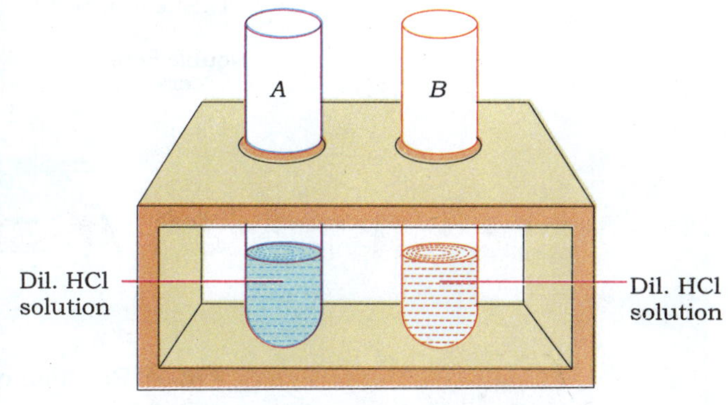

Fig. 1 Set up for litmus test

2. Reaction with Zinc (Zn) Metal

(i) Take clean zinc granules in a clean and dry boiling tube.

(ii) Add dil. HCl to the boiling tube containing zinc granules, such that zinc granules are totally submerged in the acid.

(iii) Place a cork having glass delivery tube.

(iv) Bring a burning match-stick near the mouth of a test tube.

Observation After adding dil. HCl to the test tube containing zinc granules, a vigorous reaction takes place (after 2-3 minutes) with the evolution of a colourless, odourless hydrogen gas. On bringing a burning match-stick near the mouth of gas tube, the gas burns with a pale blue flame producing a pop sound (as shown in Fig. 2).

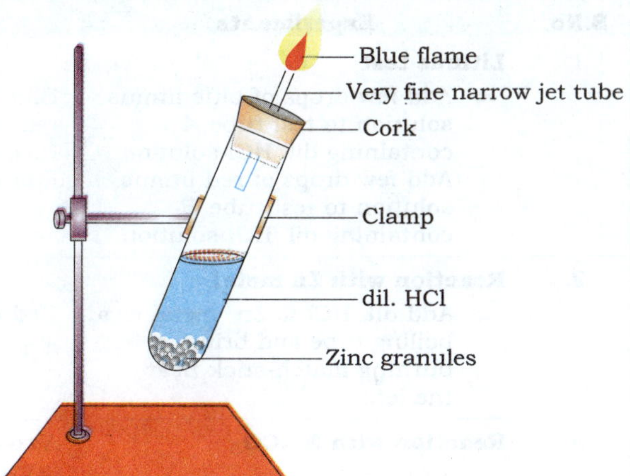

Fig. 2 Action of dil. HCl on Zn metal

3. Reaction with Solid Sodium Carbonate (Na_2CO_3)

(i) Take a small amount of solid sodium carbonate in a flat bottom flask and add some distilled water in it, shake it well.

(ii) Take a double bore cork with a thistle funnel and a delivery tube fitted in it, fit it on the open end of the flask.

(iii) Now, add dil. HCl in the flask through thistle funnel.

(iv) Pass the released gas through freshly prepared lime water with the help of delivery tube (as shown in Fig. 3).

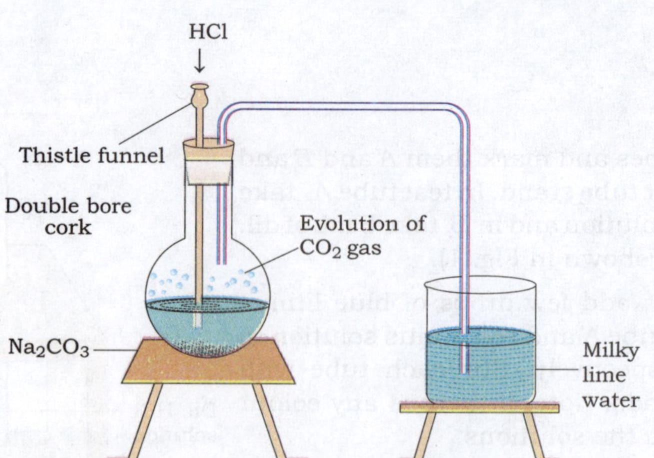

Fig. 3 Reaction of dil.HCl with sodium carbonate

Observation Dil. HCl on reacting with sodium carbonate (Na_2CO_3) liberates carbon dioxide (CO_2) gas which turns lime water milky on passing through it . While on passing the gas in excess of lime water, the milkiness disappears.

Observation Table

S.No.	Experiments	Observations	Inferences
1.	**Litmus test** ⇒ Add few drops of blue litmus solution to test tube *A* containing dil. HCl solution. Add few drops of red litmus solution to test tube *B* containing dil. HCl solution.	Blue litmus solution turns red in colour. No change in colour of red litmus solution.	HCl has .... character. HCl .... affect red litmus solution.
2.	**Reaction with Zn metal** ⇒ Add dil. HCl to Zn metal in a boiling tube and bring a burning match-stick near the jet.	Hydrogen gas evolves and a pop sound is obtained.	Zn reacts with dil. HCl and liberates .... gas. $Zn\ (s) + 2HCl(aq) \longrightarrow ZnCl_2(aq) + \ldots\uparrow$
3.	**Reaction with Na_2CO_3** ⇒ Add a few drops of dil. HCl to Na_2CO_3.	A colourless, odourless gas is evolved which turns lime water milky. On passing the gas in excess in lime water, the milkiness disappears.	.... gas is liberated on the reaction between dil. HCl and Na_2CO_3. $2HCl\ (aq) + Na_2CO_3(s) \longrightarrow 2NaCl\ (aq) + \ldots\ldots + H_2O(l)$

Results/Conclusions

1. Hydrochloric acid turns blue litmus solution/paper to red but it does not affect red litmus solution/paper.
2. It reacts with zinc metal to liberate hydrogen gas and also forms zinc chloride as a product.
3. It reacts with sodium carbonate to liberate carbon dioxide.

Hence, we conclude that hydrochloric acid (HCl) is acidic in nature.

PRECAUTIONS

1. *As HCl is corrosive in nature, it should be handled with care.*
2. *Use small quantities of chemicals.*
3. *Use small quantities of Zn and HCl, otherwise large amounts of H_2 will be formed which may cause explosion.*
4. *Use clean zinc metal, otherwise the reaction will occur very slowly.*
5. *While adding HCl to Na_2CO_3, make sure that apparatus is airtight.*
6. *Observe the milkiness in the lime water soon.*
7. *In case you allow carbon dioxide to pass for a long time through lime water, the milkiness may be removed due to the formation of soluble calcium bicarbonate as depicted in the reaction as follows:*

$$CaCO_3(s) + CO_2(g) + H_2O(l) \longrightarrow Ca(HCO_3)_2(aq)$$

8. *Shake the solutions and reaction mixtures carefully without spilling.*
9. *Care must be taken while performing combustion test with H_2.*

Suggested Experiments

1. To study the reaction of metal carbonate (calcium carbonate) with hydrochloric acid and write the observation and conclusion.
2. To study the reaction of copper oxide (a metallic oxide) with hydrochloric acid.

Viva-Voce

Q. 1 Name one metal (other than zinc) which on reacting with dil. HCl gives a colourless gas that burns with a pop sound.

Ans. Magnesium metal evolves hydrogen gas on reacting with dil. HCl. The gas burns with a pop sound.

Q. 2 When a white powder was mixed with dilute acid, a colourless and odourless gas was produced which turned lime water milky. What is this white powder?

Ans. White powder may be carbonate or bicarbonate of metals, which evolve CO_2 gas on reacting with dilute acid. This CO_2 gas turned lime water milky.

Q. 3 Why does lime water turn milky when CO_2 gas is passed through it?

Ans. Due to the formation of insoluble calcium carbonate, lime water turn milky when CO_2 gas is passed through it.

Q. 4 If a moist blue litmus paper is brought near CO_2 gas. What change would be observed on the blue litmus paper?

Ans. Blue litmus paper turns red. In the presence of moisture, CO_2 gas changes to carbonic acid.

$$\underset{\text{Carbondioxide}}{CO_2(g)} + \underset{\text{Water}}{H_2O(l)} \longrightarrow \underset{\text{Carbonic acid}}{H_2CO_3(aq)}$$

It will change the colour of blue litmus to red.

Q. 5 **A drop of red litmus solution is poured in a metal carbonate solution. The colour of litmus solution changes to blue. What is the nature of metallic carbonate solution?**

Ans. The metallic carbonate solution is alkaline in nature.

Q. 6 **Out of acetic acid and hydrochloric acid, which would have a lower pH?**

Ans. HCl would have lower pH as being a strong acid, it can easily dissociate to give more H^+ ions as compare to acetic acid.

Questions From NCERT Lab Manual

Q. 1 **What will be the colour of a blue litmus paper on bringing it in contact with a drop of dil. hydrochloric acid?**

Ans. The colour of the blue litmus paper changes to red on bringing it in contact with a drop of dil. hydrochloric acid.

Q. 2 **Explain, why hydrogen gas is not collected by the downward displacement of air?**

Ans. Hydrogen gas is not collected by the downward displacement of air because hydrogen gas is lighter than air.

Q. 3 **What will happen to a lighted candle if it is brought near the mouth of a gas jar containing hydrogen gas?**

Ans. The candle extinguishes with a pop sound and the gas burns with a pale blue flame.

Q. 4 **Which gas is produced when zinc metal reacts with hydrochloric acid?**

Ans. When zinc metal reacts with hydrochloric acid, hydrogen gas is produced.

$$Zn(s) + 2HCl(aq) \longrightarrow ZnCl_2(aq) + H_2(g)$$

Q. 5 **Which gas is liberated when sodium carbonate reacts with hydrochloric acid?**

Ans. When sodium carbonate (Na_2CO_3) reacts with hydrochloric acid, carbon dioxide (CO_2) gas is released.

$$Na_2CO_3(s) + 2HCl(aq) \longrightarrow 2NaCl(aq) + CO_2(g) + H_2O(l)$$

Q. 6 **Hydrogen gas is neutral to litmus paper. Explain how?**

Ans. Hydrogen gas is neither acidic nor basic in nature, thus it does not affect blue and red litmus paper.

Q. 7 **What is the utility of the reaction between $NaHCO_3$ and HCl in daily life situation?**

Ans. Sodium bicarbonate ($NaHCO_3$) acts as an antacid and it neutralises excess of hydrochloric acid (HCl) in our stomach.

Q. 8 **How can the deposits of carbonates and hydrogen carbonates on the metal surface be cleaned?**

Ans. The deposits of carbonates and hydrogen carbonates on the metal surface can be cleaned by dil. HCl or acetic acid.

Experiment 1 (c)

AIM

To study the properties of a base (dil. NaOH) on the basis of its their reaction with

(a) Litmus solution (blue/red) (b) Zinc metal (c) Solid sodium carbonate

Materials Required

Test tubes, test tube stand, test tube holder, litmus solution/paper strips (red and blue), dil. NaOH, solid sodium carbonate, zinc granules, Bunsen burner, distilled water, match-box, thistle funnel, flat bottom flask, delivery tube, cork, glass rods and freshly prepared lime water.

Theory/Principle

Base

A base is a substance which furnishes OH^- ions when it is dissolved in water. Sodium hydroxide (NaOH) is a strong base. Its pH is much higher than 7.

- It turns red litmus into blue and do not affect the blue litmus.
- On reacting with Zn metal, it forms a salt (sodium zincate) and hydrogen gas (H_2) is liberated.

$$\underset{\text{Zinc}}{Zn(s)} + \underset{\text{Sodium hydroxide}}{2NaOH(aq)} \longrightarrow \underset{\text{Sodium zincate}}{Na_2ZnO_2\ (aq)} + \underset{\text{Hydrogen}}{H_2(g)}$$

- Solid Na_2CO_3 does not react with NaOH because both are basic in nature.

$$\underset{\text{Sodium carbonate}}{Na_2CO_3(s)} + \underset{\text{Sodium hydroxide}}{NaOH(aq)} \longrightarrow \text{No reaction}$$

- Base (NaOH) neutralises acid (HCl) to gives salt (NaCl).

$$\underset{\text{Hydrochloric acid}}{HCl\ (aq)} + \underset{\text{Sodium hydroxide}}{NaOH(aq)} \longrightarrow \underset{\text{Sodium chloride}}{NaCl(aq)} + \underset{\text{Water}}{H_2O(l)}$$

Procedure

1. Litmus Test

(i) Take two test tubes and put them in a test tube stand (as shown in Fig. 1), mark them *A* and *B*. Take 3 mL of dil. NaOH in test tube *A* and 3 mL of dil. NaOH in test tube *B*.

(ii) Using a dropper, add few drops of blue litmus solution in test tube *A* and red litmus solution in test tube *B*. Note, if there is any colour change in the solutions in the test tubes.

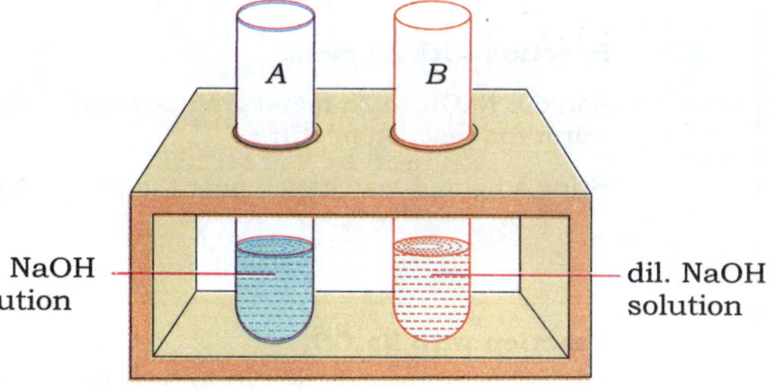

Fig. 1 Set up for litmus test

Observation Red litmus solution in test tube *B* turns into blue while there is no change observed in blue litmus solution present in test tube *A*.

2. Reaction with Zinc (Zn) Metal

(i) Take few zinc granules in a clean and dry test tube.

(ii) Add NaOH to the test tube containing zinc granules, such that zinc granules are totally submerged in the base.

(iii) Place a cork having glass delivery tube and heat the test tube.

(iv) Bring a burning matchstick near the mouth of the test tube.

Observation A vigorous reaction will take place after 2-3 minutes with the evolution of a colourless, odourless gas. On bringing a burning match-stick near the mouth of gas tube, the gas burns with a pale blue flame producing a pop sound (as shown in Fig. 2).

Fig. 2 Action of dil. NaOH on zinc metal

3. Reaction with Solid Sodium Carbonate (Na_2CO_3)

(i) Take a small amount of Na_2CO_3 in a test tube.

(ii) Add some drops of dil. NaOH solution in the test tube containing Na_2CO_3.

Observation Even after adding NaOH solution to the test tube containing Na_2CO_3, there is no change observed.

Observation Table

S. No.	Experiments	Observations	Inferences
1.	**Litmus test**		
	⇒ Add few drops of blue litmus solution to test tube *A* containing dil. NaOH solution.	No change in colour of blue litmus solution.	NaOH .... affect blue litmus solution.
	⇒ Add few drops of red litmus solution to another test tube *B* containing dil. NaOH solution.	Red litmus solution turns blue.	NaOH has .... character.
2.	**Reaction with Zn metal**		
	Add dil. NaOH to Zn metal granules and warm the reaction mixture.	Hydrogen gas evolves.	Zn reacts with dil. NaOH and liberates .... gas.
	Bring a lighted matchstick near the jet.	A pop sound is obtained.	$\underset{\text{Zinc}}{Zn(s)} + \underset{\text{Sodium hydroxide solution}}{2NaOH(aq)} \rightarrow \underset{\text{Sodium zincate}}{Na_2ZnO_2(s)} + ..\uparrow$
3.	**Reaction with Na_2CO_3** Add a few drops of dil. NaOH to Na_2CO_3.	No change is observed.	NaOH and Na_2CO_3 do not react.

Results/Conclusions

1. Sodium hydroxide turns red litmus solution/paper blue but it does not affect blue litmus solution/paper.
2. It reacts with zinc metal and liberates hydrogen gas which burns with a pop sound when burning splinter or a match stick brought near it. During this reaction, sodium zincate is also formed.
3. It does not react with sodium carbonate.

Hence, we conclude that sodium hydroxide (NaOH) is basic in nature.

PRECAUTIONS

1. *Sodium hydroxide should be handled with care because it is highly corrosive in nature.*
2. *Do not heat mixture of zinc and dilute NaOH to a boiling point.*
3. *Small quantity of chemicals should be used to perform the experiment to get best results.*
4. *Test tubes and droppers should be washed well with distilled water before use.*
5. *Do not interchange droppers while testing with acids/alkalis/indicators.*
6. *Hands must be cleaned properly after completing the experiment.*

Suggested Experiments

1. To study the neutralisation reaction of (acid) dilute hydrochloric acid with base sodium hydroxide solution.
2. To study the reaction of active metals (aluminium metal) with dilute hydrochloric acid and write the observation and conclusion.

Q. 1 What are strong bases? Give example.

Ans. Those bases which dissociate into its ions completely when present in solution and whose pH value is much greater than 7, are called strong bases, e.g. NaOH, KOH, etc.

Q. 2 A blue litmus paper was first dipped in dil. HCl and then in dil. NaOH solution. What colour would you observe on the litmus paper?

Ans. Dilute HCl turns blue litmus paper red which becomes blue again in dil. NaOH solution.

Q. 3 A teacher gave two test tubes, one containing water and the other containing sodium hydroxide solution, to the students and asked them to identify the test tube containing sodium hydroxide solution. Which substance can be used to identify the test tube?

Ans. Red litmus paper can be used as red litmus paper turns blue in the presence of sodium hydroxide solution.

Q. 4 What will be the reaction of Zn with NaOH on heating?

Ans. Zn reacts with NaOH to form sodium zincate and hydrogen gas.

$$\underset{\text{Zinc}}{Zn\,(s)} + \underset{\text{Sodium hydroxide solution}}{2NaOH\,(dil.)} \longrightarrow \underset{\text{Sodium zincate}}{Na_2ZnO_2(aq)} + \underset{\text{Hydrogen}}{H_2(g)}$$

Q. 5 **What will be the effect of litmus on hydrogen gas?**

Ans. Hydrogen gas is neutral towards litmus. It is neither acidic nor basic and therefore, it neither changes the colour of blue litmus nor red litmus.

Q. 6 **A yellow stain of turmeric turns red when rubbed with soap. What is the reason behind this change?**

Ans. The yellow stain of turmeric changes to red because soap is alkaline in nature, since turmeric (an indicator) changes to red colour in the presence of OH^- ions.

Q. 7 **When carbon dioxide is passed through lime water, it turns milky. Due to which insoluble substance milkiness is formed?**

Ans. Insoluble calcium carbonate ($CaCO_3$) makes the solution milky.

Q. 8 **What would happen when dil. HCl and dil. NaOH (same concentrations) are mixed in equal amounts? Write the equation also.**

Ans. When dil. HCl and dil. NaOH are mixed in equal amounts, neutralisation reaction takes place with formation of salt and water.

$$\underset{\text{Hydrochloric acid}}{HCl\,(aq)} + \underset{\text{Sodium hydroxide solution}}{NaOH\,(aq)} \longrightarrow \underset{\text{Sodium chloride}}{NaCl\,(aq)} + \underset{\text{Water}}{H_2O\,(l)}$$

Q. 9 **What happen if we bring a match-stick near the mouth of the test tube when NaOH is added to zinc granules?**

Ans. When zinc granules is added to sodium hydroxide, hydrogen gas is liberated. When we bring a match-stick near the mouth of the test tube, this gas burns with a pop sound.

$$\underset{\text{Zinc}}{Zn\,(s)} + \underset{\text{Sodium hydroxide solution}}{2NaOH\,(aq)} \longrightarrow \underset{\text{Sodium zincate}}{Na_2ZnO_2\,(aq)} + \underset{\text{Hydrogen}}{H_2(g)}$$

Q.10 **What are the metals (other than Zn) which react with alkalies to produce hydrogen gas? What are these metals called?**

Ans. Aluminium. These metals are called amphoteric metals.

Q. 11 **A solution of soda ash is prepared by dissolving 1 g of it in 10 mL of distilled water. A strip of blue litmus paper *A* and strip of red litmus paper *B* is dipped in this solution. What would be the colour of strip *A* and *B*?**

Ans. The soda ash (sodium carbonate) solution is alkaline in nature. Thus, only the colour of red litmus paper changes to blue when it is dipped in soda ash solution. There is no colour change in blue litmus paper.

Questions From NCERT Lab Manual

Q. 1 **A dilute solution of sodium carbonate was added to two test tubes — one containing dil. HCl (*A*) and the other containing dilute NaOH (*B*). What would you observe in test tubes?**

Ans. In test tube *A*, sodium carbonate reacts with dilute HCl to form colourless CO_2 gas.

$$\underset{\text{Sodium carbonate solution}}{Na_2CO_3(aq)} + \underset{\text{Hydrochloric acid}}{2HCl\,(aq)} \longrightarrow \underset{\text{Sodium chloride solution}}{2NaCl(aq)} + \underset{\text{Carbon dioxide}}{CO_2(g)} + \underset{\text{Water}}{H_2O\,(l)}$$

In test tube B, no reaction will take place.

Q. 2 **What will be the colour of blue litmus paper on bringing it in contact with a drop of dil. NaOH?**

Ans. The colour of the blue litmus paper remains same on bringing it in contact with a drop of dil. NaOH.

Practical Based MCQs

For Experiments 1 (b) and 1(c)

Q. 1 Which one of the following setups is the most appropriate for the evolution of hydrogen gas and its identification?

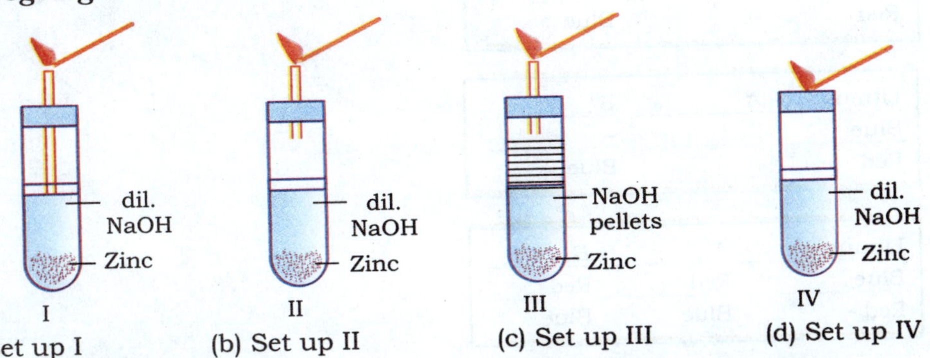

(a) Set up I (b) Set up II (c) Set up III (d) Set up IV

Q. 2 When Zn metal reacts with hydrochloric acid, then the gas evolved

(a) supports combustion.
(b) turns lime water milky.
(c) burns with a pop sound.
(d) has a pungent odour.

Q. 3 Four students were asked by their teacher to arrange the set ups I-IV as given below and identify the gas evolved in each case, if any.

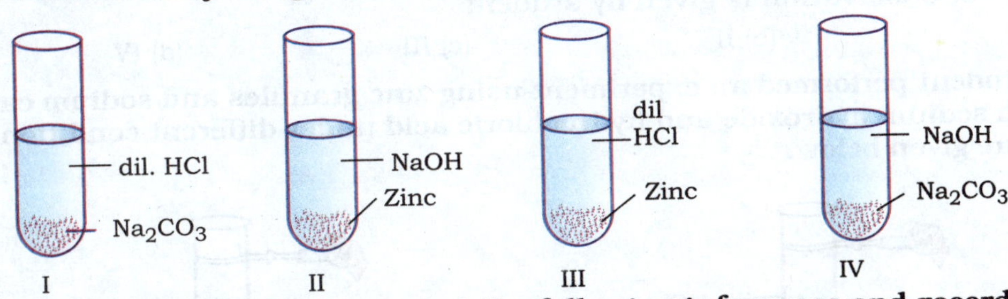

After observations, they arrived at the following inferences and recorded these in the form of a given table.

Students	I	II	III	IV
A	Hydrogen	No gas	Carbon dioxide	Hydrogen
B	Carbon dioxide	Hydrogen	No gas	Carbon dioxide
C	Carbon dioxide	Hydrogen	Hydrogen	No gas
D	No gas	Carbon dioxide	Carbon dioxide	Hydrogen

Which student has given the correct inferences?

(a) *A* (b) *B* (c) *C* (d) *D*

Q. 4 When dilute hydrochloric acid is added to solid sodium carbonate in a test tube then, it is observed that

(a) no change takes place.
(b) a loud sound is produced.
(c) the solution turns blue.
(d) brisk effervescence takes place.

Q. 5 **Four students I, II, III and IV were asked to examine the changes for blue and red litmus paper strips with dil. HCl (solution A) and dil. NaOH (solution B). The following observations were reported by the four students. The sign (–) indicating no colour change.**

I.

Litmus	*A*	*B*
Blue	–	Red
Red	–	Blue

II.

Litmus	*A*	*B*
Blue	Red	–
Red	–	Blue

III.

Litmus	*A*	*B*
Blue	Red	Red
Red	Blue	Blue

IV.

Litmus	*A*	*B*
Blue	Blue	Blue
Red	Red	Red

Correct observation is given by student

(a) I (b) II (c) III (d) IV

Q. 6 **A student performed an experiment using zinc granules and sodium carbonate with sodium hydroxide and hydrochloric acid under different conditions as shown figure given below.**

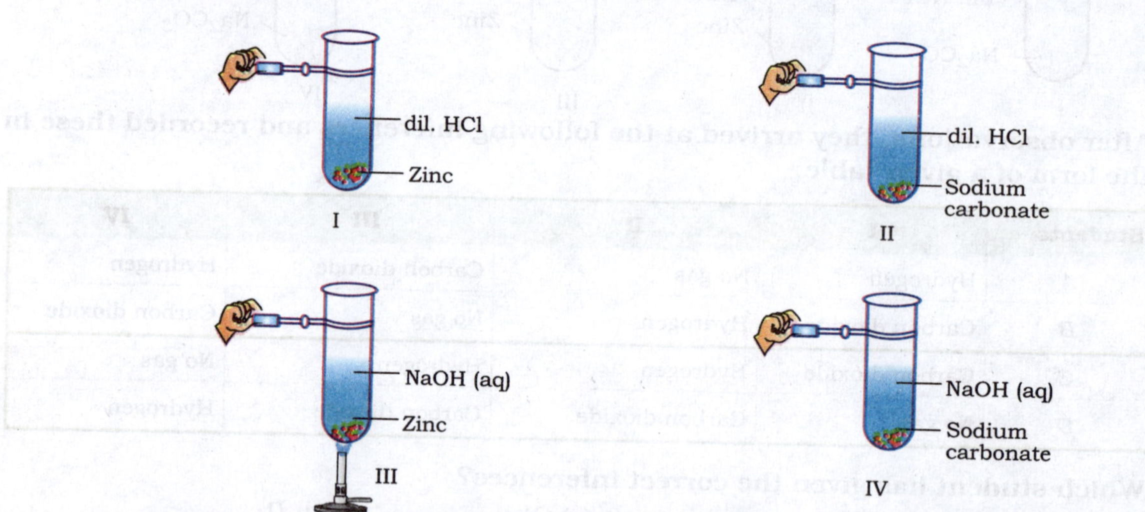

In which setup, no gas is evolved?

(a) I (b) II (c) III (d) IV

Q. 7 Given below are the observations reported by the three students I, II and III for the changes observed for different materials with dil. HCl or dil. NaOH.

Students	Materials	Dil. HCl	Dil. NaOH
I	Moist litmus paper	Blue to red	Red to blue
II	Zinc metal	React at room temperature	Reacts on warming the mixture
III	Solid sodium bicarbonate	No reaction	Brisk effervescence

Which among the given students, gave the correct observations?

(a) Student I and II
(b) Only Student II
(c) Student I and III
(d) Student II and III

Q. 8 **Given below are certain chemical properties of substances :**

I. It turns blue litmus to red.
II. It turns red litmus to blue.
III. It reacts with zinc metal and a gas evolves.
IV. It reacts with solid sodium carbonate to give brisk effervescence.

Out of these properties, which are shown by dilute hydrochloric acid?

(a) Both I and II
(b) Both I and III
(c) Both I, III and IV
(d) Both II, III and IV

Q. 9 **The following pairs of substances are available in the laboratory :**

I. Zinc and dilute hydrochloric acid.
II. Zinc and dilute sodium hydroxide solution.
III. Sodium bicarbonate and dilute hydrochloric acid.

Which of these can be used to produce a colourless and odourless gas, which gives a pop sound on burning?

(a) Only I
(b) Only II
(c) Both I and II
(d) Both I and III

Q.10 **A teacher gave two test tubes, one containing water and the other containing sodium hydroxide solution, to the students and asked them to identify the test tube containing sodium hydroxide solution. Which substance out of the following can be used to identify the test tube?**

(a) Blue litmus
(b) Red litmus
(c) Sodium carbonate solution
(d) Dilute hydrochloric acid

Answers

1. (b)	**2.** (c)	**3.** (c)	**4.** (d)	**5.** (b)	**6.** (d)	**7.** (a)	**8.** (c)	**9.** (c)	**10.** (b)

Experiment 2(a)

AIM

To perform and observe the action of water on quicklime and classify the reaction.

Materials Required

Calcium oxide (quicklime), distilled water, iron container, test tube, glass rod, dropper, red and blue litmus paper strips.

Theory/Principle

When calcium oxide (quicklime) is dissolved in water, it forms calcium hydroxide (slaked lime). The reaction is highly exothermic, i.e. a lot of heat is produced during the reaction. This reaction may be represented in the form of a chemical reaction as follows:

$$\underset{\text{Calcium oxide (quicklime)}}{CaO(s)} + \underset{\text{Water}}{H_2O(l)} \longrightarrow \underset{\text{Calcium hydroxide (slaked lime)}}{Ca(OH)_2(aq)} + \text{Heat} \quad \ldots \text{(i)}$$

Note Calcium hydroxide is basic in nature. Therefore, it turns moist red litmus paper blue. If we pass CO_2 gas through clear calcium hydroxide solution (lime water), it turns milky due to the formation of a white precipitate (insoluble calcium carbonate).

$$\underset{\text{Lime water (colourless)}}{Ca(OH)_2(aq)} + \underset{\text{Carbon dioxide}}{CO_2(g)} \longrightarrow \underset{\text{Calcium carbonate (white ppt.)}}{CaCO_3(s)} + H_2O(l)$$

In reaction (i), two compounds-quicklime and water combine to give a single product slaked lime. So, this is an example of combination reaction. Hence, it may be stated that a reaction in which two or more substances react together to form a single product, is called a **combination reaction.**

Also, it has been observed that a large amount of heat is evolved alongwith the formation of products. Such type of reactions which are accompanied by the evolution of heat, are called **exothermic reactions.**

Procedure

(i) Take a small amount of quicklime in a iron container.

(ii) Slowly add water to it as shown in Fig. 1(a).

(iii) Stir it well with a clean glass rod as shown in Fig. 1(b).

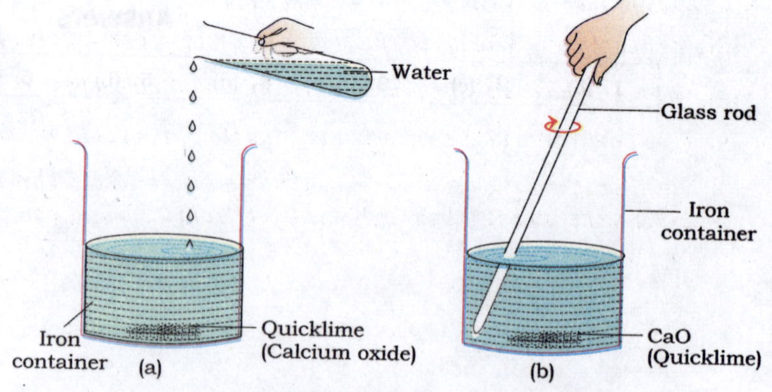

Fig. 1 (a) Addition of water to quicklime
(b) Action of water on quicklime

(iv) Using a clean dropper, take a few drops of the solution formed in the beaker and place them on red and blue litmus paper strip (as shown in Fig. 2). Make your observation.

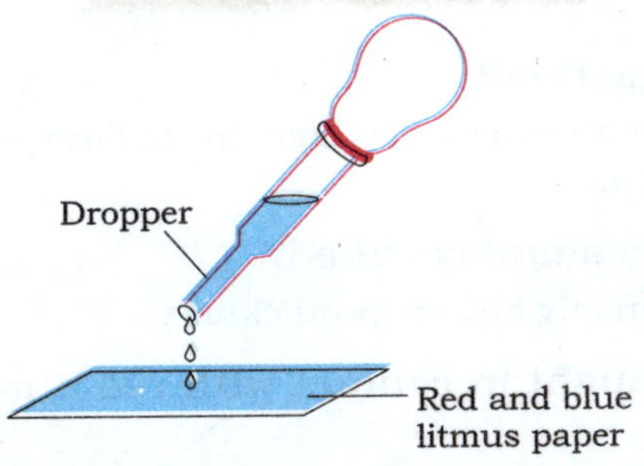

Fig. 2 Litmus paper test

Observations

The hissing sound is produced and solution becomes hot. The heat is evolved during the reaction which raises the temperature of the reaction mixture. On putting a few drops of the solution on red and blue litmus paper, it is observed that only red litmus paper turns blue, no changes occur in blue litmus paper.

Inference

- In this reaction, quicklime (CaO) and water (H_2O) combine to give a single product slaked lime [$Ca(OH)_2$].

$$\underset{\text{Calcium oxide}}{CaO\,(s)} + \underset{\text{Water}}{H_2O\,(l)} \longrightarrow \underset{\text{Calcium hydroxide}}{Ca(OH)_2\,(aq)} + \text{Heat}$$

- It is a combination reaction and the product calcium hydroxide [$Ca(OH)_2$] is basic in nature.
- As heat is evolved, the reaction is exothermic.

Result

The reaction between quicklime and water to form slaked lime is a **combination reaction** as well as **exothermic reaction**.

PRECAUTIONS

1. Always take a small amount of quicklime.

2. The reaction is highly exothermic, so do not touch the beaker having reaction mixture directly.

3. Water is added slowly to a beaker containing quicklime.

4. Quicklime can cause severe burns, therefore, it should be handled with spatula.

5. Use good quality glassware, while adding water to quicklime. This is because, the reaction is highly exothermic and the beaker if made of ordinary glass, can crack.

Suggested Experiments

1. To perform and observe chemical reaction of burning of magnesium ribbon in air and classify the reaction.
2. To perform and observe chemical reaction, when iron filings are heated with sulphur powder and classify the reaction.

Viva-Voce

Q. 1 What is combination reaction?

Ans. A reaction in which two or more substances combine to form a single product (compound) is called a combination reaction.

Q. 2 What is calcium oxide commonly called?

Ans. Calcium oxide (CaO) is commonly known as quicklime.

Q. 3 When slaked lime is brought in contact with red litmus paper, what do you observe?

Ans. We observe that red litmus paper turns blue. From this, we can conclude that slaked lime is basic in nature.

Q. 4 While adding small amount of quicklime in a beaker, water is added slowly to the beaker. What observation would you note down?

Ans. When water is added slowly in a quicklime, hissing sound is produced and the solution becomes hot.

Q. 5 Name the reaction between calcium oxide and water.

Ans. The reaction between calcium oxide and water is known as combination reaction as a single compound calcium hydroxide is formed in this reaction.

Q.6 Why should we not touch iron container in which CaO reacts with H_2O?

Ans. We should not touch iron container in which CaO reacts with H_2O because iron container will be very hot as the reaction is exothermic.

Q. 7 Write the product formed when quicklime reacts with water.

Ans. Quicklime reacts with water to give calcium hydroxide $Ca(OH)_2$, i.e. slaked lime.

$$\underset{\text{Calcium oxide}}{CaO\ (s)} + \underset{\text{Water}}{H_2O(l)} \longrightarrow \underset{\text{Calcium hydroxide}}{Ca(OH)_2(aq)}$$

Q. 8 What is the effect of temperature on the solubility of calcium hydroxide?

Ans. Solubility of calcium hydroxide or slaked lime decreases with increase in temperature.

Q. 9 Is the reaction between quicklime and water exothermic or endothermic?

Ans. As heat energy is released during the reaction, therefore it is an exothermic reaction.

Q.10 Name the chemical formula and chemical name of slaked lime.

Ans. Chemical formula of slaked lime — $Ca(OH)_2$.

Chemical name of slaked lime — Calcium hydroxide

Q.11 Most of the combination reactions are exothermic in nature. Give reason.

Ans. Most of the combination reactions are accompanied by liberation of heat energy. This is known as exothermicity. For example, when natural gas burns in the oxygen of air, it forms carbon dioxide and water vapour. A large amount of heat is also produced.

$$\underset{\substack{\text{Methane}\\\text{(natural gas)}}}{CH_4(g)} + \underset{\substack{\text{Oxygen from}\\\text{air}}}{2O_2(g)} \longrightarrow \underset{\text{Carbon dioxide}}{CO_2(g)} + \underset{\text{Water}}{2H_2O(g)} + \text{Heat}$$

Q.12 Give an example of a combination reaction.

Ans. When magnesium ribbon burns in air, it forms magnesium oxide. This is an example of combination reaction.

$$\underset{\text{Magnesium}}{2Mg(s)} + \underset{\text{Oxygen}}{O_2(g)} \xrightarrow{\text{Combination}} \underset{\substack{\text{Magnesium}\\\text{oxide}}}{2MgO\ (s)}$$

Experiment 2(b)

AIM

To perform and observe the action of heat on ferrous sulphate crystals and classify the reaction.

Materials Required

Ferrous sulphate crystals (2g), boiling tube, test tube holder, safety glass (goggle), Bunsen burner, blue and red litmus paper strips.

Theory/Principle

A type of reaction in which a single reactant breaks into two or more simpler products is called **decomposition reaction.**

This decomposition can be brought by heat, light or electricity and the reactions are correspondingly known as thermal, photo or electric decomposition.

Example Thermal decomposition of ferrous sulphate.

Heating of Ferrous Sulphate Crystals

The ferrous sulphate crystals are actually ferrous sulphate heptahydrate ($FeSO_4 \cdot 7H_2O$). They contain seven molecules of water of crystallisation. These crystals are green in colour.

When the green coloured ferrous sulphate heptahydrate crystals ($FeSO_4 \cdot 7H_2O$) are heated, they first lose seven molecules of water of crystallisation to form anhydrous ferrous sulphate ($FeSO_4$) which is white in colour.

When this anhydrous ferrous sulphate is heated, it decomposes to give ferric oxide, sulphur dioxide and sulphur trioxide.

The reactions may be represented as:

$$\underset{\substack{\text{Hydrated ferrous} \\ \text{sulphate} \\ \text{(green)}}}{FeSO_4 \cdot 7H_2O} \xrightarrow{\text{Heat}} \underset{\text{Ferrous sulphate}}{FeSO_4(s)} + \underset{\text{Water}}{7H_2O} \qquad \text{...(i)}$$

$$\underset{\substack{\text{Ferrous sulphate} \\ \text{(light green)}}}{2FeSO_4(s)} \xrightarrow{\text{Heat}} \underset{\substack{\text{Ferric oxide} \\ \text{(brown)}}}{Fe_2O_3(s)} + \underset{\substack{\text{Sulphur dioxide} \\ \text{(colourless)}}}{SO_2(g)} + \underset{\substack{\text{Sulphur trioxide} \\ \text{(colourless)}}}{SO_3(g)} \ ] \qquad \text{...(ii)}$$

Here, $FeSO_4$ decomposes to give three products Fe_2O_3, SO_2 and SO_3 on heating.

Procedure

(i) Take about 2 g ferrous sulphate crystals in a boiling tube.

(ii) Note the colour of ferrous sulphate crystals.

(iii) Hold the boiling tube in a test tube holder.

(iv) Heat the boiling tube (as shown in Fig. 1) and observe the odour of gases evolved and colour of residue formed.

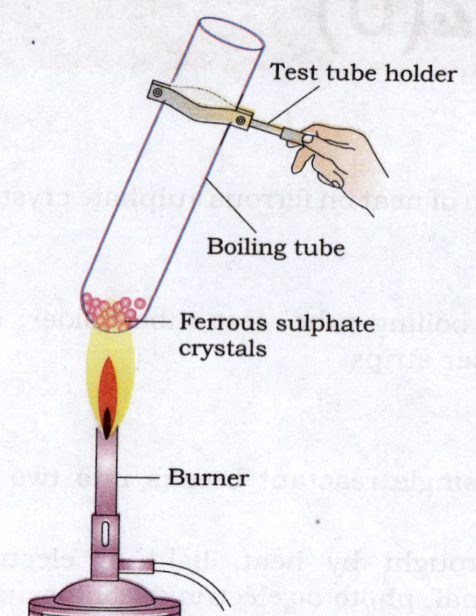

Fig. 1 Heating the ferrous sulphate crystals

(v) Steamy fumes are given out which condense to form tiny droplets of a colourless liquid at the neck of boiling tube. Test the nature of these droplets with the help of blue and red litmus paper.

(vi) Smell if any gas evolved by turning it gently towards your nose with a blow of your hand (as shown in Fig. 2).

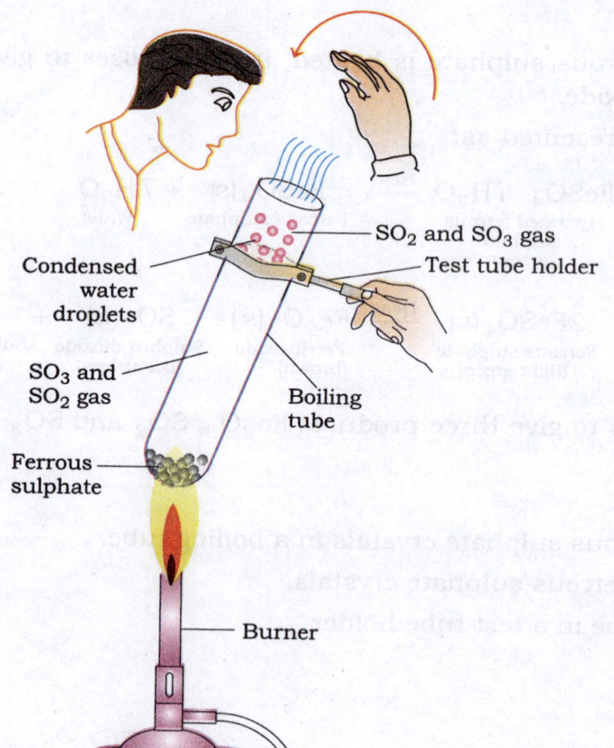

Fig. 2 Heating ferrous sulphate strongly and smelling the gas

(vii) Bring a wet blue and red litmus paper near the mouth of the boiling tube (as shown in Fig. 3) and observe the change.

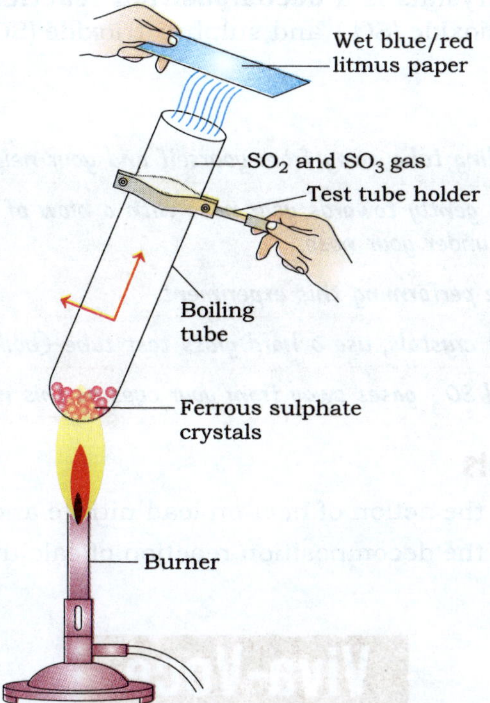

Fig. 3 Testing the nature of gas evolved

(viii) Classify the reaction.

Observations

(i) The green colour of ferrous sulphate crystals first changes to white and then a brown solid is formed (which is ferric oxide, Fe_2O_3).

(ii) Both red and blue litmus paper do not show any change in colour with tiny droplets, formed at the neck of boiling tube.

(iii) Gas having the smell of burning sulphur comes out of the boiling tube.

(iv) Moist blue litmus paper turns red when it comes in contact with evolved gas.

Inferences

- When ferrous sulphate is heated strongly, it decomposes to form ferric oxide, sulphur dioxide and sulphur trioxide, so this is a **decomposition reaction.**
- The tiny droplets, formed near the cooler parts of the boiling test tube are of water. That's why, it is neutral to red and blue litmus paper.
- Oxides of sulphur (SO_2 and SO_3) turns blue litmus paper red. Therefore, gases have acidic nature.
- The decomposition of ferrous sulphate is carried out by heating, so it is called **thermal decomposition reaction**.

Result

Heating of ferrous sulphate crystals is a **decomposition reaction** and it decomposes to give ferric oxide (Fe_2O_3), sulphur dioxide (SO_2) and sulphur trioxide (SO_3).

PRECAUTIONS

1. *Keep the mouth of the boiling tube away from yourself and your neighbour.*
2. *Smell the gas by turning it gently towards your nose with a blow of your hand and not by bringing the mouth of boiling tube under your nose.*
3. *Wear the safety glass while performing this experiment.*
4. *While heating $FeSO_4 \cdot 7H_2O$ crystals, use a hard glass test tube (boiling tube) which is perfectly dry.*
5. *Keep the fumes of SO_2 and SO_3 gases away from your eyes as this may cause irritation to the eyes.*

Suggested Experiments

1. To perform and observe the action of heat on lead nitrate and classify the reaction.
2. To perform and observe the decomposition reaction of calcium carbonate.

Viva-Voce

Q.1 What is decomposition reaction?

Ans. When a compound decomposes to give two or more simpler substances, it is a decomposition reaction. For example, when lead nitrate is heated, it decomposes as shown below:

$$\underset{\text{Lead nitrate}}{2Pb(NO_3)_2(s)} \xrightarrow{\Delta} \underset{\text{Lead oxide}}{2PbO(s)} + \underset{\text{Nitrogen dioxide}}{4NO_2(g)} + \underset{\text{Oxygen}}{O_2(g)}$$

Q.2 Write the formula of ferrous sulphate crystals.

Ans. $FeSO_4 \cdot 7H_2O$

Q.3 What is the common name of ferrous sulphate crystals?

Ans. The common name of ferrous sulphate crystals are green vitriol.

Q.4 When $FeSO_4$ crystals are strongly heated, it gives off some gases. Name these gases.

Ans. These gases are sulphur dioxide (SO_2) and sulphur trioxide (SO_3), which have suffocating smell like burning sulphur.

Q.5 The heating of ferrous sulphate ($FeSO_4 \cdot 7H_2O$) is an example of which type of reaction?

Ans. The heating of $FeSO_4 \cdot 7H_2O$ is an example of thermal decomposition reaction.

Q.6 What happens when crystals of ferrous sulphate are heated?

Ans. Ferrous sulphate crystals ($FeSO_4 \cdot 7H_2O$) lose water when heated and the colour of crystals changes. It then decomposes to ferric oxide (Fe_2O_3), sulphur dioxide (SO_2) and sulphur trioxide (SO_3). Fe_2O_3 is solid while SO_2 and SO_3 are gases.

$$\underset{\substack{\text{Ferrous sulphate}\\\text{(light green)}}}{2FeSO_4(s)} \xrightarrow{\text{Heat}} \underset{\text{Ferric oxide}}{Fe_2O_3(s)} + \underset{\substack{\text{Sulphur dioxide}\\\text{(colourless)}}}{SO_2(g)} + \underset{\text{Sulphur trioxide (colourless)}}{SO_3(g)}$$

Q.7 On heating ferrous sulphate crystals, two gases are evolved. Which gas produces fumes of sulphuric acid when it comes in contact with moist air?

Ans. Sulphur trioxide gas produces fumes of sulphuric acid when it reacts with water vapour present in the air.

Q.8 What residue is formed when hydrated ferrous sulphate crystals are heated?

Ans. The residue of ferric oxide [Iron (III) oxide] Fe_2O_3 is formed.

Q.9 Write the use of decomposition reaction.

Ans. The decomposition reactions carried out by electricity, are used to extract several metals from their naturally occurring compounds like chlorides or oxides.

Q.10 During thermal decomposition of ferrous sulphate solution, gases are produced, what is the odour of the gas?

Ans. Ferrous sulphate decomposes with the evolution of a gas having a characteristic odour of burning sulphur.

Q.11 What is the colour of the residue left in the test tube after thermal decomposition of ferrous sulphate?

Ans. Brown colour residue of ferric oxide left in the test tube after thermal decomposition of ferrous sulphate.

Q.12 Which colour of gases are produced when $FeSO_4$ crystals are strongly heated?

Ans. Colourless gases SO_2 and SO_3 are evolved.

Q 13 When $FeSO_4$ crystals are strongly heated in a test tube, what precaution should be taken and why?

Ans. When ferrous sulphate ($FeSO_4$) is heated in a test tube, precaution should be taken to ensure that the gas evolved, i.e. SO_2 should not inhaled directly because SO_2 is poisonous in nature, if one inhales this gas directly, he/she might start coughing.

Experiment 2 (c)

AIM

To perform and observe the reaction of iron nails kept in copper sulphate solution and classify the reaction.

Materials Required

Two test tubes, two iron nails, beaker, measuring cylinder, a piece of sand paper, distilled water, copper sulphate solution, thread, laboratory stand with clamp, test tube stand.

Theory/Principle

According to the **reactivity series**, a more reactive metal displaces a less reactive metal from its salt solution. Elements placed above in this series are more reactive than those placed below them.

Iron is placed above copper in the activity series, thus iron is more reactive than copper. When iron nails are placed in blue coloured copper sulphate solution, iron displaces copper from $CuSO_4$ solution to form ferrous sulphate $FeSO_4$, while the grey coloured iron nails gets covered by a brownish-red deposit of copper metal.

$$\underset{\text{Iron (grey)}}{Fe\ (s)} + \underset{\substack{\text{Copper sulphate} \\ \text{(blue)}}}{CuSO_4\ (aq)} \longrightarrow \underset{\substack{\text{Iron (II) sulphate} \\ \text{(light green)}}}{FeSO_4\ (aq)} + \underset{\substack{\text{Copper} \\ \text{(brownish red)}}}{Cu\ (s)}$$

In this reaction, since highly reactive metal displaces lower reactive metal from its compound thus, it is called a **single displacement reaction.** In the reaction between iron and copper sulphate, metallic iron is converted into ferrous iron (Fe^{2+}) and cupric ion (Cu^{2+}) is converted into metallic copper.

$$\underset{\text{Iron}}{Fe\ (s)} + \underset{\text{Copper ion}}{Cu^{2+} (aq)} \longrightarrow \underset{\text{Ferrous ion}}{Fe^{2+} (aq)} + \underset{\text{Copper}}{Cu\ (s)}$$

Procedure

(i) Take two iron nails and clean them with a sand paper.

(ii) Take 20 mL of distilled water in a clean test tube and dissolve 1.0 g of copper sulphate crystals in it. Add 2 or 3 drops of dil. sulphuric acid to it to check hydrolysis of $CuSO_4$ in water. Label this test tube as *A*.

(iii) Transfer about 10 mL of copper sulphate solution from test tube *A* to another clean test tube. Label this test tube as *B*.

(iv) Take one iron nail tied with a thread and immerse it carefully in copper sulphate solution in test tube *A* for about 15 min [as shown in Fig.1]. Keep the another iron nail separately for comparison afterwards.

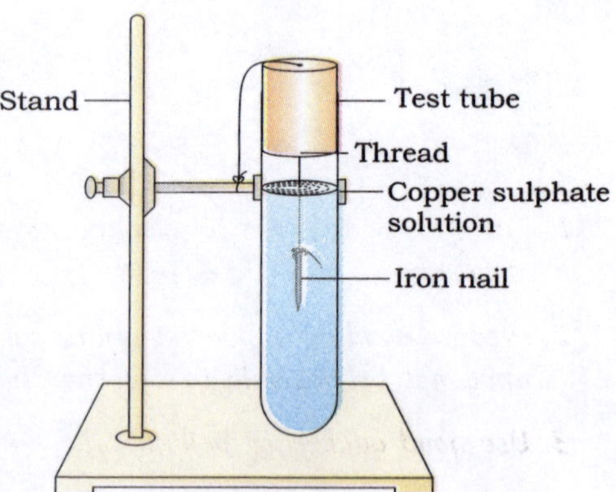

Fig. 1 Iron nails dipped in copper sulphate solution

(v) After 15 minutes, take out the iron nail from the copper sulphate solution.

(vi) Compare the intensity of blue colour of copper sulphate solution before and after the experiments in test tubes *A* and *B* and also compare the colour of iron nail dipped in copper sulphate solution with the one kept separately [Fig. 2]. Record your observations.

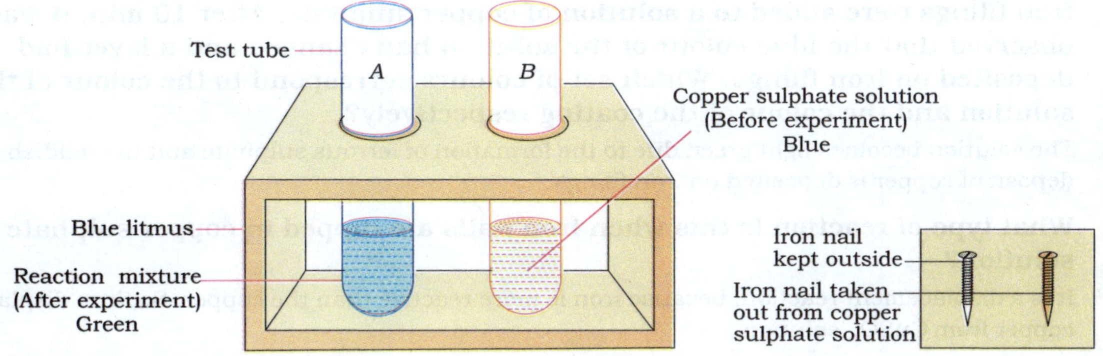

Fig. 2 Iron nails and copper sulphate solutions are compared

Observation Table

S. No.	Property	Before experiment	After experiment
1.	Colour of copper sulphate solution		
2.	Colour of iron nail		

Result

The initial colour of copper sulphate solution in the test tube is blue and iron nails are silvery grey. After being dipped in copper sulphate solution for about 15 min, the blue colour of copper sulphate solution turns light green and the surface of iron nails get covered with brownish red coating.

It is a **displacement reaction** as iron displaces copper from the copper sulphate solution to form copper and ferrous sulphate.

$$\underset{\text{Iron (grey)}}{Fe\,(s)} + \underset{\text{Copper sulphate(blue)}}{CuSO_4\,(aq)} \longrightarrow \underset{\text{Iron (II) sulphate light green}}{FeSO_4\,(aq)} + \underset{\text{Copper (brownish red)}}{Cu\,(s)}$$

PRECAUTIONS

1. *The iron nails must be cleaned properly by using sand paper before dipping them in copper sulphate solution.*
2. *Prepare a dilute copper sulphate solution in distilled water. If it is a concentrated solution, then it may not be possible to see the change its colour after the experiment.*
3. *Use good quality of boiling tube.*

Suggested Experiments

1. To study the chemical reaction and write the observation when a strip of zinc metal is placed in copper sulphate solution.
2. To perform and observe the reaction between a piece of magnesium metal kept in copper sulphate solution and classify it.

Viva-Voce

Q.1 Iron filings were added to a solution of copper sulphate. After 10 min, it was observed that the blue colour of the solution had changed and a layer had deposited on iron filings. Which set of colours correspond to the colour of the solution and the colour of the coating respectively?

Ans. The solution becomes light green due to the formation of ferrous sulphate and the reddish colour deposit of copper is deposited on iron filings.

Q.2 What type of reaction is this when iron nails are dipped in copper sulphate solution?

Ans. It is a displacement reaction, because iron is more reactive than the copper. So, iron displaces copper from $CuSO_4$ solution.

Q.3 Which metal gives reddish brown deposit on iron nails when dipped in copper sulphate solutions?

Ans. Copper metal (Cu) gives reddish brown deposit on iron nails.

Q.4 What is the correct procedure to show that iron is more reactive than copper?

Ans. To show that iron is more reactive than copper, first prepare the copper sulphate solution and dip iron nail in it.

Q.5 Why do displacement reaction occur?

Ans. Displacement reaction occurs due to the difference in reactivities of the elements.

Q.6 What is reactivity series of metal?

Ans. A series of metals in decreasing order of reactivities is called reactivity series of metals.

Q.7 If we add silver metal in copper sulphate solution, then write the observation.

Ans. No change is observed because silver being less reactive than copper is unable to displace copper from copper sulphate solution.

Q.8 What is the other name given to reaction that take place between iron metal and copper sulphate solution?

Ans. The reaction is also known as redox reaction (oxidation reduction reaction).
Because iron metal has been oxidised to Fe^{2+} ion, whereas Cu^{2+} ion has been reduced to copper metal.

Q.9 What happens when copper is added to zinc sulphate solution?

Ans. No reaction will take place as copper does not displace zinc because it is less reactive than zinc.

Q.10 In a series of reactions among metals *A*, *B*, *C* and *D* if *A* displaced *C*, *B* displaced *A* and *C* displaced *D*, then write the metals in the decreasing order of reactivity.

Ans. $B > A > C > D$

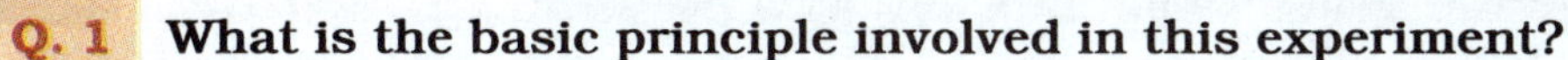

Questions From NCERT Lab Manual

Q. 1 What is the basic principle involved in this experiment?

Ans. The principle involved in this experiment is that a more reactive metal can displace a less reactive metal from its salt solution.

Q. 2 Why does the colour of copper sulphate solution change, when an iron nail is dipped in it?

Ans. Iron is more reactive than copper and hence, displaces it from its salt solution and form a new coloured compound.

$$\underset{\text{Iron}}{Fe\,(s)} + \underset{\substack{\text{Copper sulphate}\\\text{(blue)}}}{CuSO_4(aq)} \longrightarrow \underset{\substack{\text{Iron (II) sulphate}\\\text{(Pale green)}}}{FeSO_4\,(aq)} + \underset{\text{Copper}}{Cu\,(s)}$$

Q. 3 How would you devise the procedure to show that Mg > Fe > Cu in reactivity series?

Ans. Take ferrous sulphate solution in a beaker and add magnesium in it. Keep it undisturbed for about 5-10 min. Observe the change and draw conclusion. Now, take copper sulphate solution in another beaker and dip iron nail in it for 15 min. Observe the change. Since, magnesium can displace iron, it is more reactive than iron and again iron can displace copper, it is more reactive than copper.

Q. 4 Why does the following reaction takes place?

$$\underset{\text{Iodide (ion)}}{2I^-(aq)} + \underset{\text{Chlorine}}{Cl_2\,(aq)} \xrightarrow{CCl_4\,\text{(Carbon tetrachloride)}} \underset{\text{Chloride (ion)}}{2Cl^-(aq)} + \underset{\text{Iodine}}{I_2}\ \ (solvated)$$

Ans. This reaction takes place because chlorine is more reactive than iodine.

Experiment 2 (d)

AIM

To perform and observe the reaction between sodium sulphate and barium chloride solutions and classify the reaction.

Materials Required

Two test tubes, test tube stand, a conical flask, a glass rod, sodium sulphate solution, measuring cylinder and barium chloride solution.

Theory/Principle

Those reactions in which two ionic compounds in the solution react by exchange of their ions to form new compounds are called **double displacement reactions**.

The ionic compounds taken as reactants, are soluble in water. However, one of the products formed is either insoluble and separates out as a solid, called **precipitate** or it is a gas and other product is soluble in the solution.

When a solution of sodium sulphate is mixed with a solution of barium chloride, the following double displacement reaction takes place

$$\underset{\text{Sodium sulphate}}{Na_2SO_4(aq)} + \underset{\text{Barium chloride}}{BaCl_2(aq)} \longrightarrow \underset{\substack{\text{Barium sulphate}\\\text{(white ppt.)}}}{BaSO_4(s)} + \underset{\text{Sodium chloride}}{2NaCl(aq)}$$

In this reaction, sulphate ions (SO_4^{2-}) from sodium sulphate are displaced by chloride ions (Cl^-) and chloride ions from barium chloride are displaced by sulphate ions.

As a result, a white precipitate of barium sulphate is formed and sodium chloride remains in the solution.

Procedure

(i) Take two clean test tubes and label them as *A* and *B*.

(ii) In test tube *A*, take the solution of barium chloride (5 mL) and observe the colour of the solution.

(iii) In test tube *B*, take the solution of sodium sulphate (5 mL) and observe the colour of the solution (as shown in Fig. 1).

(iv) Transfer carefully the solutions of test tubes *A* and *B* in a conical flask (as shown in Fig. 2).

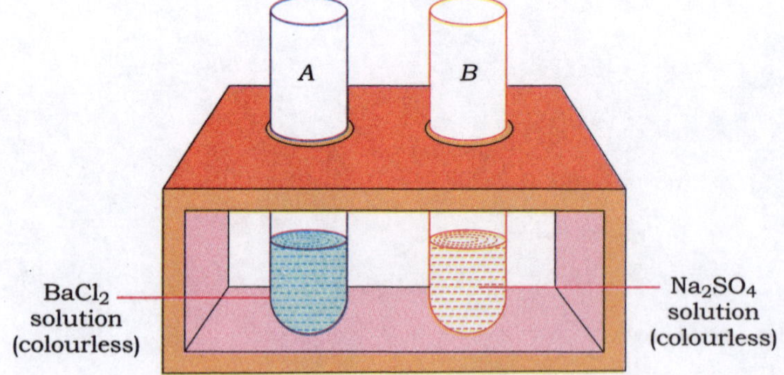

Fig. 1 Reaction mixtures before the reaction

(v) Stir the two solutions by using glass rod and leave it undisturbed for sometime.

(vi) Observe the change in colour of the solutions as per the steps given in observation table ahead.

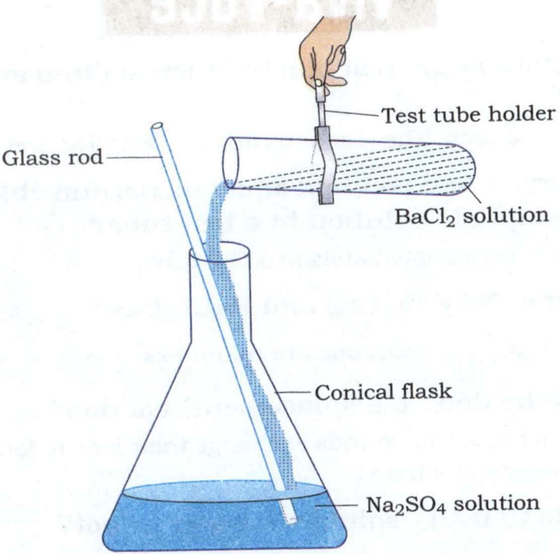

Fig. 2 Mixing of solutions of test tubes A and B

Observation Table

S.No.	Experiment	Observations
1.	Observe the colours of both solutions in test tubes *A* and *B* before mixing them.	
2.	Mix both the solutions and leave the mixture undisturbed for sometime. Does anything precipitates in the test tube? If so, what is the colour of it?	

Result

Solutions of sodium sulphate and barium chloride both are colourless. On mixing the solution of sodium sulphate and barium chloride, a white precipitate is formed. This reaction is an example of a double displacement reaction, as two different salt solutions have exchanged ions to form two new salts, i.e. barium sulphate (white ppt.) and sodium chloride.

PRECAUTIONS

1. *Test tubes, beaker and glass rod should be cleaned.*
2. *Equal volume of sodium sulphate and barium chloride solution should be used.*
3. *Add barium chloride solution very slowly to the sodium sulphate solution and stir with a glass rod.*
4. *Do not touch or taste the chemicals.*
5. *Do not fill more than one-third of the test tube with sodium sulphate solution.*

Suggested Experiments

1. To perform and observe the reaction between lead nitrate [$Pb(NO_3)_2$] and potassium chloride (KCl) solutions and classify it.
2. To perform and observe the reaction between silver nitrate ($AgNO_3$) and sodium chloride (NaCl) solutions and classify it.

Viva-Voce

Q. 1 What type of reaction is the reaction between sodium sulphate and barium chloride?

Ans. Double displacement reaction. The reaction can also be called precipitation reaction.

Q. 2 What do you observe when you mix aqueous barium chloride solution with aqueous sodium sulphate solution in a test tube?

Ans. A white precipitate is formed immediately in a test tube.

Q. 3 What is the colour of $Na_2SO_2(aq)$ and $BaCl_2(aq)$?

Ans. Both $Na_2SO_4(aq)$ and $BaCl_2(aq)$ solutions are colourless.

Q. 4 What do you mean by double displacement reaction?

Ans. Those reactions in which two compounds exchange their ions to form insoluble compound, are called double displacement reactions.

Q. 5 Is barium sulphate $(BaSO)_4$ soluble in water or not?

Ans. No, $BaSO_4$ is insoluble in water.

Q. 6 Give an example (other than given in experiment) of a double displacement reaction.

Ans. The reaction between silver nitrate and sodium chloride is also a double displacement reaction.

$$\underset{\text{Silver nitrate}}{AgNO_3(aq)} + \underset{\text{Sodium chloride}}{NaCl\,(aq)} \longrightarrow \underset{\text{Silver chloride (white ppt)}}{AgCl\,(s)} + \underset{\text{Sodium nitrate}}{NaNO_3(aq)}$$

Q. 7 What is the colour of barium sulphate precipitate?

Ans. The colour of barium sulphate precipitate is white.

Q. 8 Why is the reaction between barium chloride and sodium sulphate is called double displacement reaction?

Ans. Because in this reaction, both barium chloride and sodium sulphate exchange their ions and forms new compounds.

Q. 9 State one commercial use of barium sulphate.

Ans. Barium sulphate is used as a white pigment in paint industry.

Q.10 Out of dil. HCl, dil. H_2SO_4 and dil. HNO_3, in which acid, barium sulphate is soluble?

Ans. Barium sulphate is not soluble in any of the above acids.

Q.11 What would happen if dil. HCl is added to lead acetate $(CH_3COO)_2Pb$?

$$\underset{\text{Lead acetate}}{(CH_3COO)_2Pb(s)} + \underset{\text{Hydrochloric acid}}{2HCl\,(aq)} \longrightarrow \underset{\text{Lead chloride}}{PbCl_2(s)} + \underset{\text{Acetic acid}}{2CH_3COOH\,(aq)}$$

Ans. A white precipitate of $PbCl_2$ will be formed.

Questions From NCERT Lab Manual

Q. 1 What may happen on mixing $Pb(NO_3)_2$ and KCl solutions ? Predict (you may try to experimentally verify).

Ans. White precipitate of lead chloride ($PbCl_2$) will be formed on mixing $Pb(NO_3)_2$ and KCl solutions.

$$\underset{\text{Lead nitrate}}{Pb(NO_3)_2(aq)} + \underset{\text{Potassium chloride}}{2KCl(aq)} \longrightarrow \underset{\text{Lead chloride}}{PbCl_2(s)} + \underset{\text{Potassium nitrate}}{2KNO_3(aq)}$$

Note : You may verify this reaction experimentally by taking 5 mL of lead nitrate, ($Pb(NO_3)_2$ solution and 5 mL of Potassium chloride, (KCl) solution and follow the same procedure as given in the above experiment [2(d)].

Q. 2 Fill in the blanks

(a) Sodium sulphate and barium chloride are .... (ionic/covalent) compounds.

(b) As the white precipitate of barium sulphate is formed............. (immediately/sometime after mixing the two solutions), the reaction between .... (ionic/covalent) compounds is .... (instantaneous/slow).

Ans. (a) Ionic

(b) Immediately, ionic, instantaneous

Q. 3 What are the industrial applications of the type of reaction being studied?

Ans. Double displacement reaction is used for making compounds used in paints.

Q. 4 Why do the persons suffering from the ailment of stone formation advised not to take too much milk and tomato juice?

Ans. It is because milk contains calcium and tomato has oxalate ions which form stones.

Practical Based MCQs

For Experiments 2(a), 2(b), 2(c) and 2 (d)

Q. 1 The reaction between calcium oxide and water is known as

(a) combination reaction

(b) decomposition reaction

(c) displacement reaction

(d) double displacement reaction

Q. 2 On passing CO_2 gas through the product formed by the reaction between CaO and H_2O, solution becomes

(a) red (b) pink (c) black (d) white

Q. 3 Which of the following information about the reaction of CaO with water is not true?

(a) CaO reacts with water vigorously.

(b) During the reaction, the test tube becomes hot.

(c) CaO reacts with water to form slaked lime.

(d) During the reaction, the test tube becomes cold.

Q. 4 On heating ferrous sulphate in a test tube, it undergoes

(a) combination reaction

(b) decomposition reaction

(c) displacement reaction

(d) double displacement reaction

Q. 5 **Four groups of students were assigned separately the experiment of interaction of iron nail with a solution of copper sulphate. Each group recorded the observations as given below in the table. Which group of students recorded all the observations correctly?**

Group of students	Initial colour of solution	Final colour of solution	Change in the iron nail
A	Blue	Colourless	Grey coat
B	Green	Green	Brown coat
C	Blue	Blue	Brown coat
D	Blue	Light green	Brown coat

(a) *A* (b) *B* (c) *C* (d) *D*

Q. 6 **What type of reaction occurs, when zinc granules are dipped in copper sulphate solution?**

(a) Combination reaction (b) Decomposition reaction
(c) Displacement reaction (d) Double displacement reaction

Q. 7 **Which of the following represents a combination reaction?**

(a) Reaction of zinc metal with copper sulphate solution.
(b) Heating of lead nitrate.
(c) Reaction between silver nitrate and sodium chloride.
(d) Burning of magnesium in air.

Q. 8 **Which of the following represents the reaction between barium chloride and sodium sulphate correctly?**

(a) $NaSO_4 + BaCl \longrightarrow BaSO_4 + NaCl$
(b) $Na_2SO_4 + BaCl \longrightarrow BaSO_4 + NaCl$
(c) $Na_2SO_4 + BaCl_2 \longrightarrow BaSO_4 + 2NaCl$
(d) $NaSO_4 + BaCl \longrightarrow BaSO_4 + 2NaCl$

Q. 9 **Four students were asked to study the reaction between barium chloride and sodium sulphate. They reported their experiments as follows. Which one is a correct report?**

(a) On mixing the powder of barium chloride and sodium sulphate, the colour of the mixture changes to brown.
(b) On adding powdered sodium sulphate to barium chloride solution, solution becomes white.
(c) On adding the powder of barium chloride to sodium sulphate solution, solution turns white.
(d) On mixing solution of barium chloride and sodium sulphate, white solid substance is formed.

Answers

1. (a)	2. (d)	3. (d)	4. (b)	5. (d)	6. (c)	7. (d)	8. (c)	9. (d)

Experiment 3

AIM

(a) To observe the action of Zn, Fe, Cu and Al metals on the following salt solutions:

(i) $ZnSO_4(aq)$ (ii) $FeSO_4(aq)$ (iii) $CuSO_4(aq)$ (iv) $Al_2(SO_4)_3(aq)$

(b) To arrange Zn, Fe, Cu and Al (metals) in the decreasing order of reactivity based on the above results.

Materials Required

Aluminium foil, copper turnings, zinc granules, iron filings, ferrous sulphate solution, copper sulphate solution, zinc sulphate solution, aluminium sulphate solution, test tubes, test tube stand and four beakers of 50 mL.

Theory/Principle

Different metals have different reactivities towards chemical reagents. Some metals are more reactive than others. The metals, which can lose electron more readily to form positive ions are more reactive.

According to the reactivity series (or activity series) of metals, a more reactive metal displaces a less reactive metal from its aqueous salt solution. These reactions are called **displacement reactions.**

Displacement reactions can be used to find out the relative reactivities of metals.

Example If a piece of zinc metal is dipped in a solution of copper sulphate, zinc will displace copper from copper sulphate. The blue colour of copper sulphate solution will gradually fade and finally colourless solution of zinc sulphate will be obtained.

$$\underset{\text{Zinc}}{Zn(s)} + \underset{\substack{\text{Copper sulphate}\\ \text{solution (blue)}}}{CuSO_4(aq)} \longrightarrow \underset{\substack{\text{Zinc sulphate}\\ \text{solution colourless}}}{ZnSO_4(aq)} + \underset{\substack{\text{Copper}\\ \text{reddish brown}}}{Cu(s)}$$

It means that zinc has displaced copper from copper sulphate solution, i.e. zinc is more reactive than copper.

- Al can displace Zn, Fe, Cu from their salt solutions, therefore it is more reactive than Zn, Fe and Cu.

$$\underset{\text{Aluminium}}{2Al(s)} + \underset{\text{Zinc sulphate}}{3ZnSO_4(aq)} \longrightarrow \underset{\text{Aluminium sulphate}}{Al_2(SO_4)_3} + \underset{\text{Zinc}}{3Zn(s)}$$

$$\underset{\text{Aluminium}}{2Al(s)} + \underset{\text{Iron (II) sulphate}}{3FeSO_4(aq)} \longrightarrow \underset{\text{Aluminium sulphate}}{Al_2(SO_4)_3} + \underset{\text{Iron}}{3Fe(s)}$$

$$\underset{\text{Aluminium}}{2Al(s)} + \underset{\text{Copper (II) sulphate}}{3CuSO_4(aq)} \longrightarrow \underset{\text{Aluminium sulphate}}{Al_2(SO_4)_3} + \underset{\text{Copper}}{3Cu(s)}$$

- Zn can displace Fe and Cu from their salt solutions, therefore zinc is more reactive than Fe and Cu.

$$\underset{\text{Zinc}}{Zn(s)} + \underset{\text{Copper (II) sulphate}}{CuSO_4(aq)} \longrightarrow \underset{\text{Zinc sulphate}}{ZnSO_4(aq)} + \underset{\text{Copper}}{Cu(s)}$$

$$\underset{\text{Zinc}}{Zn(s)} + \underset{\text{Iron (II) sulphate}}{FeSO_4(aq)} \longrightarrow \underset{\text{Zinc sulphate}}{ZnSO_4(aq)} + \underset{\text{Iron}}{Fe(s)}$$

$$\underset{\text{Zinc}}{Zn(s)} + \underset{\text{Aluminium sulphate}}{Al_2(SO_4)_3(aq)} \longrightarrow \text{No reaction}$$

$$\underset{\text{Zinc}}{Zn(s)} + \underset{\text{Zinc sulphate}}{ZnSO_4(aq)} \longrightarrow \text{No reaction}$$

- Fe can displace copper from copper sulphate solution, therefore it is more reactive than copper.

$$\underset{\text{Iron}}{Fe(s)} + \underset{\text{Copper (II) sulphate}}{CuSO_4(aq)} \longrightarrow \underset{\text{Iron (II) sulphate}}{FeSO_4(aq)} + \underset{\text{Copper}}{Cu(s)}$$

$$\underset{\text{Iron}}{Fe(s)} + \underset{\text{Zinc sulphate}}{ZnSO_4(aq)} \longrightarrow \text{No reaction}$$

$$\underset{\text{Iron}}{Fe(s)} + \underset{\text{Iron (II) sulphate}}{FeSO_4(aq)} \longrightarrow \text{No reaction}$$

$$\underset{\text{Iron}}{Fe(s)} + \underset{\text{Aluminium sulphate}}{Al_2(SO_4)_3(aq)} \longrightarrow \text{No reaction}$$

- Cu cannot displace any of the above given metals from their salt solutions, therefore it is least reactive than the other given metals.
- No reaction takes place when any of the metals copper, iron, zinc and aluminium are placed in aqueous aluminium sulphate solution. From this, it can be concluded that aluminium is the most reactive and copper is the least reactive among the given four metals (Fe, Zn, Cu and Al). Thus, the decreasing order of reactivity of metals is

S. No.	Name and formulas	Colours
1.	Zinc sulphate ($ZnSO_4$)	Colourless
2.	Ferrous sulphate ($FeSO_4$)	Light green
3.	Copper sulphate ($CuSO_4$)	Blue
4.	Aluminium sulphate [$Al_2(SO_4)_3$]	Colourless
5.	Aluminium (Al)	White
6.	Iron (Fe)	Blackish grey
7.	Copper (Cu)	Reddish brown
8.	Zinc (Zn)	Silvery white (greyish)

$$Al > Zn > Fe > Cu$$

Metals and their aqueous salt solutions exhibit colours as follows

Procedure

(i) Prepare 50 mL solutions of 5% concentration (by volume) of zinc sulphate, iron(II) sulphate, copper(II) sulphate and aluminium sulphate in distilled water in four different beakers. Label these beakers as *P*, *Q*, *R* and *S* (as shown in Fig. 1).

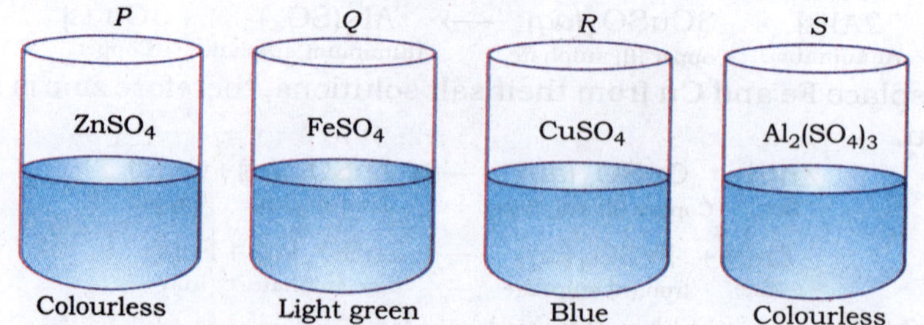

Fig. 1 Saturated aqueous solutions of $ZnSO_4$, $FeSO_4$, $CuSO_4$ and $Al_2(SO_4)_3$

(ii) Take about 10 mL of saturated solution of zinc sulphate ($ZnSO_4$), ferrous sulphate ($FeSO_4$), copper sulphate ($CuSO_4$) and aluminium sulphate [$Al_2(SO_4)_3$] in the respective test tubes (as shown in Fig. 2). Observe the colour of the solutions.

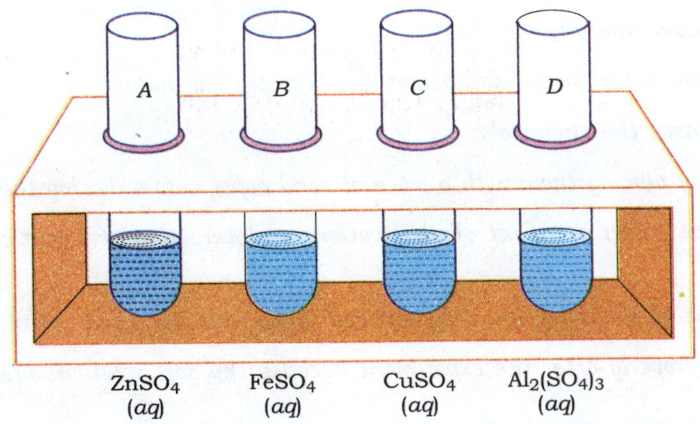

Fig. 2. Observation of colour of the solutions

(iii) Take zinc, copper, iron and aluminium metal strips and clean their surfaces with a sand paper.

(iv) Put zinc metal strip in all the four test tubes *A, B, C* and *D* and observe the change that follows.

(v) Repeat the above experiment with other metal strips by dipping them in fresh salt solutions of metals and record the observations for displacement reactions in the tabular form.

Observation Table

Metal strips	$FeSO_4$	$ZnSO_4$	$CuSO_4$	$Al_2(SO_4)_3$
Fe	—	No reaction	Displacement	No reaction
Zn	Displacement	—	Displacement	No reaction
Cu	No reaction	No reaction	No reaction	No reaction
Al	Displacement	Displacement	Displacement	—

Results

A. The action of metals on respective salt solutions are given below:

(i) Al metal is able to displace Zn, Fe and Cu from their salt solutions and therefore, Al is most reactive.

(ii) Zn metal is able to displace Fe and Cu from their salt solutions and therefore, Zn is more reactive than Fe and Cu.

(iii) Fe metal is able to displace Cu from its salt solution and therefore, Fe is more reactive than copper.

(iv) Cu is unable to displace any metal (among Al, Fe and Zn) from their salt solutions and therefore, Cu is least reactive.

B. The decreasing order of reactivity, based on the above results, follows the order

$$Al > Zn > Fe > Cu$$

PRECAUTIONS

1. *All the apparatus should be clean and dry.*
2. *Handle the chemicals carefully.*
3. *Some reactions may occur slowly, so observe the changes carefully.*
4. *Do not touch or taste the chemicals.*
5. *Clean the metals by rubbing them with a piece of sand paper before dipping them in the salt solutions.*
6. *Wash the test tubes after every set of observations of interaction of a particular metal with the four salt solutions.*
7. *For the preparation of solutions, use only distilled water and add small quantity of sulphuric acid.*
8. *Clean your hands properly after the experiment because the salt solutions are poisonous.*

Suggested Experiments

1. Observe the action of dilute hydrochloric acid on zinc and copper metals. Arrange them according to their reactivity.
2. To observe the action of lead metal, if it is placed in copper chloride solution. Observe the change and write the chemical reaction also.

Viva-Voce

Q. 1 When an aluminium strip is kept immersed in freshly prepared ferrous sulphate solution taken in a test tube, what change would you observe?

Ans. The light green colour of the solution turns colourless due to the displacement reaction.

Q. 2 Solutions of copper sulphate, iron sulphate and zinc sulphate are prepared and marked I, II and III respectively. Few pieces of aluminium are added to each solution. In which test tube would you see a change?

Ans. In all the three solutions, changes occur. Aluminium displaces all the other metals from their salt solution.

Q. 3 What does the reactivity series of metals indicate?

Ans. The reactivity series of metals indicates the reactivities of different metals in decreasing order while going from top to bottom.

Q. 4 Can we store $ZnSO_4$ in an aluminium container? Justify your answer.

Ans. No, we cannot store $ZnSO_4$ in an aluminium container because Al is more reactive than Zn.

Q. 5 A strip of copper was placed in a beaker containing zinc sulphate solution. On observing the strip next day, what was noticed by student?

Ans. On observing the strip next day, student may observe that the copper strip remained same as copper is less reactive than zinc.

Q. 6 Iron filings were added to an aqueous solution of copper sulphate. After sometime of observation it was found that the colour of the solution has changed. What change in colour is observed?

Ans. The colour of the solution has changed from blue to yellowish green as the formed iron sulphate imparts pale green colour to the solution.

Q. 7 **A thin plate of zinc metal is placed in a beaker containing aqueous ferrous sulphate solution. The zinc plate is taken out after 15 min. What change in colour of the solution is observed?**

Ans. The solution becomes colourless.

Q. 8 **Can we store copper sulphate solution in an iron container? Give reason for your answer.**

Ans. No, we cannot store copper sulphate solution in an iron container because iron is more reactive than copper therefore, it will displace copper from copper sulphate solution.

Q. 9 **Why do copper pieces not react with $FeSO_4$ solution in water?**

Ans. Copper metal is less reactive than iron in the activity series.

Q.10 **Why does blue colour of the $CuSO_4$ solution fade away on stirring with an iron rod?**

Ans. Iron being more reactive displaces copper from $CuSO_4$ solution. The deep blue colour of $CuSO_4$ fades due to the formation of light green solution of iron sulphate.

Questions From NCERT Lab Manual

Q. 1 **Name any two metals that are more reactive than iron?**

Ans. Aluminium and Zinc

Q. 2 **In the following reaction, *A* and *B* are metals and *BX* is a salt of metal *B*:**

$$A + BX \longrightarrow AX + B$$

Which one of the two metals is more reactive? Give reason.

Ans. *A* is more reactive as it displaces *B* from its salt solution *BX*.

Q. 3 **Why did the colour of copper (II) sulphate solution change, when zinc metal was dipped in it?**

Ans. Zinc is more reactive than copper, so it displaces Cu from $CuSO_4$ solution and blue colour of $CuSO_4$ turns to colourless due to the formation of $ZnSO_4$.

Q. 4 **What is your observation when copper is added to iron (II) sulphate solution?**

Ans. When copper is added to iron (II) sulphate solution, then no reaction takes place because copper is less reactive than iron.

Q. 5 **Why can we safely preserve iron (II) sulphate in a copper vessel whereas the same cannot be safely preserved in zinc vessel?**

Ans. Since, copper is less reactive than iron so, we can safely preserve iron (II) sulphate in a copper vessel. But zinc is more reactive than iron, so we cannot safely preserve iron (II) sulphate in zinc vessel.

Practical Based MCQs

Q. 1 A student puts one big iron nail each in four test tubes containing solutions of zinc sulphate, aluminium sulphate, copper sulphate and iron sulphate. A reddish brown coating was observed only on the surface of iron nail, which was put in the solution of

(a) zinc sulphate
(b) iron sulphate
(c) copper sulphate
(d) aluminium sulphate

Q. 2 Which one of the following statement is not correct for the following reaction?

$$\underset{\text{Copper}}{Cu(s)} + \underset{\text{Zinc sulphate}}{ZnSO_4(aq)} \longrightarrow \underset{\text{Copper sulphate}}{CuSO_4(aq)} + \underset{\text{Zinc}}{Zn(s)}$$

(a) This reaction does not occur.
(b) Zn is more reactive than Cu.
(c) The colourless solution is $ZnSO_4$.
(d) Zn is less reactive than Cu.

Q. 3 A more reactive metal displaces a less reactive metal from the aqueous solution of the latter. From the following sets tell which one represents a correct picture of both the possible (✓) reactions and impossible (✗) reactions between metals and the solutions of different salts?

Metal	$Al_2(SO_4)_3$	$CuSO_4$	$FeSO_4$	$ZnSO_4$
Al	✗	✓	✓	✓
Cu	✓	✗	✗	✗
Fe	✓	✓	✗	✗
Zn	✗	✓	✗	✓

(a) Al
(b) Cu
(c) Fe
(d) Zn

Q. 4 Zinc pieces were placed in each of the four test tubes containing different salt solutions as shown below :

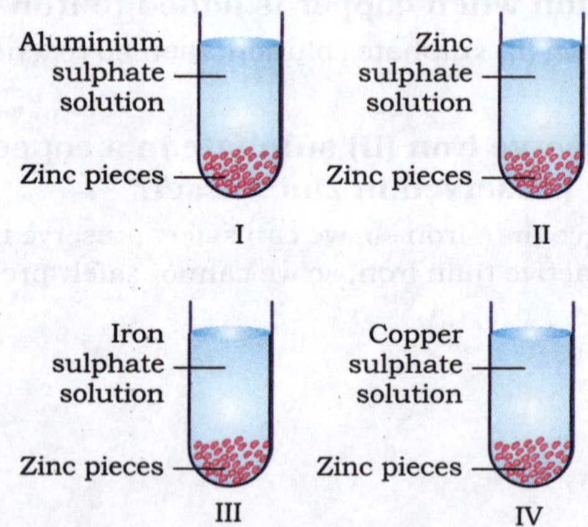

In which solutions change in colour would be observed?

(a) Both I and II
(b) Both I and III
(c) Both III and IV
(d) Both I and IV

Q. 5 **Students in a lab were assigned the experiment to study the reaction of Zn with $FeSO_4$ solution. The following set of observations were obtained. Identify the set, where all the observations were correct.**

Set	Initial colour of solution	Final colour of solution	Deposits if any
(a)	Colourless	Pale green	Black
(b)	Pale green	Colourless	Black
(c)	Colourless	Colourless	Red
(d)	Pale green	Blue	Black

Q. 6 **Aluminium sulphate and copper sulphate solutions were taken in two test tubes I and II, respectively. A few pieces of iron filings were then added to both the solutions. The four students *A, B, C* and *D* recorded their observations in the form of a table as given.**

Students	Aluminium sulphate solutions (I)	Copper sulphate solutions (II)
A	Colourless solution changes to light green.	Blue colour of the solution is retained.
B	Colourless solution does not change.	Blue colour of the solution changes to green.
C	Colourless solution changes to light blue.	Blue colour of the solution changes to green.
D	Colourless solution remains unchanged.	Blue colour of the solution fades away.

The correct set of observations have been recorded by student

(a) *A* (b) *B* (c) *C* (d) *D*

Q. 7 **Iron nails were dipped in a solution kept in a test tube. After half hour, it was observed that the colour of the solution had changed. The solution in the test tube was that of**

(a) zinc sulphate (b) copper sulphate
(c) iron sulphate (d) aluminium sulphate

Answers

1. (c)	2. (d)	3. (a)	4. (c)	5. (b)	6. (b)	7. (b)

Experiment 4

AIM

To study the dependence of potential difference (*V*) across a resistor on the current (*I*) passing through it and determine its resistance. Also, plot a graph between *V* and *I*.

Materials Required

A voltmeter and ammeter of suitable range, (fixed or known resistance) some connecting wires, a key, a dry cell (or battery eliminator), a rheostat (variable resistor) and a piece of sand paper.

Theory/Principle

Ohm's Law

According to Ohm's law, the potential difference (*V*) across the ends of a resistor is directly proportional to the current (*I*) through it provided its temperature remains the same.

i.e. $V \propto I$ or $\frac{V}{I} = \text{Constant} = R$ or $V = RI$

Here, *R* is a constant for the given resistor at a given temperature and is called its **resistance**. The SI unit of resistance is ohm (Ω).

The graph between the potential difference across the two ends of a resistor and the current passing through it is a straight line passing through the origin. The slope of this straight line graph gives the resistance *R* of the resistor.

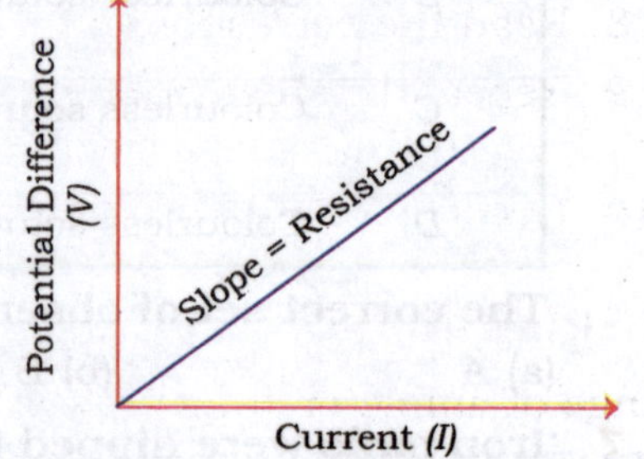

V-I Graph for an ohmic conductor.

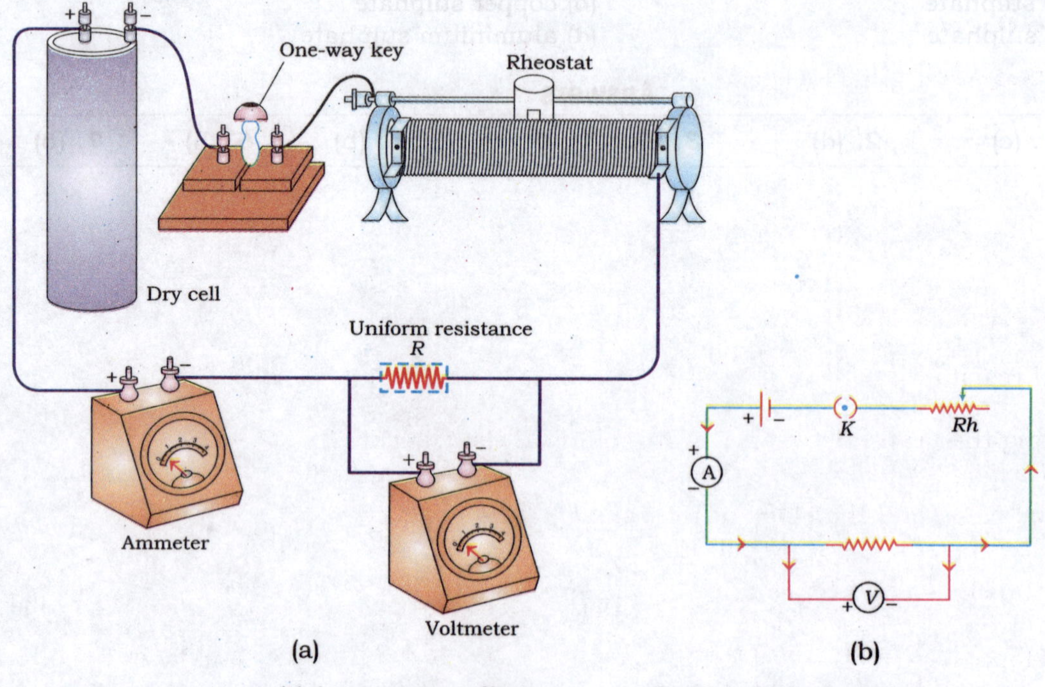

(a) (b)

Fig.1 (a) Arrangement diagram (b) Circuit diagram

Procedure

1. Before starting the experiment, note down the range, least count and zero error (if any) of the ammeter and voltmeter.
2. Wipe the ends of the connecting wires with sand paper to remove any insulating layer.
3. Connect the battery, resistor, ammeter, voltmeter, key and rheostat a shown in the figure 1(a).
4. Connect the key, the rheostat, the ammeter and the resistor in series with the connecting wires to the dry cell, as shown in the circuit diagram [Fig. 1(b)]. Ensure that positive (+) terminal of ammeter connected to the positive (+) terminal of the cell. Make neat and tight connections.
5. Connect the voltmeter in parallel with the resistor, as shown in circuit diagram. Ensure that the positive (+) terminal of the voltmeter is connected to the positive (+) terminal of the cell, and the negative (–) terminal of the voltmeter is connected to the negative (–) terminal of the cell.
6. Insert the key to allow current to flow through the circuit.
7. Adjust the rheostat, so that a small current passes through the resistor, say 0.1 A, so the reading of ammeter will be 0.1 A.
8. Read the corresponding values of potential difference from voltmeter.
9. Repeat the steps by adjusting the slider, for the values of current 0.3 A, 0.4 A, 0.5 A etc. and record the matching values of potential difference in voltmeter.
10. Lastly, plot a graph between *V* and *I* taking *V* along *Y*-axis and *I* along *X*-axis.

Observations

Range of ammeter = ... A
Least count of ammeter = ... A
Zero error of ammeter = ... A
Range of voltmeter = ... V
Least count of voltmeter = ... V
Zero error of voltmeter = ... V

S.No.	Reading of voltmeter, *V* (volt)		Reading of ammeter, *I* (ampere)		Resistance, $R = \frac{V}{I}$ (ohm)
	Observed	Corrected	Observed	Corrected	
1.					R_1 =
2.					R_2 =
3.					R_3 =

Calculations and Graph

$$\text{Mean value of resistance} = \frac{R_1 + R_2 + R_3 + R_4}{4} = ...\Omega$$

Now, by plotting the graph between *V* and *I* taking *V* along *Y*-axis and *I* along *X*-axis.

We get a straight line and the slope of *V versus I* graph gives the resistance of the resistor (as shown in Fig. 2).

i.e. $$\tan\theta = \frac{V}{I} = R = \text{Resistance}$$

$$\Rightarrow \quad \text{Slope} = \frac{BC}{AC} = \frac{V_2 - V_1}{I_2 - I_1} = R$$

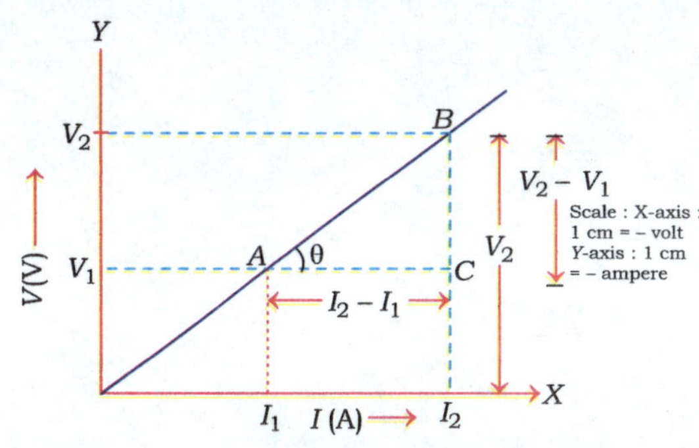

Fig. 2. *V versus I*

Results

1. The current may have flowed through the circuit for a longer period than intended. The value of resistance of the given wire was found to be approximately .... Ω. The ratio V/I remained nearly constant for different sets of the readings thus Ohm's low verified.
2. From the above calculation and observation, we have concluded that for a resistor, if temperature remains constant then current through the resistor is directly proportional to the potential difference applied across it.

PRECAUTIONS

1. *Wires should be thick and the insulation at their ends should be properly removed.*
2. *All the connections should be tight otherwise external resistance may be introduce into the circuit.*
3. *The ammeter must be connected in series with the circuit.*
4. *The voltmeter must be connected in parallel with the circuit.*
5. *The zero mark of both the ammeter and voltmeter should be checked properly.*
6. *Ensure tight connections of connecting wires.*
7. *Insert the plug key only when a reading is to be taken, and remove it immediately afterward to avoid unnecessary heating of the wires.*
8. *The positive terminals of the voltmeter and ammeter should be connected to positive terminal of the cell and vice-versa.*

Sources of Error

1. There may be a reading error of ammeter or voltmeter.
2. The cross-section area of the wire may not be uniform.
3. There may be a loose connection in the electrical circuit.

Suggested Experiments

1. Perform a similar experiment to study the dependence of current (I) on the potential difference (V) across a resistor, using a lead accumulator.
2. Perform the same experiment to verify Ohm's law using different arrangements of cells.

Viva-Voce

Q. 1 What do you mean by a battery eliminator?

Ans. A device which is used in place of battery or cells, is known as a battery eliminator.

Q. 2 What are the necessary conditions for current flow through the conductor?

Ans. There are two such conditions:

(i) There must be a closed circuit.

(ii) There must be a source of electrical energy.

Q. 3 Can a resistor store energy?

Ans. No, it only opposes or controls the flow of current.

Q. 4 Can you explain why there is no current in the circuit, if plug is removed?

Ans. As we know, air gap gives infinite resistance to the circuit. So, if the plug is removed, there will be no current in the circuit.

Q. 5 What do you understand by the term 'resistance' of a conductor?

Ans. The resistance of conductor is the property that opposes the flow of electric current through it.

Q. 6 What do you understand by the term 'emf of a cell'?

Ans. The maximum potential difference which exists across the terminals of a cell when no current is drawn out of the cell is called emf (electromotive force) of a cell.

Q. 7 What happens to resistance when thickness of wire increase?

Ans. When the thickness (i.e., the cross-sectional area) of wire increases, the resistance decrease.

Q. 8 Can resistance ever be negative?

Ans. No, resistance can never be negative for ordinary conductor.

Q. 9 Does the specific resistance of a wire depend upon the dimensions of the wire?

Ans. No, the specific resistance depends upon

(i) the nature of material of the wire and

(ii) temperature.

Questions From NCERT Lab Manual

Q. 1 **In this experiment, it is advised to take out the key from the plug when the observations are not being taken. Why?**

Ans. To avoid the unnecessary heating of wires. Heating may change the resistance of resistor.

Q. 2 **Suppose the ammeter (or voltmeter) you are using in this experiment do not have positive (+) and negative (–) terminal markings. How will you use such ammeter (or voltmeter) in the circuit?**

Ans. First of all, we connect ammeter or voltmeter arbitrary in the circuit, if deflection occurs in opposite direction. It means the connection is not proper. Now, by interchanging the terminals, we can use it in the circuit.

Q. 3 **If the resistor of known resistance value is replaced with a nichrome wire of 10 cm length. How do the values of current through the nichrome wire may change? How the values will change, if the replaced wire is of manganin in place of nichrome?**

Ans. Nichrome wire offers more resistance, so value of current decreases. As, manganin offers less resistance than nichrome, so value of current increases for the same value of potential difference.

Q. 4 **Suppose in this experiment, you see that the deflection on ammeter (or voltmeter) scale goes beyond the full scale. What will you infer from such an observation? What will you infer, if the deflection takes place in opposite direction?**

Ans. If the deflection goes beyond full scale, a higher range of ammeter is required for the circuit. Deflection in opposite direction indicates that terminal has not been joined properly and it should be reversed.

Q. 5 **Why is it advised to clean the ends of connecting wires before connecting them?**

Ans. Ends of wire should be cleaned to remove the insulation (or insulating layer) of dust particles since, presence of insulation (which is a non-conducting material) will not allow current to flow in the circuit.

Practical Based MCQs

Q. 1 **In Ohm's law experiment, the physical quantity/quantities which is/are to be kept constant while doing experiment is/are**

(a) potential difference
(b) current
(c) temperature
(d) potential difference, current and temperature

Q. 2 **The rheostat is used in the circuit to**

(a) increase the magnitude of the current
(b) decrease the magnitude of the current
(c) increase or decrease the magnitude of the current
(d) change the current in the resistor without changing the potential difference across its two ends

Q. 3 **In an Ohm's law experiment, a student plots a graph of voltage (V) *versus*. current (I) and finds a straight line that does not pass through the origin. What could be the most likely reason?**

(a) The resistor is ideal and the reading is accurate.
(b) The voltmeter has zero error.
(c) There is a contact resistance or zero error in instruments.
(d) The resistance of wire changes with temperature.

Q. 4 **A student notices that as current increases, the wire gets hot. What impact does this have on Ohm's Law?**

(a) Resistance stays the same
(b) Current keeps increasing uniformly
(c) Resistance may increase, violating Ohm's Law
(d) Voltage becomes zero

Q. 5 **In this experiment, it is advised to take out the key from the plug when the observations are not being taken. It is, so**

(a) because the resistance of wire increases with the decrease in temperature
(b) because the resistance decreases with the increase in temperature
(c) to avoid unnecessary heating of wire
(d) to allow current flowing for a longer period

Q. 6 **A student connects an ammeter in parallel instead of in series during an Ohm's law experiment. What is most likely to happen?**

(a) The current increases in the circuit
(b) The reading becomes more accurate
(c) The ammeter may get damaged
(d) The circuit will not complete

Q. 7 **What will happen to the current passing through a conductor, if potential difference across it is doubled and the resistance is halved?**

(a) Remains unchanged
(b) Becomes double
(c) Becomes half
(d) Becomes four times

Q. 8 **The correct method to connect the ammeter and voltmeter with resistance in the circuit to verify Ohm's law is**

(a) ammeter and voltmeter in series
(b) ammeter and voltmeter in parallel
(c) ammeter in series and voltmeter in parallel
(d) ammeter in parallel and voltmeter in series

Answers

1. (c)	2. (c)	3. (b)	4. (d)	5. (c)	6. (b)	7. (d)	8. (c)

Experiment 5 (a)

AIM

To determine the equivalent resistance of two resistors when connected in series combination.

Materials Required

Two standard resistance coils (or resistors), ammeter (0-1.5 A), voltmeter (0-1.5 V), one-way plug key switch, rheostat (variable resistor), connecting wires, sand paper and cell or battery eliminator.

Theory/Principle

When two or more resistors are connected end-to-end such that there is only one path for the electric current to flow, the combination is said to be in series.

In a series connection

The same current flows through all the resistors. The total voltage across the combination is equal to the sum of the voltages across individual resistors.

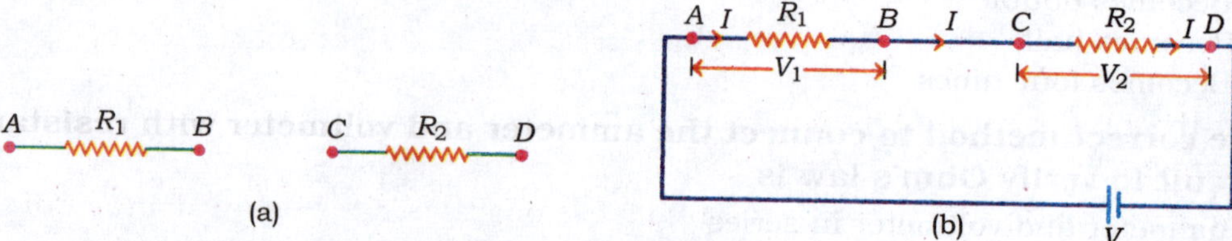

Fig.1 Two resistors *AB* and *CD* are placed one after the other

If V_1 and V_2 be the potential differences measured by the voltmeter across each resistor, then

$$V = V_1 + V_2 \quad \text{...(i)}$$

According to Ohm's law,

$$V_1 = IR_1,\ V_2 = IR_2$$

and

$$V = IR_s \quad \text{...(ii)}$$

where, R_s = Equivalent resistance of R_1 and R_2 in series combination.

From Eqs. (i) and (ii), we get

$$IR_s = IR_1 + IR_2$$

$$\Rightarrow \quad R_s = R_1 + R_2$$

Thus, the equivalent resistance of the series combination is equal to the sum of the individual resistances connected in the series circuit.

Procedure

1. Draw a neat circuit diagram as shown in the below figure 2(b).
2. Clean the ends of connecting wires using a sand paper.
3. Connect all components as shown in the figure 2(b).
4. Adjust the rheostat to vary the current.
5. Note the least count and the zero error (if any) of the given ammeter and voltmeter.
6. Use Ohm's law to calculate the resistance each time.

6. Connect the resistor in series as shown in block diagram or circuit diagram given in Fig. 2(b).

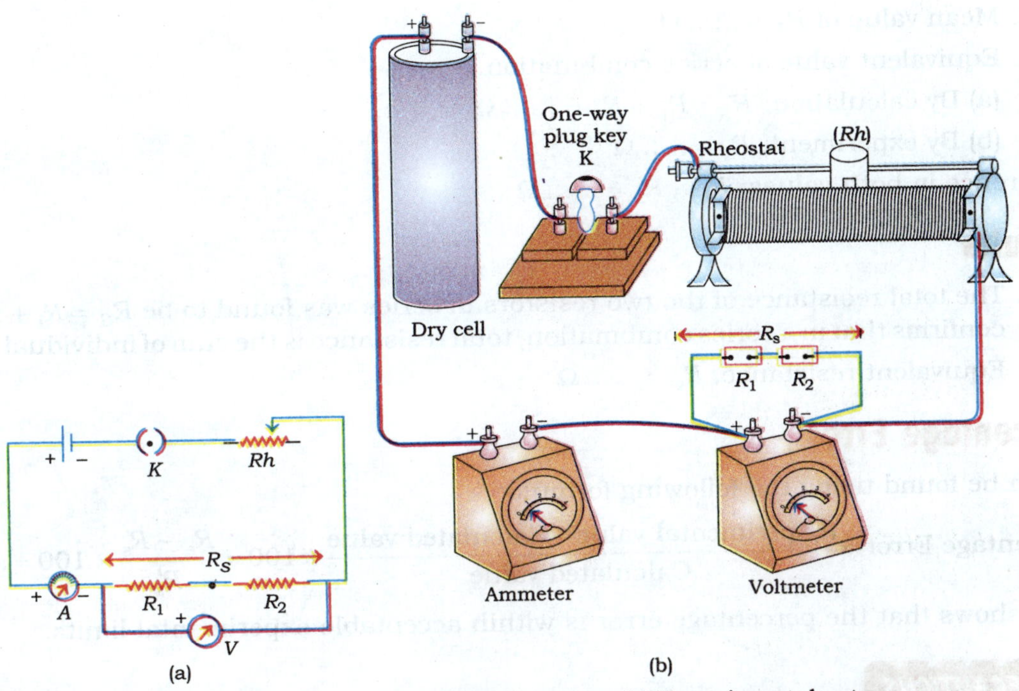

Fig.2 (a) Circuit diagram of resistors in series (b) Experimental setup

7. Insert the plug into the key and take the readings of ammeter and voltmeter (as done in Experiment 4).
8. Repeat the step 7 three times by changing the position of the sliding contact of the rheostat (as done in Experiment 4).
9. Record the readings and calculate the ratio of V and I this will give the equivalent resistance of the series combination.

Observations

1. Least count of ammeter = ... A
2. Zero error of ammeter = ... A
3. Least count of voltmeter = ... V
4. Zero error of voltmeter = ... V
5. Zero correction in ammeter reading = ... A
6. Zero correction in voltmeter reading = ... V

Resistor used	Observations	Voltmeter reading (volt)	Ammeter reading (ampere)	$R = \frac{V}{I}$ (ohm)	Mean value of resistance (ohm)
R_1	(a)				
	(b)				
	(c)				
R_2	(a)				
	(b)				
	(c)				
$R_s = R_1 + R_2$	(a)				
	(b)				
	(c)				

Calculations

1. Mean value of R_1 = ... Ω
2. Mean value of R_2 = ... Ω
3. Equivalent value of series combination,
   (a) By calculation, $R'_s = R_1 + R_2$ = ... Ω
   (b) By experiment, R_s = ...Ω

Difference in both values, $R_s - R'_s$ = ... Ω

Results

1. The total resistance of the two resistors in series was found to be $R_S = R_1 + R_2$ =...Ω. This confirms that in a series combination, total resistance is the sum of individual resistances.
2. Equivalent resistance, R_s = ... Ω

Percentage Error

It can be found using the following formula:

$$\text{Percentage Error} = \frac{\text{Experimental value} - \text{Calculated value}}{\text{Calculated value}} \times 100 = \frac{R_s - R'_s}{R'_s} \times 100 = \text{...........} \%$$

This shows that the percentage error is within acceptable experimental limits.

PRECAUTIONS

1. *Remove dust and insulating particles from the ends of connecting wires using Sand paper.*
2. *Ensure all connections are tight and properly made as per the circuit diagram.*
3. *Remove the plug from the one-way key between two observations.*
4. *Use a low-resistance rheostat to allow large variations in current.*
5. *Use thick copper connecting wires in the circuit.*
6. *Connect the positive terminals of the ammeter and voltmeter to the positive terminal of the battery or battery eliminator.*
7. *Never connect the two terminals of the cell directly without any resistance.*

Sources of Error

1. Observational errors may occur while reading the ammeter or voltmeter pointer.
2. Thick connecting wires might not be available during the experiment.
3. The cross-sectional area of resistance wire may not be uniform along its length.
4. A high-resistance rheostat may be mistakenly used.
5. Current may be allowed to flow for too long during observation.
6. Terminal screw of instruments may not be tightened properly.

Suggested Experiments

1. Take two bulbs, one fused and the other in working condition. Connect them in a series combination and also to a power source. Check whether the second (non-defective) bulb glows or not.
2. Try to find the resultant resistance of two resistor 3 Ω and 5 Ω connected in series analyse the result.

Viva-Voce

Q. 1 Two resistors in series show no voltage drop across one of them. What can you say about that resistor?

Ans. It must have zero resistance (i.e., behaves like a conductor), or it is short-circuited.

Q. 2 What is the relationship between voltage (V) and resistance (R) in a series combination?

Ans. In a series combination, the voltage is directly proportional to the resistance.

Q. 3 What happens to the resistance of the resistor, if the current through it increases?

Ans. It remains unchanged because the resistance does not depend on the current flowing through it.

Q. 4 When two unequal resistors are connected in series, what is the potential difference across each?

Ans. The potential difference across each resistor will be different, depending on its resistance.

Q. 5 What happens to the ammeter reading if two resistors of equal value are connected in series?

Ans. The deflection in ammeter will reduce.

Q. 6 Why does resistance increase in a series combination?

Ans. In a series combination, the total length of the path for current increases. Since resistance is directly proportional to length, the total resistance increases.

Q. 7 If one of the resistors in a series circuit is removed, what happens to the current in the circuit?

Ans. The circuit becomes open, so the current becomes zero - no current flows.

Q. 8 Why is the series combination not preferred in household wiring?

Ans. Because if one device fails (breaks the circuit), the current stops for all other device.

Q. 9 Why should current be passed through the circuit for a short time while taking observations?

Ans. Passing current for a long time may cause heating, which can alter the resistance of the resistors and affect the accuracy of the experiment.

Questions From NCERT Lab Manual

Q. 1 If two resistors having resistances of 2Ω and 4Ω, respectively are connected in a series combination in an electric circuit, what will be the net resistance in the circuit?

Ans. According to series combination, $R_{net} = R_1 + R_2$

$$\Rightarrow \quad R_{net} = (2 + 4)\,\Omega \quad \Rightarrow \quad R_{net} = 6\,\Omega \qquad \left[\because \begin{matrix} R_1 = 2\,\Omega \\ R_2 = 4\,\Omega \end{matrix}\right]$$

Q. 2 In an electric circuit, a resistor of 5Ω resistance is connected to a battery (5 V), through an ammeter and a plug key. Now in this circuit, an another resistor of 10 Ω is connected in series with the 5Ω resistor. Will there be any change in the ammeter reading? How much?

Ans. Resistors are added in series, therefore there will be a change in the current.

$$I_1 = \frac{V}{R} = \frac{5}{5} = 1\text{ A} \quad \text{and} \quad I_2 = \frac{V}{R_1 + R_2} = \frac{5}{10 + 5} = \frac{1}{3}\text{ A}$$

Therefore, change in ammeter reading will be from 1 A to 0.33 A.

Q. 3 In the above question, what is the potential difference across two ends of the resistor of 5 Ω resistance, when it is alone in the circuit? What is the potential difference across the two ends of resistor of 5 Ω resistance, when it is connected in series with the resistor of 10 Ω resistance? What is the potential difference across the series combination?

Ans. Consider V_1 be the potential difference across two ends of the resistor of 5 Ω resistance, when it is connected alone.

$$\Rightarrow \quad V_1 = I_1 R = 1 \times 5 = 5\text{ V}$$

Consider V_2 be the potential difference across two ends of resistor of 5 Ω resistance, when it is connected to 10 Ω resistor in series.

$$\Rightarrow \quad V_2 = I_2 R = \frac{1}{3} \times 5 = \frac{5}{3}\text{ V}$$

Potential difference across the series combination is $V_3 = I_2 R_s = \frac{1}{3} \times (5 + 10) = \frac{1}{3} \times 15 = 5\text{V}$

The potential difference across series combination is equal to applied potential difference.

Experiment 5 (b)

AIM

To determine the equivalent resistance of two resistors when connected in parallel combination.

Materials Required

Two standard resistance coils (or resistors), ammeter (0-1.5 A), voltmeter (0-1.5 V), one-way key, a low resistance rheostat, connecting wires, a piece of sand paper and cell or battery eliminator.

Theory/Principle

A parallel combination of resistors is an arrangement in which two or more resistors are connected between two common points such that the potential difference across each resistor is the same.

As shown in figure, two resistors with resistances R_1 and R_2 are connected in paraller two points A and B. Let the potential difference applied by the DC source a cross the this combination be V.

Let I_1 and I_2 be the currents measured by an ammeter connected in series with each resistor R_1 and R_2

then $$I = I_1 + I_2 \quad \text{...(i)}$$

According to Ohm's law, $$I_1 = \frac{V}{R_1} \quad \text{and} \quad I_2 = \frac{V}{R_2} \quad \text{... (ii)}$$

If R_p be the equivalent resistance of the parallel combination,

then $$I = \frac{V}{R_p} \quad \text{...(iii)}$$

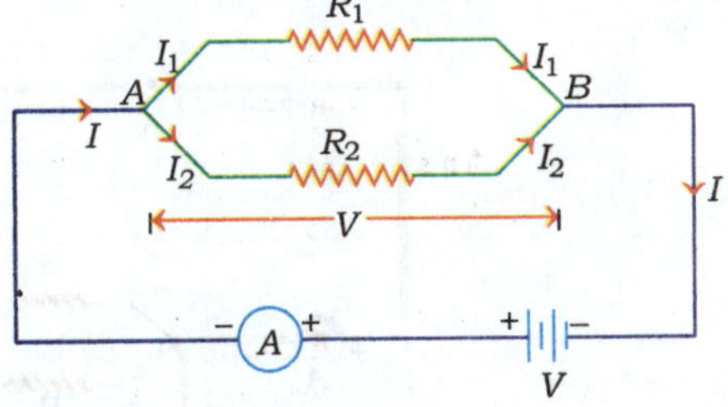

Fig. 1. Two resistors are connected in a parallel combination

From Eqs. (i), (ii) and (iii), we get

$$\frac{V}{R_p} = \frac{V}{R_1} + \frac{V}{R_2} \quad \text{or} \quad \frac{1}{R_p} = \frac{1}{R_1} + \frac{1}{R_2}$$

or $$R_p = \frac{R_1 R_2}{R_1 + R_2}$$

This shows that for resistor in parallel, the reciprocal of the equivalent resistance is equal to the sum of the reciprocals of the individual resistances.

Procedure

1. Draw a neat and clean circuit diagram as shown in Fig. 2 or Fig. 3 (a).
2. Clean the ends of connecting wires using sand paper.
3. Note down the least count and zero error (if any) of the given ammeter and voltmeter.
4. Adjust the rheostat to vary the current.

5. Find the values of two given resistances R_1 and R_2 by the procedure given in Experiment 4.

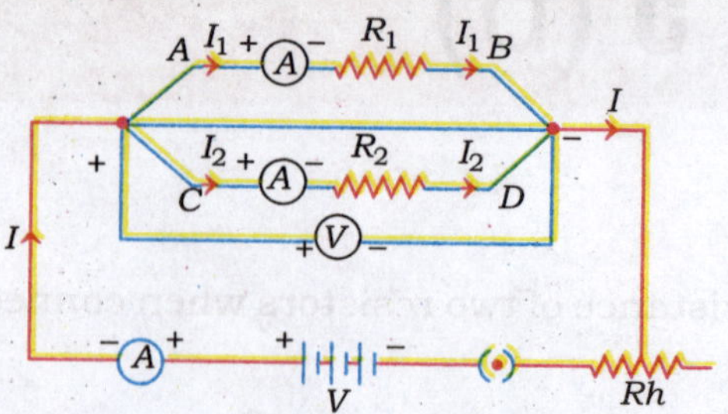

Fig. 2 Parallel combination

6. Use Ohm's law to calculate the resistance each time.
7. Connect the given resistors in parallel combination between the terminals of the voltmeter (as shown in Fig. 3).

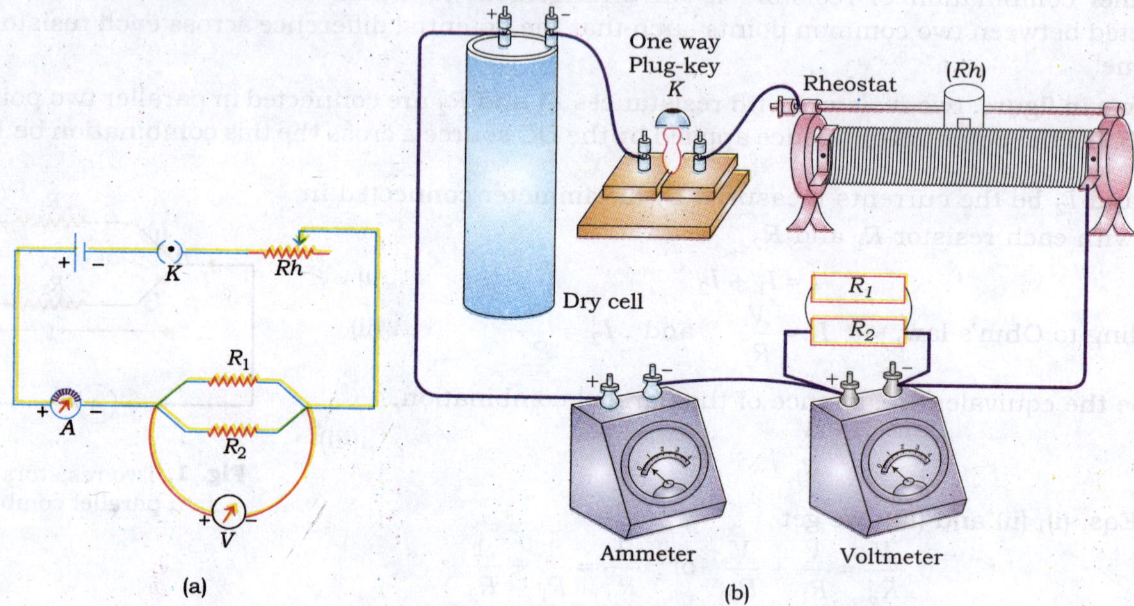

Fig. 3 (a) Circuit diagram for resistors in parallel (b) Experimental setup

8. Insert the plug into the key to complete the circuit and take the readings of both the ammeter and voltmeter following the same procedure used in.
9. Repeat the measurement process at least three times. Each times change the position of the sliding contact on the reheostat to vary the current in the circuit.
10. Record all the readings and calculate the ratio of V and I. This ratio will give the equivalent resistance of the parallel combination.

Observations

1. Least count of ammeter = ...A
2. Zero error of ammeter = ...A
3. Least count of voltmeter =......... V
4. Zero error of voltmeter = ... V
5. Zero correction in ammeter reading = ... A
6. Zero correction in voltmeter reading = ... V

Resistor used	Observations	Voltmeter reading (volt)	Ammeter reading (ampere)	$R=\frac{V}{I}$ (ohm)	Mean value of resistance (ohm)
R_1	(a) (b) (c)				
R_2	(a) (b) (c)				
$R_p = \frac{R_1 R_2}{R_1 + R_2}$	(a) (b) (c)				

Calculations

1. Mean value of R_1 = ...Ω
2. Mean value of R_2 = ...Ω

   Equivalent value of parallel combination,

   (a) By calculations, $R'_p = \frac{R_1 R_2}{R_1 + R_2}$ = ...Ω

   (b) By experiment, R_p = ...Ω

Results

1. The equivalent resistance of parallel combination, R_p =..........Ω.
2. There is close agreement between the calculated value and the value obtained by the experiment. Hence , $\frac{1}{R_p} = \frac{1}{R_1} + \frac{1}{R_2}$ is verified.

Percentage Error

It can be found by using the following relation

$$\text{Percentage error} = \frac{\text{Experimental value} - \text{Calculated value}}{\text{Calculated value}} \times 100$$

$$= \frac{R_p - R'_p}{R'_p} \times 100 = ...\%$$

It shows that percentage error is within the experimental error.

PRECAUTIONS

1. *It is to be properly checked that ammeter is connected in series and voltmeter is connected in parallel.*
2. *The connecting wires should be thick and must have tight connection at the joints.*
3. *The ends of connecting wires should be cleaned properly using sand paper.*
4. *The ammeter and voltmeter should be of appropriate range and have suitable least count.*
5. *The current should be passed for very short time, otherwise heating effect may alter the actual result.*

Sources of Error

1. Reading errors may occur while observing the pointer of the ammeter and voltmeter.
2. The cross-sectional area of the resistance wire may not be uniform along the entire length.
3. A high resistance rheostat might be used, which could affect the results.
4. Current may be allowed to flow through the circuit for a longer duration than required.
5. The terminal screws of the instruments may not be properly tightened.

Suggested Experiments

1. **You are given two wires** of known area of cross-section and length. Perform an activity to determine out the equivalent resistance, when they are connected between two common points.
2. Perform an activity to demonstrate that whether the intensity of the bulb's glow decreases or increases, when two resistors of resistance 2 Ω are connected in parallel at the junction *AB*, in the given electrical circuit.

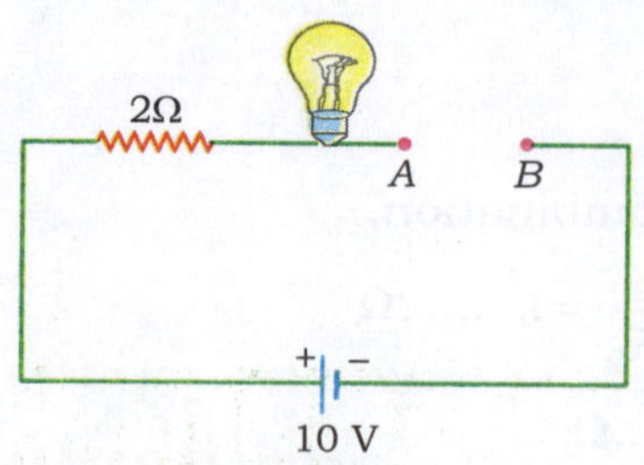

Viva-Voce

Q. 1 State the law for the equivalent resistance, when resistors are connected in parallel combination.

Ans. This law states that the reciprocal of equivalent resistance is equal to the sum of the reciprocal of individual resistances.

Q. 2 Why does a bulb glow brighter in a parallel circuit than in series, even if the same battery is used?

Ans. Because in parallel, each bulb gets full voltage; in series, voltage is divided.

Q. 3 What is the ratio in which current divides itself in the parallel combination?

Ans. The current divides itself in the inverse ratio of resistance in parallel combination (i.e. $I \propto \frac{1}{R}$).

Q. 4 Can you explain why voltmeter is connected in parallel across the conductor?

Ans. It is connected in parallel across the conductor to measure the maximum potential drop.

Q. 5 If the resistance of one branch in a parallel circuit becomes infinite, how does it affect the parallel resistance?

Ans. The total resistance increases, but current still flows through other branches.

Q. 6 Name the quantity which remains same in parallel combination of resistors.

Ans. In parallel combination of resistors, voltage (V) remains same.

Q. 7 State some disadvantages of parallel circuit.

Ans. (i) As one fuse controls all light, fans, and other electric appliances of a single room, circuit all of them will be put off when the fuse blow off.

(ii) It is difficult to install a new circuit for new installation of electrical appliances.

Q. 8 If two resistors of resistances R_1 and R_2 respectively are connected in parallel, how will you find the equivalent resistance?

Ans. If two resistors of resistances R_1 and R_2 respectively are connected in parallel, then equivalent resistance can be given as $\frac{1}{R_p} = \frac{1}{R_1} + \frac{1}{R_2}$

Q. 9 Suppose in a combination, we find that the equivalent resistance is smaller than the smallest resistance used in the circuit. Which type of combination is present in the circuit?

Ans. It is a parallel combination.

Q.10 What is the effect of temperature on the value of resistance of a conductor?

Ans. The resistance of conductor increases with increase in temperature.

Q.11 Can we use a low-resistance ammeter in parallel? Why or why not?

Ans. No, a low-resistance ammeter in parallel creates a short circuit, drawing huge current and damaging the device.

Questions From NCERT Lab Manual

Q. 1 If two resistors having resistances of 3 Ω and 6 Ω respectively are connected in parallel, what will be the net resistance in the circuit?

Ans. The net resistance or equivalent resistance of the circuit is given by

$$R_{eq} = \frac{R_1 R_2}{R_1 + R_2} = \frac{3 \times 6}{9} = 2\,\Omega$$

Q. 2 Two resistors having resistances of 4 Ω and 6 Ω respectively are connected in a circuit. It was found that the total resistance in the circuit is less than 4 Ω . In what way, the resistances would have been connected?

Ans. As we know that, for parallel combination, net resistance is less than that of individual resistance. So, they are connected in parallel with each other.

Q. 3 Two resistors are connected in series and then in parallel. What effect will it have on the readings of voltmeter and ammeter?

Ans. As the applied voltage remains same, so there will be no change in the reading of voltmeter. Ammeter reading will be less in case of series and more in case of parallel.

Q. 4 In what way, household appliances should be connected?

Ans. Household appliances must be connected in parallel.

Practical Based MCQs

For Experiments 5(a) and 5 (b)

Q. 1 **While doing the experiment, on finding the equivalent resistance of two resistors connected in series, three students *A, B* and *C* set up their circuits as shown below.**

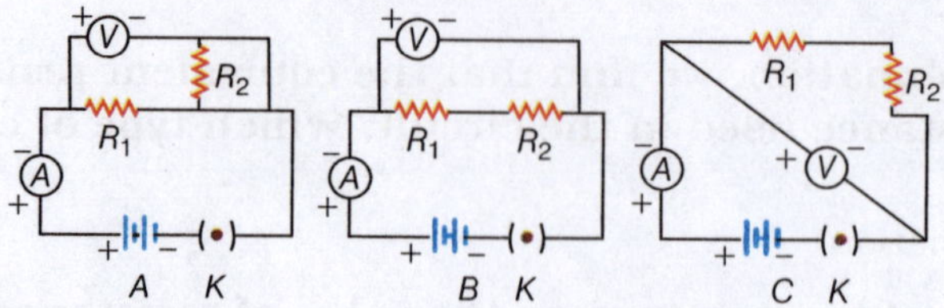

The correct set up is that of

(a) *A* and *B* (b) *B* and *C* (c) *C* and *A* (d) All the three students

Q. 2 **Which is most correct about the readings of ammeters A_1, A_2 and A_3 connected in the following circuit (currents reading are shown by I_1, I_2 and I_3, respectively)?**

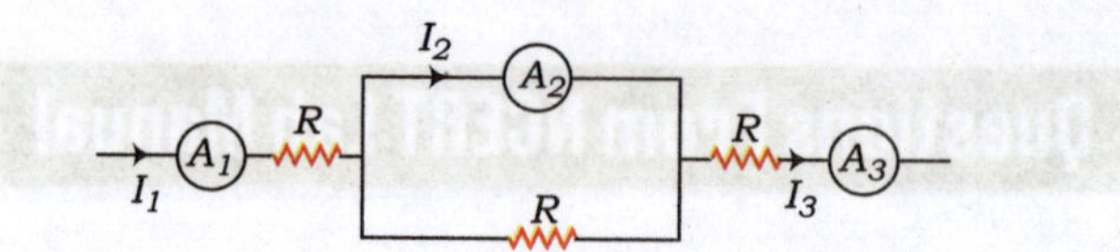

(a) $I_1 < I_2$ (b) $I_3 < I_2$
(c) $I_1 = I_2 = I_3$ (d) $I_1 = I_3$

Q 3 **Two students set up their circuits for finding the equivalent resistance of two resistors connected in series in two different ways as shown in figure.**

The circuit (s) likely to be labelled as incorrect

(a) are neither of the two circuits
(b) is only circuit I
(c) is only circuit II
(d) are both the circuits

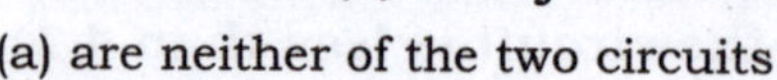

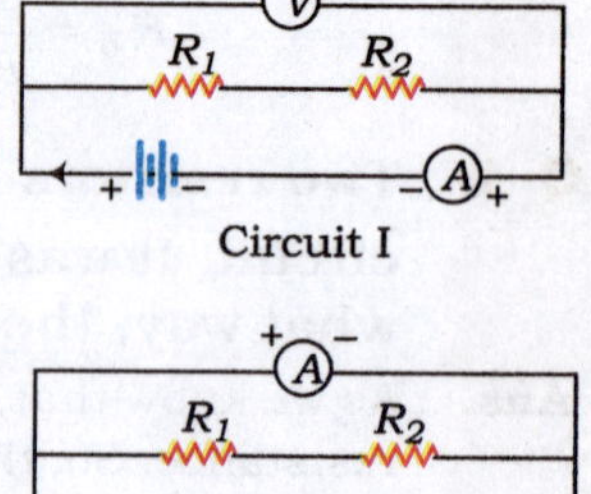

Q. 4 **The diagram shows a network of four resistors which is connected to an electric source. Identify the resistors which are connected in series in this network.**

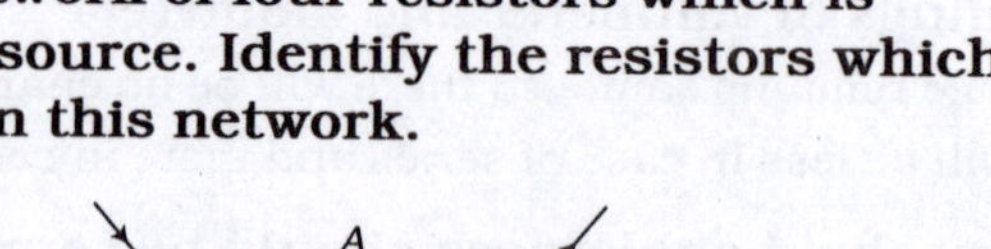

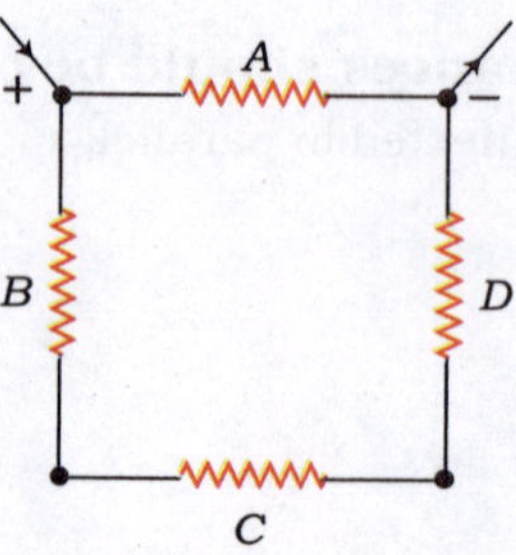

(a) *B, A* and *D* (b) *B, C* and *D* (c) *C, D* and *A* (d) *A, B* and *C*

Q. 5 **In an electric circuit, three resistors R_1, R_2 and R_3 are connected in series such that $R_2 = R_3$.**

If V_1, V_2 and V_3 are the voltages across R_1, R_2 and R_3 respectively, then

(a) $V_1 = V_2$ (b) $V_2 = V_3$ (c) $V_1 = V_3$ (d) $V_1 = V_2 = V_3$

Q. 6 **In a practical experiment on a parallel circuit, the voltmeter connected across a resistor reads zero. What does this indicate?**

(a) Resistor is short-circuited
(b) Resistor has infinite resistance
(c) Circuit is open
(d) Ammeter is not working

Q. 7 **Which combination gives a lower equivalent resistance than any of the individual resistors?**

(a) Series connection of equal resistors
(b) Parallel connection of unequal resistors
(c) Parallel connection of equal resistors
(d) Both B and C

Q. 8 **In a lab setup, why is it dangerous to connect a resistor of very low value (e.g., 0.1 Ω) in parallel with others?**

(a) It will make voltage zero
(b) It will short the circuit
(c) It will increase resistance
(d) It will break the ammeter

Answers

1. (b)	2. (d)	3. (c)	4. (b)	5. (b)	6. (a)	7. (d)	8. (b)

Experiment 6

AIM

To prepare a temporary mount of a leaf peel to show stomata.

Materials Required

Fresh leaves from a dicot (either *Petunia, Dianthus* or *Solanum*) plant, needle, forceps, brush, glycerine, watch glass, slide, cover slips, safranin solution, a piece of blotting paper, distilled water, razor blade and a compound microscope pencil, pen, sharpner, eraser, notebook etc.

Theory/Principle

The leaves of a plant are flat, green part originating from the nodes of stems and its branches they functions as the kitchen of the plants by preparing food, using sunlight carbon-dioxide and water.

In plants, physiological processes such as respiration and photosynthesis involve exchange of gases between plant tissues and the external atmosphere. This occurs through minute microscopic pores called **stomata** (singular, stoma) present in the leaf.

The stomata are elliptical pore, which are found on the surface of leaves, i.e. both the upper and lower epidermis. These minute pores are enclosed by two kidney-shaped guard cells on its either side which possess chloroplasts.

These guard cells have a thin outer and thick inner walls and they regulate the opening and closing of the stomatal pores, i.e. when guard cells are turgid, the stomata will be open [Fig. 1(a)] and when guard cells become flaccid, the stomata will close [Fig. 1(b)].

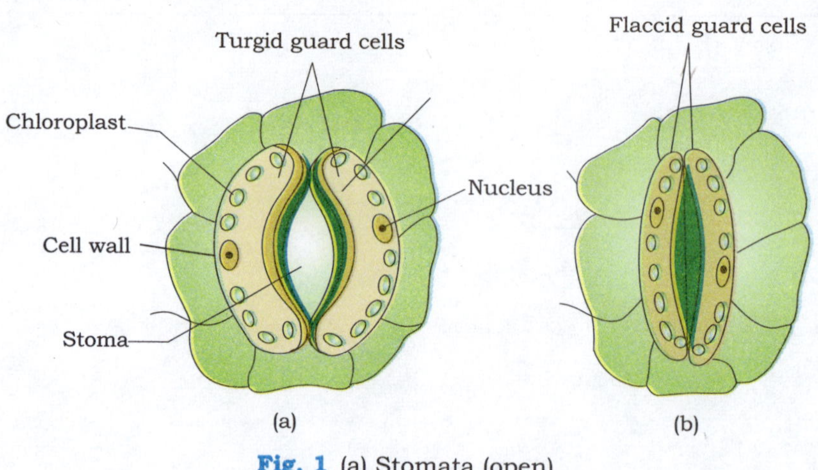

Fig. 1 (a) Stomata (open)
(b) Stomata (closed)

The number, distribution and the type of stomata varies in different plants. Even the variation is visible between the upper and the lower epidermis of a single leaf as in dicots, lower epidermal surface has more number of stomata than upper surface to facilitate maximum exchange of oxygen with minimum water loss due to transpiration. But in monocot plants, leaves have almost equal number of stomata present on both the surfaces. However, the type of stomata remains the same in a particular plant species. In case of submerged hydrophytes or aquatic plants like *Hydrilla*, the stomata are absent or reduced.

Procedure

A. Preparation of Leaf Peel

1. Take few freshly plucked leaves.
2. Fold the plucked leaf and then tease it apart, to produces a thin, transparent and membraneous peel (repeat this step to obtain 4-5 peels) [Fig. 2(b)]. The leaf peels can also be obtained by carefully scratching the leaf surface with a razor blade.
3. Take the peel and place it in a watch glass containing few drops of distilled water with the help of a forcep.

Fig. 2 Preparation of temporary mount of leaf peel

B. Staining and Mounting of Leaf Peel

4. Add 1-2 drops of safranin on the watch glass containing leaf peel and wait for 1-2 minutes.
5. With the help of a brush, transfer this stained peel in the centre of a clean and dry slide.
6. Add one drop of glycerine just over the peel, present in the centre of the slide.
7. Using a needle, very gently place a cover slip over the peel.
8. Wipe off excess glycerine using a piece of blotting paper.
9. Place the slide under the microscope and first observe it under low magnification(10x), then under higher magnification (45x).

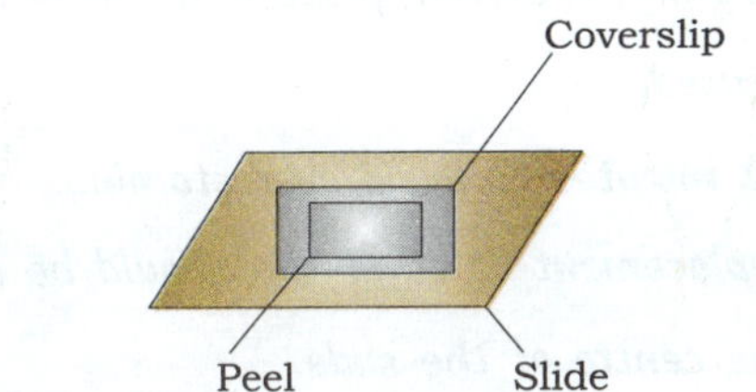

Fig. 3 Mounting and Staining of the Peel

10. Draw a well labelled diagram of stoma as seen in microscopic field and write down your observations in record book/Notebook.

Observations

1. The epidermal cells may be irregular or rectangular depending upon the leaf used for leaf peeling.
2. A stomatal pore is present in the epidermis and is surrounded by two guard cells.
3. Inner wall of guard cell is thicker than the outer wall.
4. Each guard cell has a nucleus and many chloroplasts.
5. Some stomata are open, while some are closed.

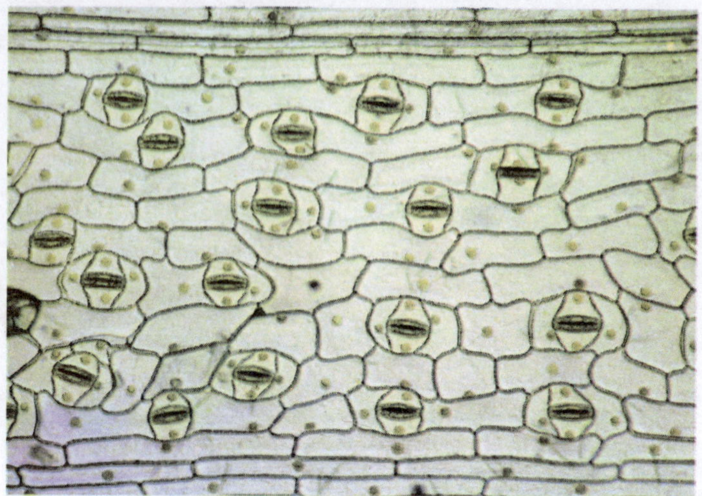

Fig. 4 Open and closed stomata (Under low power)

Results

Stomata are tiny openings or pores in plant tissue that allow gaseous exchange.

PRECAUTIONS

1. *Always use a freshly plucked leaf for isolating a peel.*
2. *The peel should not be allowed to dry, therefore place it in water soon after removing.*
3. *A clean and dry slide should be used.*
4. *Keep the sample in stain for 1-2 minutes to avoid over-staining.*
5. *Formation of air bubbles during placement of cover slip should be avoided.*
6. *Ensure that peel is placed on the centre of the slide.*
7. *While wiping off the excess water, place the blotting sheet on slide and use very soft/gentle press.*

Suggested Experiments

1. (i) Pluck leaves from any green plant at two different times, i.e. day and night.
   (ii) Prepare a temporary peel mount from both the leaves. The mount prepared from leaf plucked during the day is labelled as '*A*' and during the night is labelled as '*B*'.
   (iii) Observe both the slides under the microscope first under low and then high power and record your observations.
   (iv) Did you notice any difference between the stomata of slide '*A*' and '*B*'.
   (v) Compile a report with a neat and labelled diagram of both conditions and discuss the result with your teacher.
2. Calculation of stomatal index.
   (i) Count the number of stomata and epidermal cells per microscopic field of both surfaces of different leaves.
   (ii) Using, Stomatal Index = $\frac{S}{E} \times 100$ %, find out the index.
   (iii) This gives a fair idea about the shape, size, number and distribution of stomata on the two surfaces of different leaves.
   Note S = Number of stomata,
   E = Number of epidermal cells
   (Both per microscopic field).

Viva-Voce

Q. 1 The number of stomata is same in all plants. True/false, give reason supporting your answer .

Ans. False. All plants have different number of stomata. It depends on the habitat and type of plant. Even the number of stomata are different within a single leaf like in a dicot leaf where upper surface has less number of stomata than lower surface.

Q. 2 What happens, if we do not keep the isolated peel in water?

Ans. The peel will dry up and become useless.

Q. 3 Before conducting this experiment, if the plant is kept in dark, what will be the condition of stomata?

Ans. Stomatal pore will be closed.

Q. 4 Staining of the leaf peel plays what role in the observations?

Ans. The leaf peel is transparent, thus the cells present in it, will also be transparent. Staining helps in precise observation of cells.

Q. 5 Name a plant in which stomata are absent.

Ans. *Hydrilla* (Aquatic plant).

Q. 6 Why do guard cells bend, when they swell up?

Ans. The guard cells bend because of the differential thickenings of its inner and outer walls. The inner wall of guard cell is thicker and less stretchable as compared to the outer wall.

Q. 7 Why glycerine is used as mounting medium while preparing slides?

Ans. Glycerine prevents the drying up of plant material.

Questions From NCERT Lab Manual

Q. 1 What is the function of guard cells in stomata?

Ans. Guard cells regulate the opening and closing of the stomata depending on the state they are in, i.e. whether they are turgid or flaccid.

Q. 2 Why are stomata absent in roots?

Ans. Roots are present underground in the soil hence, the stomatal functions will be blocked. Also, stomata are used for transpiration hence, there presence is observed in leaves.

Q. 3 What is the shape of guard cells in stoma of grass leaf?

Ans. Grass is a monocot plant in which, the guard cell is dumb-bell shaped.

Q. 4 Do guard cells have a rigid or elastic walls? Justify your answer.

Ans. Guard cells have unevenly thickened walls, i.e., the inner walls are rigid (thicker) and the outer walls are more elastic (thinner), which enables them to open and close stomata effectively

Practical Based MCQs

Q. 1 Green colour of leaf is due to the pigment

(a) xanthophyll
(b) carotene
(c) chlorophyll
(d) phycocyanin

Q. 2 In the sketch of the stomatal apparatus given below:

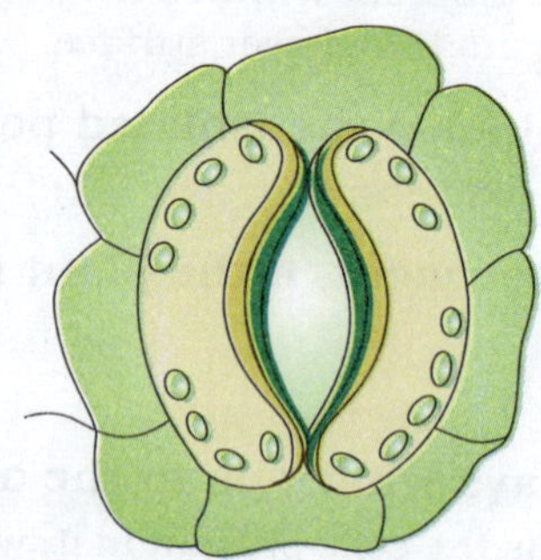

Which one of the following is missing?

(a) Cell membrane of the cells
(b) Cell walls of the cells
(c) Nuclei in the guard cells
(d) Chloroplasts in the guard cells

Q. 3 Plant in which stomata are usually absent is

(a) *Opuntia*
(b) *Hydrilla*
(c) *Grass*
(d) Potato

Q. 4 A student focused on the leaf epidermal peel under a low power microscope, but could not see all parts. He should

(a) use the coarse adjustment knob to focus the slide.
(b) use the fine adjustment knob to increase magnification.
(c) focus under high power using the coarse adjustment knob.
(d) focus under high power using the fine adjustment knob.

Q. 5 Leaf peels are mounted in glycerine to

(a) prevent it from drying
(b) keep it fixed
(c) keep it for longer time
(d) All of these

Q. 6 The shape of guard cells in monocot plants is

(a) kidney-shaped
(b) shaped
(c) apple-shaped
(d) None of these

Q. 7 Pressure responsible for opening and closing of stomata is

(a) wall pressure
(b) diffusion pressure deficit
(c) turgor pressure
(d) root pressure

Q. 8 What happens to the guard cells, when they gain water?

(a) Remain same
(b) Become turgid
(c) Become flaccid
(d) None of these

Q. 9 A well-stained leaf peel preparation when focused under high power microscope showed a structure similar to the figure shown below.

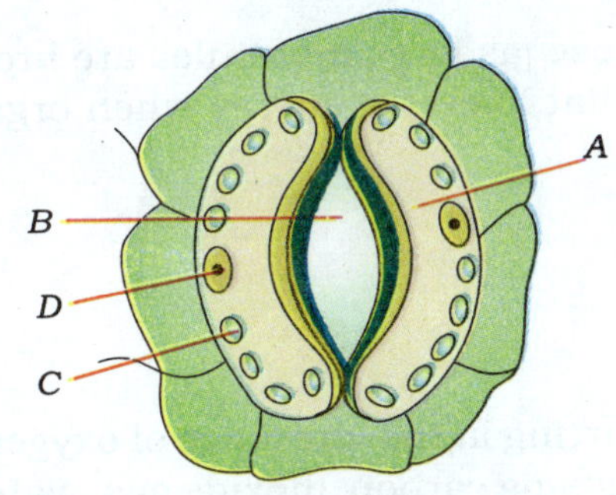

The correct labelling, out of the following, is

(a) A – Guard cell, B – Stoma, C – Chloroplast, D – Nucleus
(b) A – Cytoplasm, B – Nucleus, C – Stoma, D – Chloroplast
(c) A – Guard cell, B – Starch, C – Nucleus, D – Stoma
(d) A – Cytoplasm, B – Chloroplast, C – Stoma, D – Nucleus

Q.10 In which of the following plants, there will be no transpiration?

(a) Plants on hilly areas
(b) Aquatic, submerged plants
(c) Plants in deserts
(d) Aquatic plants with floating leaves

Answers

1. (c)	2. (c)	3. (b)	4. (d)	5. (a)	6. (b)	7. (c)	8. (b)	9. (a)	10. (b)

Experiment 7

AIM

To show that carbon dioxide is given out during respiration.

Materials Required

A conical 100 mL flask, soaked and germinating seeds of gram, freshly prepared KOH (potassium hydroxide) solution, vaseline, bent delivery tube (a tube bent twice at right angles), moist cloth (cotton/wool or moist blotting paper), water, thread, beaker (250 mL), test tube and rubber cork with one hole.

Theory/Principle

Respiration is a **catabolic process** (as large molecules are broken down into smaller units) and can be defined as the process that liberates energy when organic molecules are oxidised.

Respiration is of two types:

(a) Aerobic

(b) Anaerobic

(a) Aerobic Respiration

It is the respiration process occurring in the presence of oxygen. A complete oxidation of glucose (carbohydrates) takes place, releasing carbon dioxide gas, water and a large amount of energy in the form of ATP (i.e. adenosine triphosphate).

The reaction of this process is represented by the following equation:

$$\underset{\text{Glucose}}{C_6H_{12}O_6} + \underset{\text{Oxygen}}{6O_2} \longrightarrow 6CO_2 + 6H_2O + \text{Energy (38 ATP)}$$

(b) Anaerobic Respiration

It is the respiration process occurring in the absence of oxygen. It leads to incomplete oxidation of organic food (glucose) releasing carbon dioxide and ethyl alcohol and a very less/insignificant amount of energy. It is more commonly called as **fermentation** in micro-organisms. The reaction of this process is represented by the following equation:

$$\underset{\text{Glucose}}{C_6H_{12}O_6} \xrightarrow{\text{Yeast}} \underset{\text{Ethyl alcohol}}{2\,C_2H_5OH} + 2CO_2 + \text{Energy (2 ATP)}$$

Method I

Procedure

1. Take about 30-40 seeds of gram soaked in water and allow them to germinate by placing them on a moist cotton/wool or blotting paper or moist cloth for 2-5 days.
2. Transfer the germinating seeds (seeds with a whitish outgrowth) into a conical flask and add few drops of water to keep the seeds moist.

3. Take the freshly prepared solution of KOH in a test tube and suspend it in the conical flask using a thread just above the germinating seeds.
4. The mouth of the conical flask is closed by placing the rubber cork with one hole. Ensure that the thread tied to KOH containing tube is firmly placed and held at a correct distance.
5. Take a bent delivery tube, insert one of its end in the conical flask through the hole in the rubber cork. The other end of the delivery tube is placed in a beaker containing water.
6. Seal all the connections of the experimental set up (Fig. 1) with vaseline (petroleum jelly) to make the apparatus airtight.

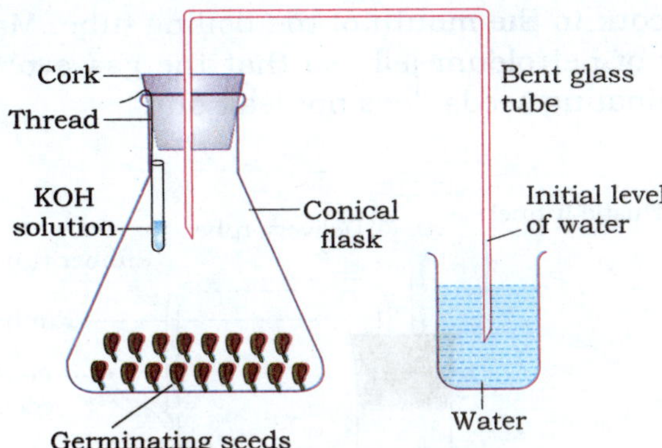

Fig. 1 Initial set up

7. Mark the initial level of water in the delivery tube and leave the set up undisturbed in bright sunlight for 1-2 hours approx.
8. Observe the change in the level of water in the delivery tube immersed in water inside the beaker.

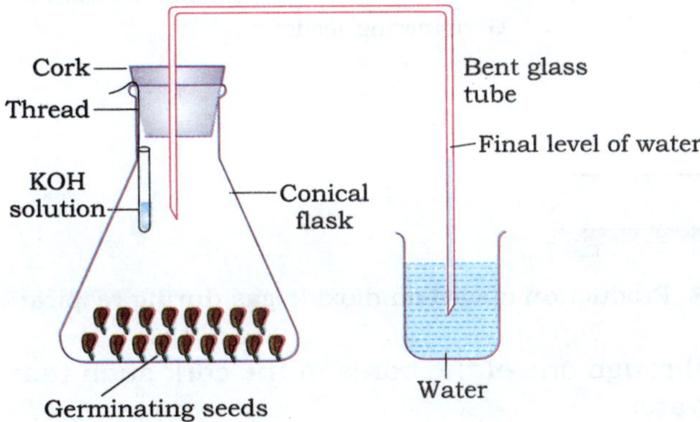

Fig. 2 Setup showing rise in the level of water

Observations

After 2 hours, it was observed that the level of the water has risen up, in bent delivery tube dipped in the beaker, from the initial marked level (Fig. 2).

Note : Germinating seeds in the conical flask release CO_2 during respiration which is absorbed by KOH solution kept in the test tube. Due to the absorption of CO_2, a vacuum is created in the flask which causes the rise in level of water in the delivery tube.

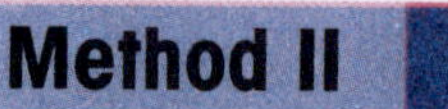

Method II

Another method can also be used to show that CO_2 releases during respiration by plants.

Materials Required

Germinating gram seeds, phenol red indicator, vaseline, a thistle funnel, a delivery tube, a rubber tubing, rubber cork with two holes, pinch cock, a boiling tube, a stand with clamp, water and test tube.

Procedure

1. Place about twenty germinating seeds in a boiling tube containing some water in it .
2. Fit a two-bore rubber cork to the mouth of the boiling tube. Make the set up air-tight by applying a thin smear of petroleum jelly so that the gas evolved during the process of respiration of the germinating seeds does not leak out.

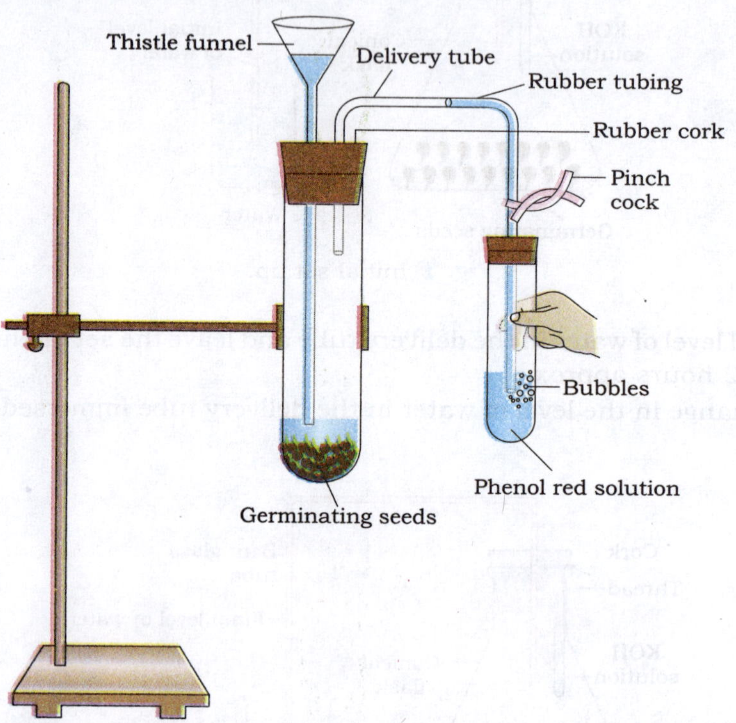

Fig. 3 Production of carbon dioxide gas during respiration

3. Fix a thistle funnel through one of the bores in the cork such that the lower end of thistle funnel must dip in water.
4. Pass a delivery tube through the second bore of the cork. Attach a rubber tubing to the delivery tube, fold it backwards and fix a pinch cock on it. Using a clamp, fix the boiling tube to a stand as shown in Fig. 3.
5. Place the set up in bright sunlight for about one hour.
6. Take about 1 mL of water in a test tube. Add two drops of phenol red indicator to it and shake. Note the colour.
7. Dip the free end of rubber tubing into the test tube containing phenol red indicator solution and release the pinch cock.

8. Pour a few mL of water through the thistle funnel into the boiling tube containing germinating gram seeds.
9. Observe bubbles of the gas emerging from the rubber tube dipped in the phenol red indicator solution. Shake the test tube vigorously and note the change in the colour of indicator. Record your observations.

Observations

The colour of dilute phenol red indicator in the beginning of experiment is red. After keeping the boiling tube in bright sunlight for about an hour and on passing the evolved gas from the boiling tube through the indicator, the colour of phenol red indicator changes to pale yellow.

Results

The germinating seeds of gram perform active respiration and release CO_2 which can be seen as:

(i) The increased level of water in the bent shaped delivery tube in method 1.

(ii) Colour change of phenol red from pink colour to pale yellow in method 2.

PRECAUTIONS

1. Germinating seeds should be kept moist at all times.

2. All the experiment setup connections must be air tight.

3. Freshly prepared KOH solution must be used. KOH is corrosive, handle it carefully.

4. The end of the delivery tube present in the beaker should be completely immersed in Phenol red indicator.

5. The ends of bent tube should not touch the germinating seeds as well as the bottom of beakers.

Viva-Voce

Q. 1 In which form energy is produced and utilised in our body?

Ans. ATP (Adenosine triphosphate).

Q. 2 The germinating seeds are required to be kept moist during the experiment. Why so?

Ans. Germinating seeds require water as they are in growing stage. If water is not available, the seeds will dry up and rate of respiration will slow down.

Q. 3 Aerobic respiration is different from anaerobic respiration. How?

Ans.

	Aerobic respiration	Anaerobic respiration
(i)	Occurs in the presence of O_2.	Occurs in the absence of O_2.
(ii)	H_2O, CO_2 and energy are produced.	Ethyl alcohol, CO_2 and very little energy is produced.
(iii)	High yield of energy.	Very low or insignificant energy yield.
(iv)	Complete oxidation of molecules.	Incomplete oxidation occurs.

Q. 4 When we say that plants and animals respire, where exactly is the process occurring?

Ans. The process of respiration occurs in the cytoplasm and mitochondria of the cell.

Q. 5 Does respiration occur in plants only at a specific time?

Ans. No, plants perform respiration at all the times.

Questions From NCERT Lab Manual

Q. 1 What is the role of KOH in this experiment?

Ans. The KOH solution in the flask absorbs the CO_2 released by germinating seeds.

Q. 2 Why do we use germinating seeds in this experiment?

Ans. Germinating seeds are active and they exchange respiratory gases, i.e. carbon dioxide and oxygen.

Q. 3 Why germinating seeds or flower buds are ideal materials for this experiment?

Ans. Germinating seeds or flower buds are used as their cells are metabolically active and they actively exchange the respiratory gases (CO_2 and O_2) as the oxidation of food takes place in these cells.

Q. 4 Why do we pour water into the boiling tube containing germinating seeds through a thistle funnel?

Ans. Thistle funnels is used to add small amount of liquids (water) to an exact position. Thus, water is poured through a thistle funnel into the boiling tube containing germinating seeds as water is required for germination.

Q. 5 Which gas that reacts with phenol red indicator (or with the lime water)?

Ans. Carbon dioxide (CO_2).

Q. 6 How do germinating seeds respire—aerobically or anaerobically? Analyse.

Ans. Germinating seeds respire aerobically. As CO_2 water and energy are produced as an end product, when respiration occurs in the presence of oxygen.

Q. 7 Arrange the following steps in correct sequence for this experiment.

I. The colour of phenol red indicator (or line water) changes;

II. Remove the pinch-cock attached to the rubber tubing;

III. Take a few germinating seeds in the boiling tube;

IV. Place the set-up in bright sunlight.

(a) I,II, III and IV
(b) III, IV , II and I
(c) IV, II, III and I
(d) III, II, IV and I

Ans. (b) III, IV, II and I

Q. 8 Drop a NaOH (or KOH) pellet into the pale yellow phenol red indicator and observe? Reason out the cause of the change.

Ans. Pale yellow phenol red indicator (acidic medium) will turn into pink on addition with NaOH or KOH. As phenol red gives pink colour on addition of a base.

Q.9 Why is respiration called a catabolic process?

Ans. Respiration is called catabolic process, as in this process, larger molecules of food are broken down into smaller units to release energy.

Practical Based MCQs

Q 1 What will happen if instead of moist seeds, boiled seeds are used for the experiment?

(a) Germination will occur
(b) Germination will not occur
(c) Amount of germination of seeds will increase
(d) None of the above

Q 2 KOH is commonly used to

(a) increase the number of germinating seeds
(b) absorb water
(c) absorb CO_2
(d) avoid foul smell of germinating seeds

Q 3 What will happen if the KOH solution will not be placed in the experimental setup?

(a) CO_2 will not be released
(b) CO_2 will not be absorbed
(c) Level of water will not increase
(d) Both (b) and (c)

Q 4 Anaerobic respiration is also called

(a) glycolysis
(b) only respiration
(c) fermentation
(d) fragmentation

Q 5 What is the reason for taking the germinating seeds for the experiment?

(a) They respire continuously
(b) They respire slowly
(c) They respire actively at a faster rate
(d) They do not show any effect

Q 6 Which of the following is not a product of respiration in plants?

(a) Carbon dioxide
(b) Water
(c) Energy
(d) Oxygen

Q 7 The correct equation for aerobic respiration is

(a) $C_6H_{12}O_6 + 6CO_2 \longrightarrow 6O_2 + 6\ H_2O$ + 38 ATP
(b) $C_6H_{12}O_6 + 6O_2 \longrightarrow 6CO_2 + 6\ H_2O$ + 38ATP
(c) $C_6H_{12}O_6 + 6O_2 \longrightarrow 6\ CO_2 + 6\ H_2O$ + 37 ATP
(d) $C_6H_{12}O_9 + 6O_2 \longrightarrow 6CO_2 + 6H_2$ + 38 ATP

Q 8 Which of these is not the end product of anaerobic respiration?

(a) Acetic acid
(b) CO_2
(c) Energy
(d) Ethyl alcohol

Q 9 **Four sets of three precautions to be taken while setting up the experiment to show that CO_2 is evolved during respiration, are given below. Find the correct set of precautions.**

(a) Airtight setup, delivery tube dipped in water in beaker, germinating seeds in flask
(b) Thread holding KOH pellets, airtight flask, delivery tube just above the water level in the beaker
(c) Germinated seeds completely under the water in the flask, experimental setup not airtight, delivery tube above water level
(d) Delivery tube touching the bottom of the beaker, KOH pellets kept along with germinating seeds at the bottom of the flask, seeds are not germinating

Q.10 **Which process does not depend on respiration?**

(a) Conduction of nerve impulse
(b) Diffusion of glucose
(c) Active uptake of ions
(d) Contraction of muscles

Q.11 **The diagram shows an investigation into the respiration of germinating seeds.**

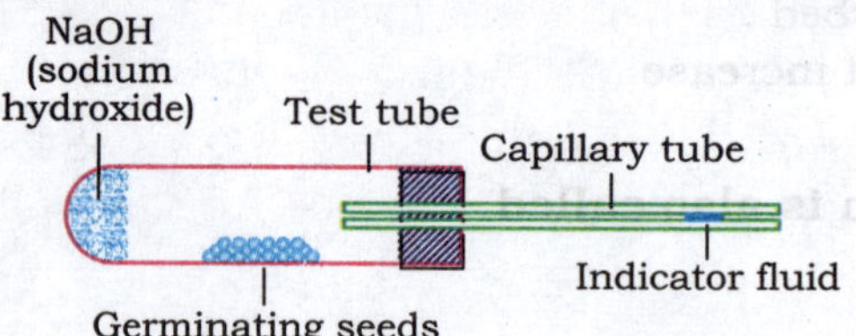

The indicator fluid in the capillary tube shown in the diagram above will

(a) move away from the test tube because of oxygen output by the seeds
(b) move towards the test tube because of oxygen intake by the seeds
(c) move towards the test tube because of carbon dioxide by the seeds
(d) remain stationary, because carbon dioxide output and oxygen intake are equal

Answers

1. (b)	**2.** (c)	**3.** (d)	**4.** (c)	**5.** (c)	**6.** (d)
7. (b)	**8.** (a)	**9.** (a)	**10.** (b)	**11.** (b)	

Experiment 8

AIM

To study the following properties of acetic acid (ethanoic acid):

(i) Odour (ii) Solubility in water

(iii) Effect on litmus (iv) Reaction with sodium hydrogen carbonate

Materials Required

Test tubes, delivery tube, glass rod, acetic acid, blue and red litmus paper or solution, distilled water, sodium hydrogen carbonate ($NaHCO_3$), freshly prepared lime water.

Theory

An organic compound containing the carboxylic group (— COOH) is known as **carboxylic acid.** Acetic acid is an organic acid with the chemical formula CH_3COOH. Its IUPAC name is **ethanoic acid**.

Acetic acid is present in vinegar. It can be obtained by wood tar distillation. It is sour in taste and has a vinegar like smell. Vinegar, commonly called 'Sirka', is a dilute (4-5 per cent) solution of acetic acid.

Acetic acid is highly soluble in water because it gets ionised in aqueous solution and exhibits acidity.

$$\underset{\text{Acetic acid}}{CH_3COOH\,(l)} + \underset{\text{Water}}{H_2O\,(l)} \longrightarrow \underset{\text{Acetate ion}}{CH_3COO^-\,(aq)} + \underset{\text{Hydronium ion}}{H_3O^+\,(aq)}$$

The acidic property of acetic acid is due to the presence of carboxylic group (— COOH), which upon dissociation provide H^+ (or H_3O^+) ions. It turns blue litmus to red but does not affect red litmus.

Acetic acid reacts with sodium hydrogen carbonate and sodium carbonate to evolve carbon dioxide gas.

$$\underset{\text{Acetic acid}}{CH_3COOH(l)} + \underset{\text{Sodium hydrogen carbonate}}{NaHCO_3(s)} \longrightarrow \underset{\text{Sodium acetate}}{CH_3COONa\,(aq)} + \underset{\text{Carbon dioxide}}{CO_2(g)} + \underset{\text{Water}}{H_2O(l)}$$

On reacting with sodium hydroxide, acetic acid produce sodium ethanoate and water.

$$\underset{\text{Acetic acid}}{CH_3COOH(l)} + \underset{\text{Sodium hydroxide}}{NaOH(aq)} \longrightarrow \underset{\text{Sodium acetate}}{CH_3COONa\,(aq)} + \underset{\text{Water}}{H_2O(l)}$$

Procedure

1. Odour

(i) Take 5 mL of acetic acid in a test tube.

(ii) Observe the colour and odour of given acid and note them in observation table.

2. Solubility in Water

(i) Take 2 mL of water in a test tube and add 1 mL of acetic acid in it and shake it properly.

(ii) Observe the changes occur and write it in the observation table.

3. Effect on Litmus

(i) Take a blue litmus paper strip and put a drop of acetic acid over it using a clean glass rod as shown in Fig. 1.

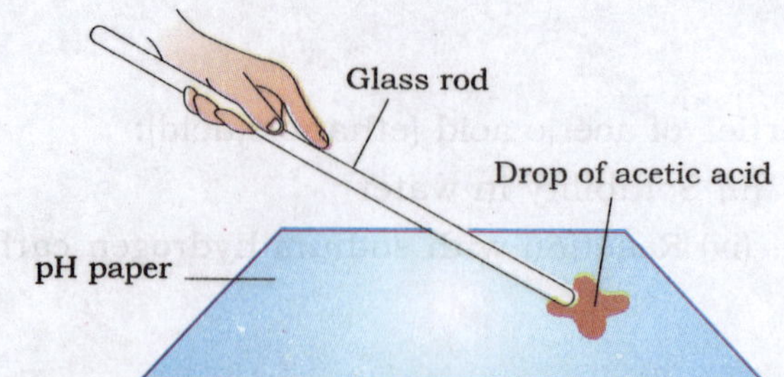

Fig. 1 Testing the colour change of the litmus paper

(ii) Observe the colour change of the litmus paper and write it in the observation table.

(iii) Repeat above two steps with red litmus paper.

4. Reaction with Sodium Hydrogen Carbonate

(i) Take a clean test tube and add 2 mL of acetic acid to it.

(ii) Add a pinch of sodium hydrogen carbonate to the test tube and shake it properly.

(iii) On the test tube, put a cork carrying a delivery tube, so that its other end dips in another test tube containing lime water. Allow the gas evolved to pass through lime water (Fig. 2) and write your observation in the observation table.

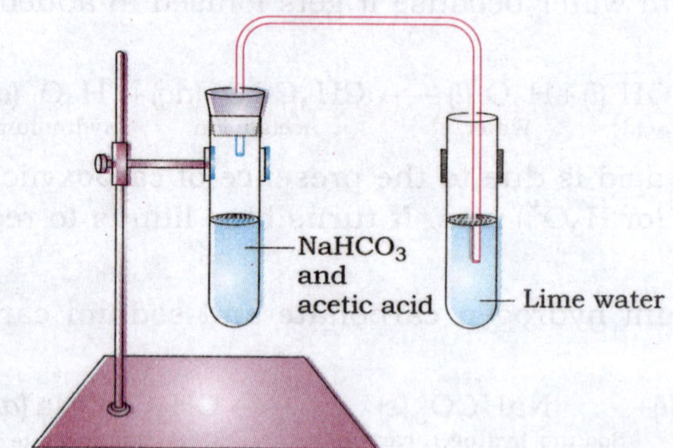

Fig. 2 Set up for the reaction of sodium hydrogen carbonate with acetic acid

Observation Table

S.No.	Experiments	Observations	Inferences
1.	**Odour**	It gives a pungent smell of vinegar.	Acetic acid smells like a vinegar.
2.	**Solubility test**	A homogeneous solution is formed.	Acetic acid is highly soluble in water.
3.	**Effect on litmus**	(i) Blue litmus paper turns red. (ii) No change in red litmus paper.	(i) Acetic acid is acidic in nature. (ii) Acetic acid does not have the quality of base.
4.	**Reaction with sodium hydrogen carbonate**	A colourless, odourless gas is evolved which turns lime water milky. On passing the gas in excess through the lime water, the milkiness disappears.	CO_2 gas is liberated on the reaction between acetic acid and sodium bicarbonate. $\underset{\text{Acetic acid}}{CH_3COOH\,(l)} + \underset{\text{Sodium bicarbonate}}{NaHCO_3(s)} \longrightarrow \underset{\text{Sodium acetate}}{CH_3COONa\,(aq)} + \underset{\text{Carbon dioxide}}{CO_2(g)} + \underset{\text{Water}}{H_2O(l)}$

Results

1. Acetic acid has a pungent odour of vinegar.
2. Acetic acid is completely soluble in water.
3. It turns blue litmus paper to red.
4. It evolves CO_2 gas when reacts with sodium bicarbonate.

PRECAUTIONS

1. Ethanoic acid should be handled carefully.
2. Do not taste or touch ethanoic acid.
3. Do not taste or touch sodium hydrogen carbonate.
4. Use small quantities of sodium hydrogen carbonate to control the intensity of CO_2 evolved.
5. Use clean and dry test tubes.
6. Do not inhale vapours of pure acetic acid directly.
7. Freshly prepared lime water should be used.

Suggested Experiments

1. To demonstrate that carboxylic acids react with sodium carbonate solution, write your observation and inference.
2. To compare the strength of dilute hydrochloric acid (strong acid) and dilute acetic acid (weak acid).

Viva-Voce

Q. 1 When Shweta smells acetic acid, she observes that acid smells like vinegar which is used for preserving pickles. Why does she found the odour of both substances to be similar?

Ans. Vinegar is 5-8% aqueous solution of acetic acid. Hence, both substances have acetic acid as a common constituent. Thus, both have same odour.

Q. 2 Acetic acid was added to small pieces of marble and the gas evolved was tested with a burning splinter. What do you observe?

Ans. CO_2 gas is evolved and when it is tested with a burning splinter then the gas does not burn but extinguishes the flame.

Q. 3 Blue and red litmus papers were dipped separately in dilute acetic acid. What colour would you observe on the litmus papers?

Ans. Dilute acetic acid turns blue litmus red but does not show any change/effect on red litmus paper.

Q. 4 When a white powder was mixed with acetic acid, a colourless and odourless gas was produced which turns lime water milky. What is this white powder?

Ans. White powder is sodium hydrogen carbonate ($NaHCO_3$) which evolves CO_2 gas on reacting with acetic acid. This CO_2 gas evolved which turns lime water milky.

Q. 5 Is acetic acid an inorganic acid?

Ans. No, acetic acid is an organic acid.

Q. 6 **What is glacial acetic acid?**

Ans. Pure (100%) ethanoic acid is called glacial acetic acid.

Q. 7 **A salt *X* is formed and a gas is evolved when ethanoic acid reacts with sodium hydrogen carbonate. Name the salt *X* and the gas evolved.**

Ans.
$$\underset{\text{Acetic acid}}{CH_3COOH(l)} + \underset{\text{Sodium hydrogen carbonate}}{NaHCO_3(s)} \longrightarrow \underset{\text{Sodium ethanoate }(X)}{CH_3COONa(aq)} + \underset{\text{Carbon dioxide}}{CO_2(g)\uparrow} + \underset{\text{Water}}{H_2O(l)}$$

Salt X = Sodium ethanoate

Gas evolved = Carbon dioxide

Q. 8 **A student added blue litmus solution to a solution of acetic acid, it turns red. What change will be observed when a few drops of dil. HCl are added to it?**

Ans. The colour of mixture will not change, i.e. it remains red as HCl is also an acid.

Q. 9 **A student added acetic acid to a unknown solid *A* which was already kept in a test tube. A colourless and odourless gas *B* was evolved. The gas was passed through lime water which turned milky. Identify *A* and *B*.**

Ans. Solid A is sodium carbonate or sodium hydrogen carbonate, and gas B is carbon dioxide.

Questions From NCERT Lab Manual

Q. 1 **Which gas is evolved when ethanoic acid reacts with sodium hydrogen carbonate?**

Ans. Carbon dioxide (CO_2) gas is evolved when ethanoic acid reacts with sodium hydrogen carbonate.

$$\underset{\text{Acetic acid}}{CH_3COOH\ (aq)} + \underset{\text{Sodium hydrogen carbonate}}{NaHCO_3(s)} \longrightarrow \underset{\text{Sodium acetate}}{CH_3COONa\ (aq)} + \underset{\text{Water}}{H_2O\ (l)} + \underset{\text{Carbon dioxide}}{CO_2(g)}$$

Q. 2 **How will you test that the liberated gas is carbon dioxide?**

Ans. Carbon dioxide gas turns lime water milky and the milkiness disappears if excess of CO_2 is passed through the solution.

$$\underset{\text{Calcium hydroxide}}{Ca(OH)_2(aq)} + \underset{\text{Carbon dioxide}}{CO_2\ (g)} \longrightarrow \underset{\substack{\text{Calcium carbonate} \\ \text{(white ppt)}}}{CaCO_3\downarrow} + \underset{\text{Water}}{H_2O\ (l)}$$

$$\underset{\substack{\text{White ppt} \\ \text{(insoluble)}}}{CaCO_3\ (s)} + \underset{\text{Carbon dioxide}}{CO_2\ (g)} + \underset{\text{Water}}{H_2O\ (l)} \longrightarrow \underset{\substack{\text{Calcium bicarbonate} \\ \text{(soluble)}}}{Ca(HCO_3)_2(aq)}$$

Q. 3 **How will you show that ethanoic acid is acidic in nature?**

Ans. The acidic nature of ethanoic acid can be shown by using blue litmus paper. Dip the blue litmus paper in ethanoic acid. If it turns red, it means ethanoic acid is acidic in nature.

Q. 4 **Where do you find the use of ethanoic acid in day-to-day food products?**

Ans. Ethanoic acid is the main constituent of vinegar which is used as a preservative.

Q. 5 **What is the common name of ethanoic acid as sold in the market in form of its dilute solution?**

Ans. A dilute solution of ethanoic acid is vinegar.

Practical Based MCQs

Q. 1 A blue and red litmus paper were dipped separately and completely in the dilute acetic acid using a tong. The observed colour of the two litmus papers after the dip will be

(a) blue and red respectively
(b) red and blue respectively
(c) both red
(d) both blue

Q. 2 When a white powder was mixed with acetic acid, a colourless and odourless gas was produced which turns lime water milky. What is this white powder?

(a) $NaHCO_3$
(b) NaCl
(c) CH_3COONa
(d) $Ca(OH)_2$

Q. 3 What is the common name of ethanoic acid as sold in the market in the form of 5-8% dilute solution?

(a) Acetic acid
(b) Formic acid
(c) Vinegar
(d) Ester

Q. 4 Lime water turns milky upon reaction with carbon dioxide gas due to formation of white precipitate. Identify the white precipitate which gives milky colour to the solution.

(a) $Ca(OH)_2$
(b) $CaCO_3$
(c) CaO
(d) CH_3COONa

Q. 5 Shweta smells a colourless liquid and observed that it smells like vinegar which is used for preserving pickles. The colourless liquid is

(a) concentrated acetic acid
(b) dilute acetic acid
(c) pure acetic acid
(d) a kind of ester which smells the same

Q. 6 By which of the following names, the reaction between ethanoic acid and sodium hydrogen carbonate is known

(a) carboxylation
(b) decarboxylation
(c) oxidation
(d) combustion

Q. 7 The reaction between acetic acid and sodium hydrogen carbonate is

(a) slow
(b) fast
(c) vigorous
(d) explosive

Q. 8 Acetic acid is added to a solid *X* kept in a test tube. A colourless, odourless gas *Y* evolves. The gas is passed through lime water which turned milky. What could be *X* and *Y* possibly?

	X	*Y*
(a)	CH_3COOH	H_2O
(b)	$NaHCO_3$	CO_2
(c)	CH_3COOH	$NaHCO_3$
(d)	$NaHCO_3$	CH_3COONa

Q. 9 When acetic acid is added to water, it forms

(a) homogeneous mixture
(b) heterogeneous mixture
(c) immiscible layers
(d) micelles like fat droplets

Q.10 **Colour and odour of acetic acid respectively is**

(a) Colourless; ester like
(b) Bluish; vinegar like
(c) Bluish; ester like
(d) Colourless; vinegar like

Q.11 **7 mL of acetic acid was added to equal volume of water and the mixture was shaken well for one minute and allowed to settle. Which of the following figure represents the correct observation?**

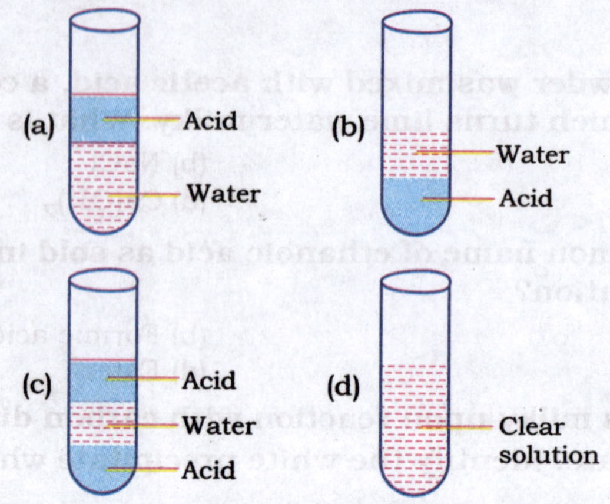

Answers

1. (c)	**2.** (a)	**3.** (c)	**4.** (b)	**5.** (b)	**6.** (b)
7. (c)	**8.** (b)	**9.** (a)	**10.** (d)	**11.** (d)	

Experiment 9

AIM

To study the comparative cleaning capacity of a sample of soap in soft and hard water.

Materials Required

Tap water (or well water), distilled water, calcium hydrogen carbonate or calcium sulphate, soap sample, three test tubes, test tube stand, a physical balance and weight box, glass rod, three beakers, measuring cylinder (50 mL) and a measuring scale.

Theory/Principle

Hardness of water is due to the presence of the salts of calcium and magnesium (hydrogen carbonates, chlorides and sulphates) in water. Hardness is of two types, i.e. temporary hardness and permanent hardness.

Temporary hardness of water is due to the presence of calcium and magnesium bicarbonates in water and can be removed by boiling or by adding Na_2CO_3.

Permanent hardness of water is due to the presence of chlorides and sulphates of calcium and magnesium and can be removed by using ion exchange method.

When soap is added to hard water, it forms a scum by reacting with the salts of magnesium and calcium ions. This scum is insoluble and floats on the surface of water.

The scum is formed due to the formation of insoluble calcium or magnesium salts of the fatty acid used in the soap formation. The soap in solution then becomes ineffective.

$$\underset{\text{Calcium bicarbonate}}{Ca(HCO_3)_2(aq)} + \underset{\substack{\text{Sodium Stearate}\\ \text{(Soap)}}}{2\,(C_{17}H_{35}COONa)(aq)} \longrightarrow \underset{\text{+Scum}}{Ca(C_{17}H_{35}COO)_2(s)} + \underset{\text{Sodium hydrogen carbonate}}{2NaHCO_3(aq)}$$

$$\underset{\text{Calcium sulphate}}{CaSO_4(aq)} + \underset{\text{Sodium stearate (soap)}}{2(C_{17}H_{35}COONa)(aq)} \longrightarrow \underset{\text{(Scum)}}{Ca(C_{17}H_{35}COO)_2(s)} + \underset{\text{Sodium sulphate}}{Na_2SO_4(aq)}$$

Note
- When soap is shaken in soft water which does not contain Ca^{2+} and Mg^{2+} ions, lot of lather is formed which helps in cleaning clothes.
- When soap is shaken with hard water which contains Ca^{2+} and Mg^{2+} ions, very less lather is formed and cleaning of clothes does not take place.

Procedure

(i) Take three beakers and label them as *A*, *B* and *C*.

(ii) Add 20 mL of distilled water in beaker *A*, 20 mL of underground water in beaker *B* and 20 mL of distilled water in beaker *C* (Fig. 1).

(iii) Add 2 g of calcium sulphate (or calcium hydrogen carbonate) to 20 mL of distilled water taken in beaper *C*.

(iv) Stir the contents of beaker *C* with the help of clean glass rod till calcium sulphate (or calcium hydrogen carbonate) dissolves in water.

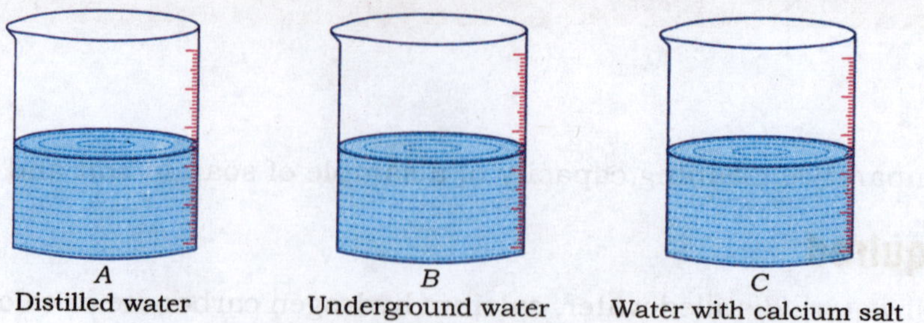

Fig. 1 Beakers containing different types of water

(v) Add equal amount of weighed soap (about 1g) to all three beakers *A*, *B* and *C*.

(vi) Stir the contents of these beakers with separate clean glass rods.

(vii) Place three test tubes in a test tube stand and label them as *P*, *Q* and *R* (Fig. 2).

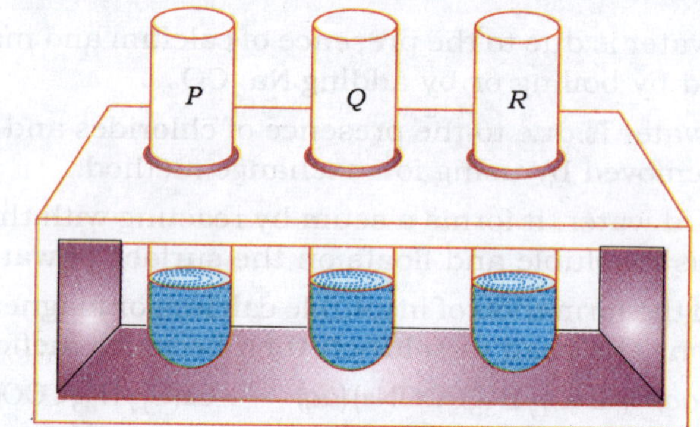

Fig. 2 Test tubes containing different soap solutions

(viii) Pour 5 mL of the above prepared soap solution from the beakers in the corresponding test tubes.

(ix) Take test tube *P* and shake it ten times by placing thumb on its mouth (Fig. 3).

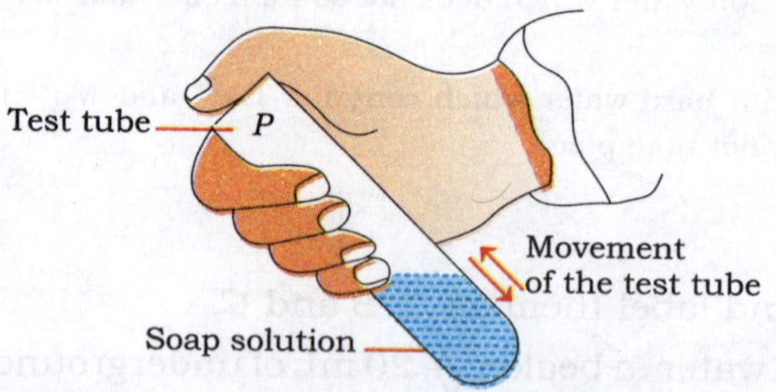

Fig. 3 Showing the shaking of test tube

(x) On shaking the test tube, foam or lather will be formed. Measure the length of foam produced immediately with the help of a measuring scale (Fig. 4).

(xi) Similarly, repeat steps (ix) and (x) with the remaining two samples.

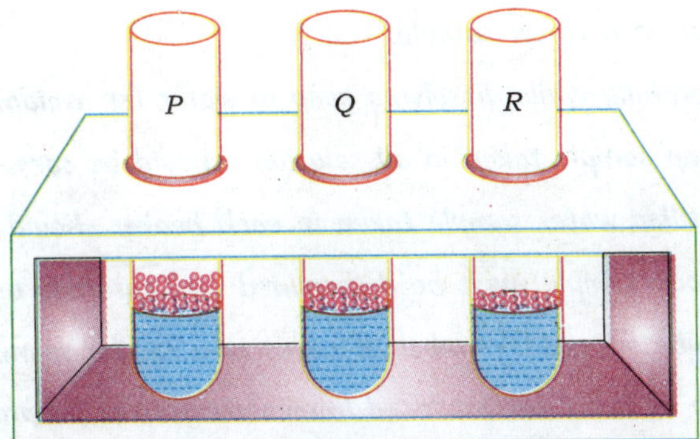

Fig. 4 To compare the foaming capacity of different samples of soap

Observations

1. Mass of sample of soap taken in each beaker = ... g.
2. Volume of distilled water and underground water added in each beaker = ...mL
3. Volume of soap sample taken in each test tube = ...mL
4. Number of times each test tube shaken = ...

Calculations

S. No.	Mixture (water + soap)	Test tube reading		Length of foam produced (cm) = Final length – Initial length
		Initial length before shaking (solution) (cm)	Final length after shaking (solution + foam) (cm)	
1.	Mixture of soap in distilled water (soft water in test tube *P*)			
2.	Mixture of soap in well water or underground water (hard water in test tube *Q*)			
3.	Mixture of soap in distilled water containing calcium sulphate (or calcium hydrogen carbonate)(very hard water in test tube *R*)			

Results

1. Soap solution in test tube *P* produces the maximum length of foam. Thus, distilled water (soft water) has the most cleansing capability.
2. Soap solution in test tube *Q* produces smaller length of foam as compare to test tube *P*. Thus, underground water has less cleansing capability than soft water.
3. Soap solution in test tube *R* produces minimum length of foam. Thus, distilled water with calcium hydrogen carbonate has least cleansing capability.

PRECAUTIONS

1. Use similar soap for each water sample.
2. Stir the mixture carefully while dissolving soap in water for avoiding spilling of soap solution.
3. The quantity of soap sample taken in all solutions should be same.
4. The amount of distilled water sample taken in each beaker should be same.
5. The mass of the soap sample must be determined very carefully using a physical balance.
6. Shake every test tube for equal number of times in a similar manner in order to avoid any disparity.
7. Measure the length of the foam produced immediately after its production.
8. Use wire gauze for warming beaker containing soap solution if needed.
9. For the experiment of cleansing capacity of a soap, always use cloth washing soap and not bathing soap or the synthetic detergent.

Suggested Experiments

1. To study the comparative cleansing capacity of a sample of soft and hard water to remove stain of blue ink on white cloth using soap.
2. To demonstrate that hard water produces foam with detergent but curdy white precipitate with soap.

Viva-Voce

Q. 1 What is soft water?

Ans. The water which has few or low mineral content like calcium (Ca) or magnesium (Mg) ions and produces lather on mixing soap to it is called soft water.

Q. 2 What is hard water?

Ans. The water that has high mineral content (like magnesium and calcium ions) and produces scum on addition of soap is called hard water.

Q. 3 Which salts cause hardness in water?

Ans. The hydrogen carbonates, chlorides and sulphates of calcium and magnesium cause hardness in water.

Q. 4 What can be used instead of soap to wash clothes in hard water?

Ans. Synthetic detergents can be used to wash clothes in hard water, as they do not produce the insoluble scum.

Q. 5 Why do detergents not produce scum with hard water?

Ans. The calcium and magnesium salts of detergents are soluble in water. Hence, detergents can be used effectively even in hard water.

Q. 6 Tanu tried to dissolve the soap in water completely but it does not dissolve and gives no lather also. What conclusion can you drawn from this observation?

Ans. The soap does not dissolve in water completely, this suggests that the water taken by Tanu is hard, i.e. it contains salts of calcium and magnesium (generally bicarbonates, chlorides or sulphates).

Q. 7 When soap is added to hard water, a white curdy substance is observed which floats on the surface of hard water. Name this white curdy substance.

Ans. When soap is added to hard water, it forms an insoluble white curdy substance called scum which floats on the surface of water.

Q. 8 When soap is added to ethanol solution, will micelles formed or not?

Ans. Soap gets completely soluble in ethanol and forms a clear solution. Thus, it does not form micelles.

Q. 9 A student observed that when Na_2CO_3 is added to hard water, it produces lather with soap. What could you conclude from this observation?

Ans. When Na_2CO_3 (sodium carbonate) is added to hard water, it reacts with calcium and magnesium ions and gets precipitated out as carbonates thereby, increasing the foaming capacity of soap and hence, soap produces lather with this type of water.

Q.10 Why the formation of foam by soap is considered important?

Ans. Formation of foam by soap is responsible for cleansing action of soap. It forms an emalsion with dirt present on the clothes and in turn makes the cloth free of dirt.

Q.11 What is foaming capacity of a soap?

Ans. It is the measure of the formation of lather by a soap when dissolved in water.

Q.12 On what factors, the foaming capacity of a soap depends?

Ans. The foaming capacity of a soap depends on

(a) Nature of soap
(b) Nature of water (hard or soft)
(c) Concentration of soap in the sample of water
(d) pH of water
(e) Temperature

Q.13 Why did we add calcium hydrogen carbonate (or calcium sulphate) to beaker *C*?

Ans. Beaker *C* contains distilled water which is free of Ca^{2+} and Mg^{2+} ions. When calcium hydrogen carbonate (or calcium sulphate) is added to distilled water, the water becomes hard. On addition of soap, these ions react with soap thereby reducing lather capacity of soap by forming scum.

Questions From NCERT Lab Manual

Q. 1 What is the reaction between soap molecules and ions present in hard water?

Ans.

$$\underset{\text{Sodium stearate (soap)}}{2C_{17}H_{35}COONa} + \underset{\text{Calcium ion (from hard water)}}{Ca^{2+}} \longrightarrow \underset{\text{Calcium stearate}}{(C_{17}H_{35}COO)_2Ca} + \underset{\text{Sodium ion}}{2Na^+}$$

$$\underset{\text{Sodium stearate (soap)}}{2C_{17}H_{35}COONa} + \underset{\text{Magnesium ion (from hard water)}}{Mg^{2+}} \longrightarrow \underset{\text{Magnesium stearate}}{(C_{17}H_{35}COO)_2Mg} + \underset{\text{Sodium ion}}{2Na^+}$$

Q. 2 Do both hard water and soft water produce foam with soap?

Ans. No, only soft water produces foam with soap.

Q. 3 Why is scum formed when hard water is treated with soap?

Ans. Hard water contains bicarbonate, chloride or sulphate salts of calcium and magnesium which reacts with soap to form insoluble precipitate called scum.

Q. 4 Was there any difference in the length of the foam formed in test tube *C* having water containing calcium hydrogen carbonate (or calcium sulphate) and test tube *B* containing well water or underground water?

Ans. Yes, test tube *B* contains larger length of foam while *C* contains smaller length of foam because test tube *C* contains calcium hydrogen carbonate (or calcium sulphate) dissolved in distilled water. This calcium hydrogen carbonate (or calcium sulphate) reduces the foaming capacity of soap.

Q. 5 **With their prolong use, white scales get deposited in the interior of boilers and electric kettles. What is the reason for this observation? How can these scales be removed?**

Ans. On prolong use, scales get deposited in the interior of boilers and electric kettles due to the precipitation of $CaCO_3$ and $CaSO_4$. The precipitation of $CaCO_3$ is also caused due to the thermal decomposition of bicarbonate ions. Descaling agent (like white vinegar contains acetic acid) can be used to remove scaling.

Q. 6 **What do you understand by temporary and permanent hardness of water?**

Ans. Temporary hardness of water is due to the presence of calcium and magnesium bicarbonates in water and can be removed by boiling or by adding Na_2CO_3 to hard water.

Permanent hardness of water is due to the presence of chlorides and sulphates of calcium and magnesium and can be removed by using an ion exchanger.

Practical Based MCQs

Q. 1 **What happens when calcium hydrogen carbonate is added to beaker containing soap solution?**

(a) More than expected lather is formed. (b) Lather formed as expected.
(c) Less than expected lather is formed. (d) No lather is formed.

Q. 2 **When soap is added to hard water, a white curdy substance is formed which floats on the surface of hard water. Name this white curdy substance.**

(a) Lather (b) Scum (c) Filler (d) Soap curd

Q. 3 **Rajesh tried to dissolve the soap in water but the soap does not dissolve and gives no lather or foam. The conclusion drawn from this observation will be**

(a) Water can be hard. (b) Water can be soft.
(c) It can be distilled water. (d) The soap may have excess fillers used to it.

Q. 4 **The scum formed in hard water is chemically**

(a) sodium hydrogen carbonate (b) calcium hydrogen carbonate
(c) sodium salt of fatty acid (d) calcium salt of fatty acid

Q. 5 **On what factors, the amount of foam produced by the soap depends?**

(a) Type of cations (Na or K) present in soap (b) Free availability of hydrophobic part of soap.
(c) Amount of fillers in the soap. (d) All of the above

Q. 6 **In hard water, ... portion of soap is trapped due to the formation of scum.**

(a) hydrophobic (b) hydrophilic
(c) Both of the above (d) None of the above

Q. 7 **Which of the following might be present in soft water?**

(a) NaCl (b) $Ca(HCO_3)_2$ (c) $CaSO_4$ (d) $MgSO_4$

Q 8 **Scum is formed upon reaction of soap with hard water which**

(a) is soluble in water. (b) sediments in water.
(c) forms emulsion with water. (d) floats at water surface.

Q 9 **Which kind of soap will be more effective as a cleansing agent?**

(a) Soap salt having larger hydrocarbon chain. (b) Soap salt having shorter hydrocarbon chain.
(c) Soap salt consisting of Na^+ ion. (d) Soap salt consisting of K^+ ion.

Answers

1. (c)	**2.** (b)	**3.** (a)	**4.** (d)	**5.** (b)	**6.** (a)	**7.** (a)	**8.** (d)	**9.** (a)

Experiment 10 (a)

AIM

To determine the focal length of concave mirror by obtaining the image of a distant object.

Materials Required

A concave mirror, a mirror holder, a small screen fixed on a stand, a measuring scale and a distant object (a tree visible clearly through an open window).

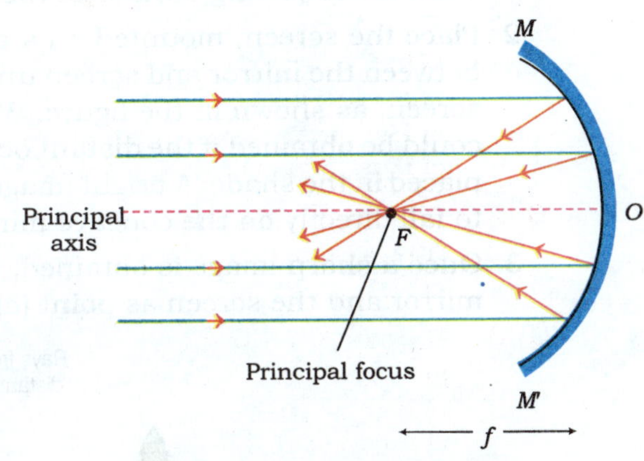

Incident parallel rays of light are parallel to principal axis

Theory/Principle

The spherical mirror with inward curved reflecting surface is called concave mirror. A beam of light generally converges after reflection from its surface, hence it is also called **convergent mirror**.

Reflection by Concave Mirror

A concave mirror obeys the laws of reflection of light. In a concave mirror, rays of light are parallel to its principal axis and meet at a single point on the principal axis, after reflection from the mirror. This point is the **principal focus** of the mirror.

The distance between the pole and principal focus of mirror is called, focal length of the mirror.

Image of Distant Object

When a parallel beam of light coming from a distant object, such as tree or pole is incident on the reflecting surface of a mirror, then after reflection, the rays converge at its principal focus as shown in the figure.

A distant object (at infinity) when reflected by a concave mirror, forms a real, diminished, and inverted image at the focus of the mirror.

As the distance between the pole *O* of the concave mirror and the focus *F* is the focal length of the concave mirror. Thus, the focal length of a concave mirror can be estimated by obtaining a real image of a distant object at its focus.

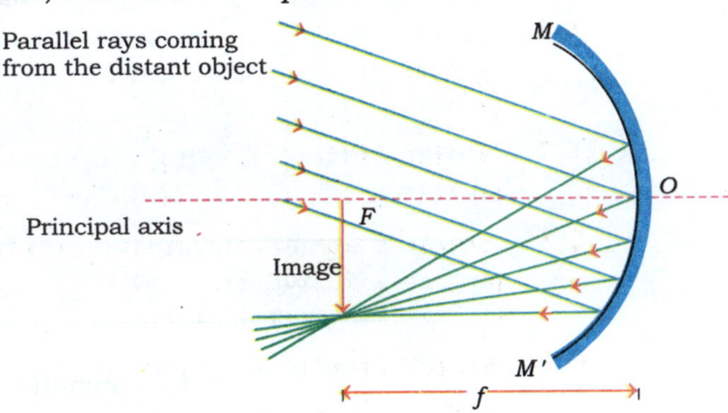

Incident parallel rays are not parallel to principal axis

To obtain the position of image for a given object distance and focal length of a mirror, the following mirror formula is used.

$$\frac{1}{f} = \frac{1}{v} + \frac{1}{u}$$

where, u = object distance,

v = image distance

f = focal length.

All u, v and f should be taken according to sign the convention.

This formula is applicable to both concave and convex spherical mirrors.

Procedure

1. Fix a concave mirror in a mirror holder and place it on the table near an open window. Turn the reflecting surface of the mirror towards a distant object (suppose a tree).
2. Place the screen, mounted on a stand, infront of the concave mirror. Adjust the distance between the mirror and screen until a clear and sharp of the distant object is formed on the screen, as shown in the figure. We can infer from the figure that a clear and bright image could be obtained if the distant object (a tree) is illuminated with sunlight and the screen is placed in the shade. A bright image of the Sun could also be obtained, if the sunlight is made to fall directly on the concave mirror.
3. Once a sharp image is obtained, mark the position of the centre of the stand holding the mirror and the screen as point (a) and (b), respectively (see the figure).

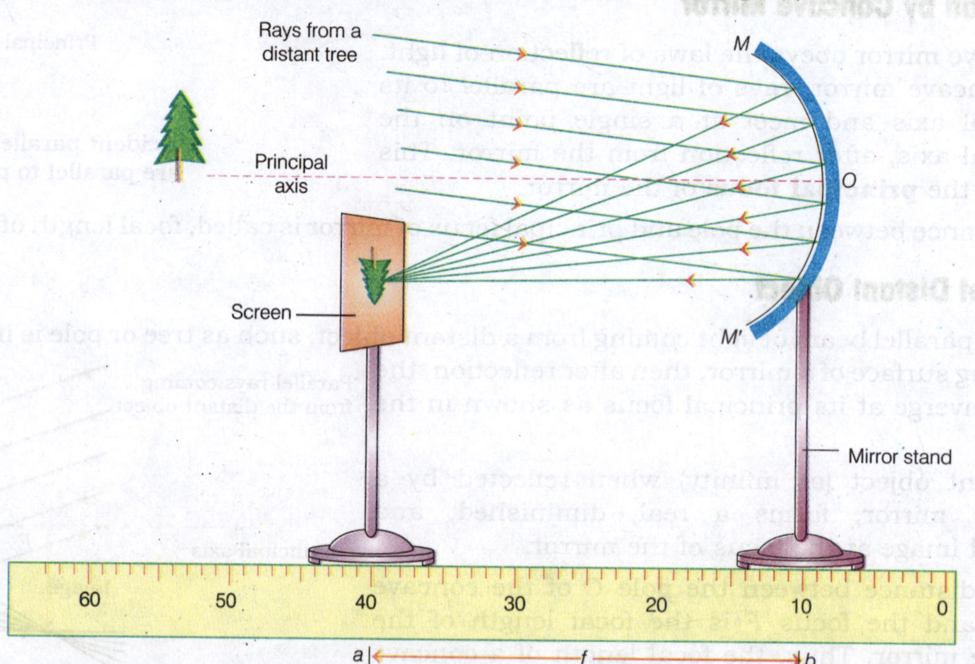

Determination of focal length of a concave mirror

4. Measure the horizontal distance between the centre of the concave mirror and the screen using a help of a measuring scale. This distance gives the approximate focal length of the mirror.
5. Record the observations in the observation table.

6. Repeat the experiment atleast two more times using different distant objects and measure the distance between the concave mirror and the screen in each case. Record the observation table.
7. Calculate the mean value of the focal length for all the observations for different objects.

S. No.	Name of the distant object	Distance between the concave mirror and the screen (f)		Mean focal length of the concave mirror (f)
		in (cm)	in (m)	in (m)

Observations and Calculations

Least count of scale used = $\frac{\text{Range}}{\text{No. of divisions}}$ .... mm = ... cm

Focal length for first object (f_1) = ... m

Focal length for second object (f_2) = ... m

Focal length for third object (f_3) = ... m

Mean focal length = $\frac{f_1 + f_2 + f_3}{3}$ = ...m

Result

The approximate value of focal length of the given concave mirror is .... m.

PRECAUTIONS

1. Concave mirror should be placed near an open window through which sufficient sunlight enters, with its polished surface facing the distant object.

2. There should not be any obstacle in the path of rays of light incident on the concave mirror.

3. If the image of the sun has to be formed, then it should be focused on the screen only. The image of the sun should never be seen directly with the naked eyes. Sunlight should never be focused on any part of the body as it can burn it.

4. In order to obtain a sharp and clear image of the distant object on the wall/ground, it must be ensured that the object is well illuminated, so that amount of light incident on the concave mirror is sufficient to produce a well illuminated and distinct image.

5. The measuring scale should be parallel to the base of both the stands.

6. The mirror holder along with the mirror should be kept perpendicular to the measuring scale for precise measurements.

Sources of Error

1. The measuring scale may not be parallel to the base of both the stands.
2. The mirror holder, along with the mirror, may not be kept perpendicular to the measuring scale.
3. Least count of measuring scale may not be correctly noted.
4. Measurement of distance from pole may not be made accurate.

Suggested Experiments

1. Observe the surface of the mirror at your home and try to conclude, whether an inner or outer surface in your mirror, is a reflecting surface. Discuss the result.
2. Consider two different spherical mirrors with reflecting surface towards your face, are lying on the table. Try to distinguish between them just by looking.

Viva-Voce

Q. 1 If the image formed is virtual, can we still determine the focal length using a screen? Why or why not?

Ans. No, because a virtual image cannot be projected on a screen. It forms on the same side as the object.

Q. 2 Give the position of an object to obtain a virtual, erect and an image larger than the object using a concave mirror.

Ans. The object should be placed between the focus and pole of the mirror.

Q. 3 Why do we obtain blurred image from a concave mirror sometimes?

Ans. The reason behind the blurred image is that the mirror is away from the object.

Q. 4 How can we find the focal length of a concave mirror, when the image is obtained by using a concave mirror?

Ans. Focal length can be found out by measuring the distance between the mirror and the screen.

Q. 5 Why do we use a screen for obtaining an image from a concave mirror?

Ans. The image formed by the concave mirror is real, so we need a screen to obtain the image.

Q. 6 If you mistakenly measure distances from the edge of the mirror instead of the pole, how will it affect your result?

Ans. The focal length will be incorrect. All measurements must be taken from the pole for accurate results.

Q. 7 Which surface of a shining spoon should be polished, to use the spoon as a concave mirror?

Ans. The surface of the spoon which is curved inward should be polished to use the spoon as a concave mirror.

Q. 8 When the light of the sun is directed on a sheet of paper with the help of a mirror, then the paper starts burning. Why?

Ans. The light from the sun is converged at a point, as the sharp, bright spot by the mirror. Actually, this spot of light is the image of the sun on the sheet of paper. The heat produced due to concentration of sunlight ignites the paper.

Questions From NCERT Lab Manual

Q. 1 How will you distinguish between a concave and a convex mirror?

Ans. A concave mirror is the spherical mirror with inward curved reflecting surface, whereas a convex mirror is the spherical mirror with outward curved reflecting surface. A concave mirror is called a converging mirror because it reflects lights rays inward to a point (focus), where a convex mirror is a diverging mirror as it spreads the reflected rays outward.

Q. 2 To determine the focal length of a concave mirror, a student focuses a classroom window, a distant tree and the sun on the screen with the help of a concave mirror. In which case will the student get more accurate value of focal length?

Ans. Student will get more accurate value of focal length in the case of sun.

Q. 3 What will be the nature of the image formed by a concave mirror for a distant object?

Ans. The nature of the image formed by a concave mirror for a distant object is real and inverted.

Q. 4 In reflector type solar cookers, special concave (parabolic) mirrors are used. In such cookers, what should be the preferable position of food vessel for cooking?

Ans. In reflector type solar cookers, the preferable position of food vessel should be at focus of the concave mirror.

Q. 5 What type of mirror is used in a torch? Give reasons.

Ans. In torch, concave spherical or parabolic mirror is used because the bulb (source) is kept at the focus of a concave mirror, parallel beam of light is obtained which remains parallel for large distance.

Q. 6 What type of mirror is used as a shaving mirror or in vanity boxes?

Ans. Concave mirror is used as a shaving mirror or in vanity boxes because a concave mirror can form a magnified upright image when the object (your face) is placed close to the mirror (within its forcus. This help to see a larger and clearer image.

Experiment 10 (b)

AIM

To determine the focal length of convex lens by obtaining the image of a distant object.

Materials Required

A thin convex lens, a lens holder, a small screen fixed on a stand and a measuring scale.

Theory/Principle

A lens which is thicker at the centre and thinner at its ends is called convex lens. Convex lenses are of three types (as shown in figure below.)

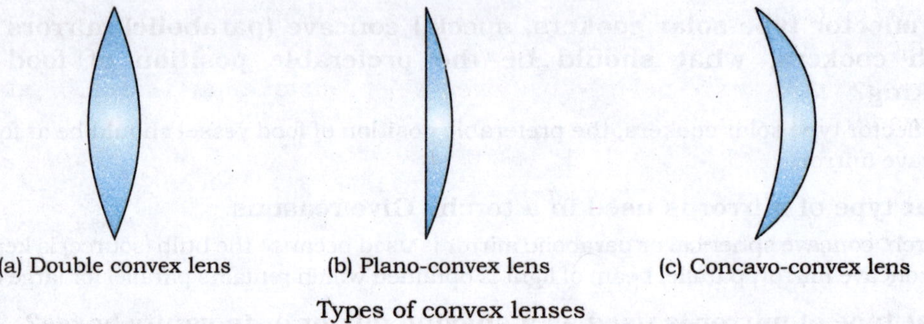

Types of convex lenses

Note A convex lens is also known as converging lens because it converges a parallel beam of light rays passing through it. A double convex lens is simply called convex lens.

The distance between the optical centre *O* of the convex lens and the focus F_1 or F_2 is its focal length (see figure below).

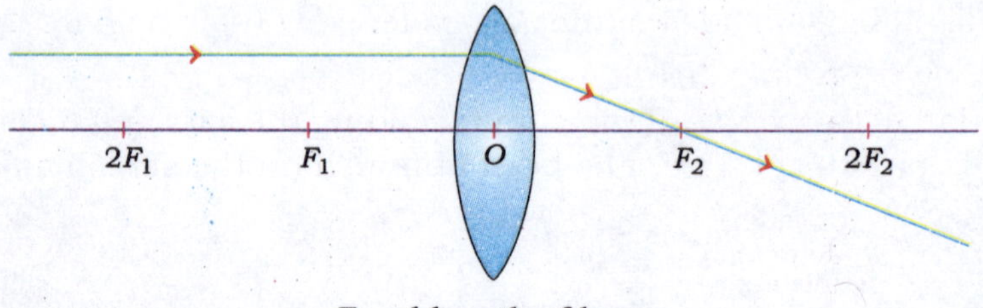

Focal length of lens

Reflection by Convex Lens

When the parallel beam of light coming from a distant object (such as the sun, a building, a tree, etc.) falls on a convex lens, the rays after refraction, converge at a point on its other side. This point is one of the two foci of the lens.

Formation of Image

When a parallel beam of light comes from a distant object, then a real, inverted image of very small size is formed at the focus of the lens as shown in the figure.

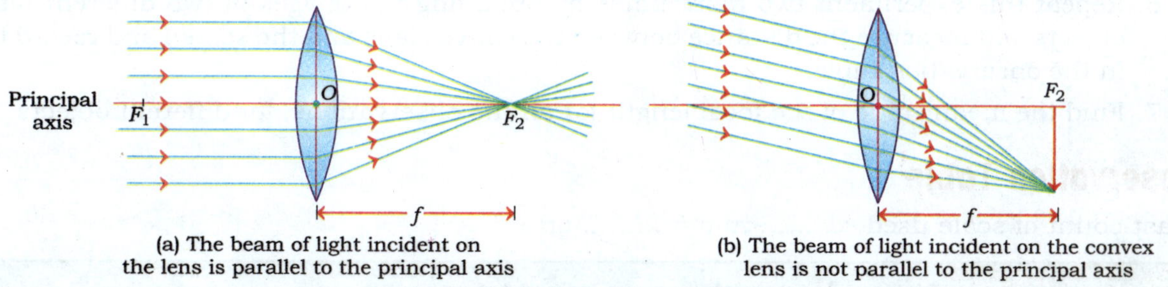

(a) The beam of light incident on the lens is parallel to the principal axis

(b) The beam of light incident on the convex lens is not parallel to the principal axis

Image formation of a distant object by a convex lens

Since, the image formed by the lens is real, so it can also be obtained on a screen as that of concave mirror. As, the focal length of a convex lens is equal to the distance between optical centre and any of its focus. Therefore focal length can be determined by obtaining a real image of a distant object at its focus.

To determine the position of image for a given object distance and focal length of a lens, the following lens formula can be used.

$$\frac{1}{f}=\frac{1}{v}-\frac{1}{u}$$

where, u = object distance, v = image distance and f = focal length.

All u, v and f must follow according to sign convention.

This expression is valid for both types of lenses, i.e. convex and concave.

Procedure

1. Fix a thin convex lens on the lens holder and place it on the table same as that done in the case of concave mirror.
2. Place the screen fixed to a stand on the other side of the lens. Adjust the position of screen by moving it back and forth in front of the convex lens to obtain a sharp and clear image of the distant object.
3. Mark the position of the centre of the stands holding the lens and the screen, when a sharp image of the distant object (tree) has been obtained on the screen as shown in figure.

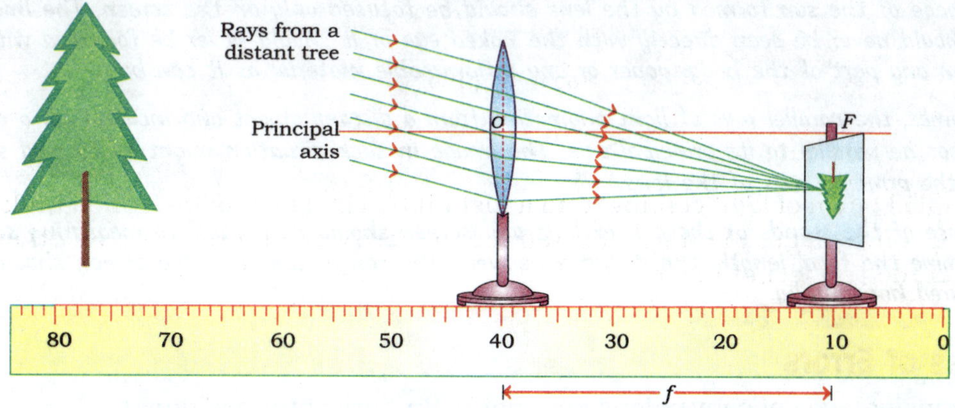

Determination of focal length of a thin convex lens

4. Now, measure the horizontal distance between the centre of the convex lens and the screen with the help of a measuring scale.
5. Record the observations in the observation table.
6. Repeat this experiment two more times by obtaining the images of two different distant objects and measure the distance between the convex lens and the screen and record them in the observation table.
7. Find the mean value of the focal length for all the observations, for different objects.

Observation Table

Least count of scale used =........ mm = ... cm

Name of the distant object	Distance between the convex lens and the screen (f)		Mean focal length of the convex lens (f) (in m)
	(in cm)	(in m)	

Calculations

Focal length for first object (f_1) = ... m, Focal length for second object (f_2) = ... m

Focal length for third object (f_3) = ... m

Mean focal length or approximate focal length of lens (f) = $\frac{f_1 + f_2 + f_3}{3}$ = ... m

Result

From the above observations and calculations, the approximate value of focal length of the given convex lens is .... m.

PRECAUTIONS

1. *The principal axis of the convex lens should be horizontal, i.e. the lens should be placed vertically.*
2. *There should be no obstacle in the path of rays of light from the distant object incident on the convex lens.*
3. *The image of the sun formed by the lens should be focused only on the screen. The image of the sun should never be seen directly with the naked eye or it should never be focussed with a convex lens on any part of the body, paper or any inflammable material as it can burn*
4. *Sometimes, the parallel rays of light originating from a distant object and incident on a convex lens may not be parallel to its principal axis. The image in such situation might be formed slightly away from the principal axis of the lens.*
5. *The base of the stands of the convex lens and screen should be parallel to measuring scale. To determine the focal length, the distance between the convex lens and the screen should be measured horizontally.*

Sources of Errors

1. The principal axis of convex lens may not be in horizontal position.
2. There may be some obstacle in the path of light ray, coming from the distant object.

Suggested Experiments

1. Perform an experiment to observes, what happens to the image, when half of the convex lens is covered, in case the object is placed at centre of curvature.
2. Conduct a similar experiment for concave lens.

Viva-Voce

Q. 1 Describe the nature of image so formed in this experiment.

Ans. The nature of image formed in this experiment is as follows

(a) Real (b) Inverted (c) Diminished (d) At focus

Q. 2 When a ray of light emerges out from a denser medium of the lens, how will it bend into the rarer medium of air?

Ans. It bends away from the normal at the point of incidence on the interface.

Q. 3 How does a ray of light behave when it enters a convex lens from a denser medium.

Ans. It bends towards the normal at the point of incidence on a denser medium of lens.

Q. 4 What happens to a ray of light when it passes through the optical centre of a lens?

Ans. When a ray of light passes through the optical centre of a lens, it goes without bending.

Q. 5 State whether the nature of image formed by a convex lens depends on the position of object.

Ans. Yes, it forms virtual image only when placed between focus and optical centre and for all other positions, it forms real image.

Q. 6 On which factor, does the ability of a lens to converge or diverge the light rays depend?

Ans. It depends upon the focal length of the lens.

Q. 7 If the lens used in the experiment is a plano-convex lens, then what is the radius of curvature of the plane surface?

Ans. The radius of curvature of the plane surface of plano-convex lens is infinity.

Questions From NCERT Lab Manual

Q. 1 How will you distinguish between a convex and concave lens?

Ans.

Convex lens	Concave lens
Its focal length is positive.	Its focal length is negative.
It converges light rays towards principal axis.	It diverges light rays away from principal axis.
Image formed may be real or virtual.	Always forms virtual image.

Q. 2 To determine the focal length of a convex lens, a student focuses a classroom window, a distant tree and the Sun on the screen. In which case, will the student is closer to accurate value of focal length?

Ans. In the case of sun, because it works as an infinite object and rays will be perfectly parallel to the principal axis giving a precise focal point.

Q. 3 What is the nature of an image formed by a thin convex lens for a distant object? What change do you expect, if the lens were rather thick?

Ans. The nature of an image is real, inverted and diminished. If lens becomes thicker, only focal length of lens decreases.

Q. 4 You are provided with two convex lenses of same aperture and different thickness. Which one of them will be of shorter focal length?

Ans. A thick convex lens has shorter focal length.

Q. 5 If we cover one-half of the convex lens, while focusing a distant object, in what way will it affect the image formed?

Ans. If we cover one-half of the convex lens, there will be no change in the nature of lens, only intensity of the image formed decreases.

Q. 6 Can this method be used to find the approximate focal length of the concave lens?

Ans. No, this method cannot be used to find the approximate focal length of the concave lens because concave lens always forms a virtual image.

Q. 7 Which type of lens is used by the watchmakers, while repairing parts of a wrist watch?

Ans. Watchmakers use convex lens and to obtain enlarged image, they place the object between optical centre and focal length.

Practical Based MCQs

For Experiments 10 (a) and 10 (b)

Q. 1 All the rays, after reflection, from a concave mirror, meet at a point in front of the mirror. This point is

(a) centre of curvature of mirror
(b) focal point of mirror
(c) pole of mirror
(d) between pole and focal point of mirror

Q. 2 In an experiment to determine the focal length of concave mirror, the image of a distant object formed by a mirror is obtained on a screen. The focal length can be estimated by measuring the distance between

(a) the mirror and the object
(b) the object and the screen
(c) the mirror and the screen
(d) the mirror and the screen and also between the object and the screen

Q. 3 The type of mirror used to obtain a full length image of a distant tall building or tree is

(a) concave mirror
(b) convex mirror
(c) both concave and convex mirrors
(d) plane mirror

Q. 4 In an experiment to obtain a virtual, erect and magnified image of an object, using a concave mirror, the object should be placed

(a) at focus
(b) at centre of curvature
(c) between focus and centre of curvature
(d) between focus and pole of the mirror

Q. 5 Your school laboratory has a large window. To determine the focal length of a concave mirror using one of the walls as the screen, the experiment must be performed by the student

(a) on the same wall as the window
(b) on the wall adjacent to the window
(c) near the wall opposite to the window
(d) only on the table as per the laboratory arrangement for the experiment

Q. 6 **In an experiment to determine the focal length of a concave mirror, a student obtained a sharp image of a distant building on the screen. To obtain the sharp image of a window grill of the laboratory on the same screen, in which direction should he move the screen?**

(a) Very far away from the mirror
(b) Very close to the mirror
(c) Slightly farther away from the mirror
(d) Slightly closer to the mirror

Q. 7 **Radha has to an experiment to determine the focal length of a given concave mirror by using a distant object.**
Out of the following set ups (I, II, III and IV) available to her, which set up is most likely to give her the best result is

I. A mirror holder, a screen holder and a scale.
II. A screen, a mirror holder and a scale.
III. A screen holder and a scale.
IV. A mirror holder and a screen holder.

(a) I (b) II (c) III (d) IV

Q. 8 **What happens to the ray of light passing through the optical centre of the convex lens?**

(a) Ray passes through principal focus or appears to come from it
(b) Ray retraces its path
(c) Ray passes undeviated
(d) Ray becomes parallel to the principal axis

Q. 9 **In an experiment to determine the focal length of convex lens, the image of a distant object formed on the screen. The focal length can be estimated by measuring the distance between**

(a) the lens and the object
(b) the object and the screen
(c) the lens and the screen
(d) the temperature difference between object and the lens

Q.10 **In an experiment to determine the focal length of a convex lens by using the sun as an object at infinity, Ram could not find a screen with a stand. Which of the following method is the most appropriate and safe to be used by him as a screen?**

(a) He should focus the image of the sun on his shirt
(b) He should focus the image of the sun on his hand
(c) He should focus the image of the sun on a carbon paper
(d) He should focus the image of the sun on a wall of the room

Q.11 **A student obtained a sharp inverted image of a distant building on the screen behind the convex lens, Then he removed the screen and looked through the lens directly in the direction of the object. He observed**

(a) a blurred image of the building on the wall of the laboratory
(b) an inverted image of the building at the focus of the lens
(c) no image as the screen has been removed
(d) an erect image of the building on the lens

Q.12 **Radhika wants to perform an experiment to find the focal length of a given convex lens by using a distant object. She can also perform her experiment, if she is provided with**

(a) a lamp and a scale
(b) a lamp and a screen
(c) a scale and a screen
(d) only a screen

Answers

1. (b)	**2.** (c)	**3.** (a)	**4.** (d)	**5.** (a)	**6.** (c)
7. (b)	**8.** (c)	**9.** (c)	**10.** (d)	**11.** (b)	**12.** (c)

Experiment 11

AIM

To trace the path of a ray of light passing through a rectangular glass slab for different angles of incidence. Measure the angle of incidence, angle of refraction, angle of emergence and interpret the result.

Materials Required

Some drawing pins, a white sheet of paper, a rectangular glass slab, a protractor, a measuring scale, a drawing board, a sharp pencil and adhesive tape.

Theory/Principle

Refraction of Light

Change in path of a light ray as it passes from one medium to another medium is called refraction of light. When light travels from a rarer medium to a denser one, it bends towards the normal ($i > r$) and when travels from a denser medium to a rarer one, it bends away from the normal ($i < r$) (as shown in figure).

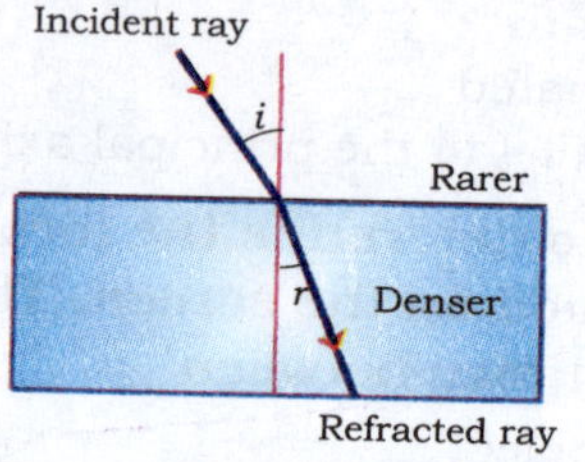

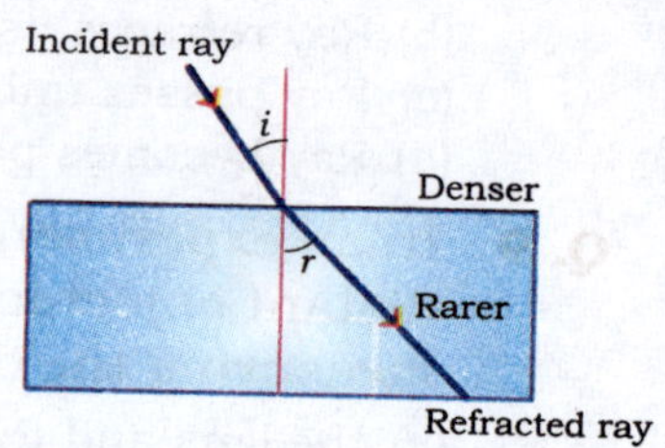

Refraction of light

where, i = angle of incidence and r = angle of refraction

Note A medium in which the speed of light is more is known as optically rarer medium and the medium in which speed of light is lesser is known as optically denser medium.

Cause of Refraction

Speed of light is different in different media. It is lesser in denser medium and higher in rarer medium. So, when light enters a denser medium, its speed reduces and it bends towards the normal and when it enters rarer medium, its speed increases and it bends away from the normal.

Refraction through a Rectangular Glass Slab

When a light ray enters in a glass slab, then the emergent ray is parallel to the incident ray but it is shifted side ways slightly. In this case, refraction takes place twice; first when ray enters glass slab from air and second when exits from glass slab to air.

Both refractions have been shown in figure(here glass slab is denser medium and air is rarer medium). The extent of bending of the ray of light at opposite parallel faces AB and CD of rectangular glass slab is equal and opposite. So, the ray emerging from face CD is parallel to incident ray but shifted sideward slightly.

Here, i = angle of incidence, r = angle of refraction and e = angle of emergence

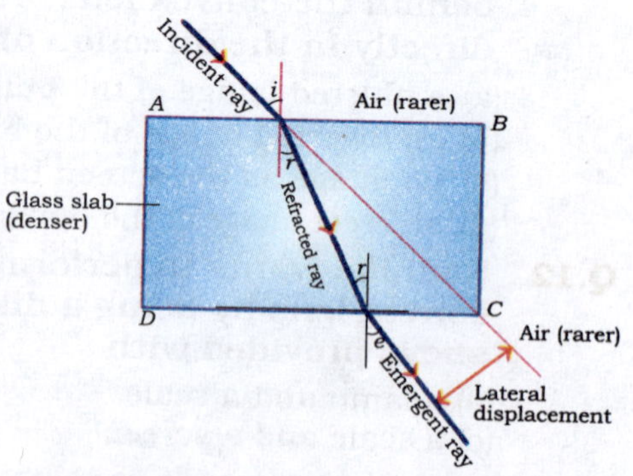

Refraction through a rectangular glass slab

Lateral Displacement

The perpendicular distance between the emergent ray and incident ray when the light passes through a glass slab is called lateral displacement.

Lateral Displacement Increases With :

(i) an increase in the thickness of the medium.

(ii) an increase in the angle of incidence.

(iii) an increase in the refractive index of the medium.

(iv) a decrease in the wavelength of light.

Note Angle of incidence = angle of emergence, i.e. $\angle i = \angle e$

If the incident ray falls normally perpendicular on the surface of glass slab, then there is no bending of light, the ray passes straight through without any deviation.

Procedure

1. Fix a white sheet of paper on a drawing board.
2. Place the rectangular glass slab in the middle of the paper and mark its boundary *ABCD* using a pencil as shown in figure.

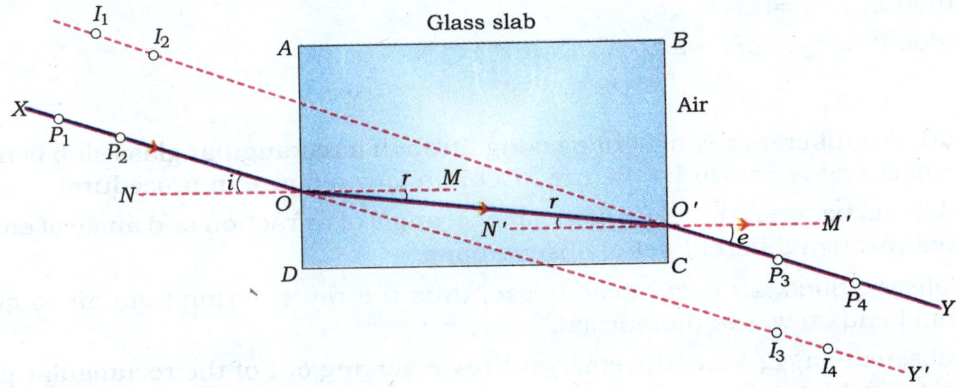

The images of pins P_1 and P_2 appear to be at I_1 and I_2 when viewed through the face *BC* while I_3 and I_4 show the position of the images of pins P_3 and P_4 when viewed through the face *AD*

3. Remove the glass slab. Draw a straight line *XO* inclined at the face *AD* of the glass slab at any angle preferably between 30° and 60°. Choose point *O* approximately at the centre of the face *AD*. Replace the glass slab exactly over the boundary marked on the paper.
4. Fix two pins P_1 and P_2 vertically about 5 cm apart by gently pressing their heads with thumb on the line *XO*.
5. Observe the images of pins P_1 and P_2 through the opposite face *BC* of the rectangular glass slab. While observing the images of the pins P_1 and P_2 through the face *BC* of the glass slab, align two more pins at points P_3 and P_4 such that feet of all four the pins appear to be in a straight line. In other words, the pins P_3 and P_4 are collinear with the images of pins P_1 and P_2.
6. Remove all the pins and the glass slab and mark the positions of the feet of all the four pins. Join the points that mark the positions of the pins P_3 and P_4 and extend the line until it meets face *BC* at point *O'*. Also, join the points *O* and *O'* as given in the Figure, where *XOO'Y* show the path of a ray of light passing through the glass slab. The line XP_1P_2O represents the incident ray. Line *OO'* shows the path of refracted ray in glass slab while line $O'P_3P_4Y$ shows the emergent ray.

7. Draw the normal *NOM* to the face *AD* at the point of incidence *O* and similarly, the normal *M′O′N′*, to the face *BC* at point *O′*. Measure the angle of incidence *XON* ($\angle i$), angle of refraction *MOO′* ($\angle r$) and angle of emergence *M′O′Y* ($\angle e$).
8. Record the values of $\angle i$, $\angle r$ and $\angle e$ in the observation table.
9. Repeat the experiment for two more angles of incidence in the range 30° to 60° and record the values of angles *r* and *e* in each case.

Observations and Calculations

S.No.	Angle of incidence ($\angle i$)	Angle of refraction ($\angle r$)	Angle of emergence ($\angle e$)
1.			
2.			
3.			

And we know that,

Angle of deviation ($\angle\delta$) = Angle of incidence – Angle of emergence

For observation 1, $\angle\delta_1 = \angle i_1 - \angle e_1 =$ ....

For observation 2, $\angle\delta_2 = \angle i_2 - \angle e_2 =$ ....

For observation 3, $\angle\delta_3 = \angle i_3 - \angle e_3 =$ ....

Result

1. The path of a different ray of light passing through a rectangular glass slab is traced on the plane sheet and is shown by the ray *XOO′Y* in (given figure in procedure)
2. The relations between the angle of incidence, angle of refraction and angle of emergence are obtained through different set of observations.
3. From observations, $\angle r < \angle i$ in each case, thus the ray entering from air to glass (denser medium) bends towards the normal.
4. From observation, $\angle i = \angle e$, the emergent ray emerging out of the rectangular glass slab, is parallel to, but laterally displaced with respect to the incident ray.
5. Angle of refraction ($\angle r$) increases with increase in angle of incidence ($\angle i$).

PRECAUTIONS

1. The glass slab should be perfectly rectangular with all its faces smooth.

2. The tips of pins P_1, P_2, P_3 and P_4 should be sharp. If the pins fixed on the paper are not perpendicular, their fat may appear off. Hence always observe the feet of the pins and their images carefully to ensure proper alignment.

3. The distance of 5 cm between the pins P_1 and P_2 or P_3 and P_4 must be carefully maintained to obtain an accurate direction of incident ray and emergent ray.

4. Take the angle of incidence preferably between 30° and 60°.

5. Thin lines should be drawn using a sharp pencil to obtain accuracy.

6. Angles should be measured accurately using a good quality protractor clear markings by keeping the eye above the marking.

Sources of Error

1. Drawing board may be hard.
2. Drawing pins may not be fixed perpendicularly.
3. Eyes may not be kept along the plane of paper in line, while observing the images.

Suggested Experiments

1. Perform an activity which shows that in case of glass slab, if angle of incidence is taken large (i.e. greater than 60°), the emergent light ray passes through the side face.
2. Deduce the expression, how lateral shift depends on the thickness of glass slab.

Viva-Voce

Q. 1 Give the relation between angle of incidence ($\angle i$), angle of refraction ($\angle r$), angle of emergence ($\angle e$), in this experiment.

Ans. In this experiment, the relations between $\angle i$, $\angle r$ and $\angle e$ are

$$\angle e = \angle i \text{ and } \angle r < \angle i$$

Q. 2 What happens to the refraction angle, when angle of incidence decreases?

Ans. On decreasing angle of incidence, angle of refraction also decreases

Q. 3 What distance should be maintained between the pins P_1 and P_2 or P_3 and P_4 to obtain the accurate result?

Ans. The distance between the pins should be maintained at 5 cm, to obtain the accurate result.

Q. 4 Why is it necessary to observe the feet of the pins for collinearity of the points in this experiment?

Ans. The pins fixed on the sheet of paper may not be exactly perpendicular to the plane of paper. Thus, if their heads appear to be collinear, their feet may not be. So, it is important to observe the collinearity by looking at the feet.

Q. 5 Define an angle of emergence.

Ans. The angle made by the emergent ray with the normal to the glass-air interface is called an angle of emergence. It is denoted by $\angle e$.

Q. 6 State some precautions that one should take while performing the experiment on tracing the path of a ray of light passing through a rectangular glass slab for different values of angle of incidence.

Ans. 1. Pins should be fixed exactly vertical.
2. Angles should be fixed between 30° and 60°.
3. Glass slab should be placed well within the outline marked.

Q. 7 When a ray of light refracts through glass slab with parallel surfaces, what is the difference between angle of incidence and angle of emergence?

Ans. When a ray of light refracts through glass slab with parallel surfaces, then the difference between angle of incidence and angle of emergence is zero.

Questions From NCERT Lab Manual

Q. 1 Why are the incident and emergent rays parallel to each other, in case of refraction though a rectangular glass slab?

Ans. As the angle of incidence ($\angle i$) is equal to the angle of emergence ($\angle e$) in case of glass slab, so incident ray is parallel to emergent ray.

Q. 2 Why does a ray of light bend towards the normal, when it enters from air into glass slab and bends away from the normal, when it emerges out into air?

Ans. It bends towards the normal, when it travels from rarer to denser medium or speed of light decreases in denser medium and *vice-versa.*

Q. 3 How does the lateral displacement of the emergent ray depend on the width of the glass slab and angle of incidence?

Ans. Lateral displacement is directly proportional to the width or thickness of the glass slab. It is also directly proportional to the angle of incidence.

Q. 4 Draw the path of a ray of light, when it enters perpendicular to the surface of a glass slab.

Ans.

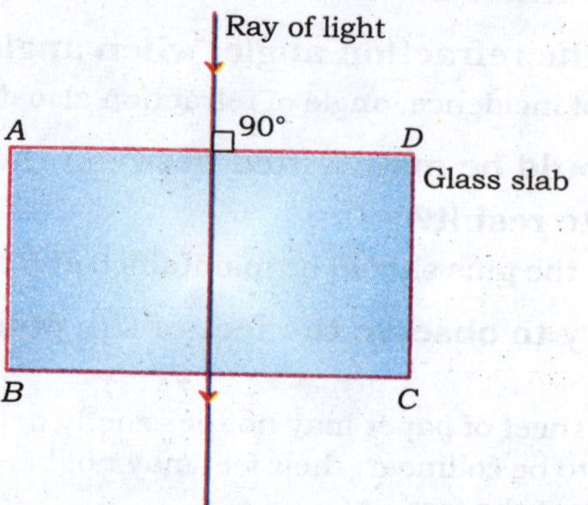

Q. 5 While tracing the path of ray of light through a glass slab, the angle of incidence is generally taken between 30° and 60°. Explain the reason on the basis of your performing this experiment for different angles of incidence.

Ans. These are following reasons

1. If the angle of incidence is less than 30°, bending of light at glass-air interface will be very less.
2. If the angle is too large (more than 60°), the emergant ray may deviate significantly and exit through the sides of the glass slab making measurement difficult and inaccurate.

Practical Based MCQs

Q. 1 **What should be the range of angle of incidence while performing the experiment of tracing the path of ray of light passing through the glass slab, to get the best result?**

(a) 20° to 50° (b) 30° to 80°
(c) 30° to 60° (d) 20° to 50°

Q. 2 **The relation between angle of incidence $\angle i$, angle of refraction $\angle r$ and angle of emergence $\angle e$ in the glass slab experiment is**

(a) $\angle e > \angle i$ and $\angle r < \angle i$
(b) $\angle e = \angle i$ and $\angle r < \angle i$
(c) $\angle e < \angle i$ and $\angle r > \angle i$
(d) $\angle e < \angle i$ and $\angle r = \angle i$

Q. 3 **The refracted ray in the ray diagram of an experiment to trace the path of a ray of light passing through a rectangular glass slab as shown below is**

(a) *PQ*
(b) *QR*
(c) *RS*
(d) *MN*

Q. 4 **What happens to the ray of light, when it emerges out from glass slab to air in the glass slab experiment?**

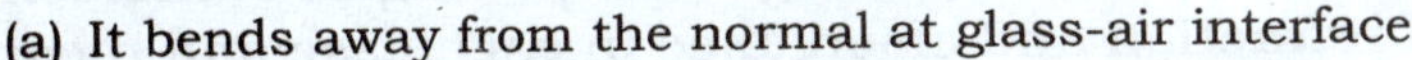

(a) It bends away from the normal at glass-air interface
(b) It bends towards the normal at glass-air interface
(c) It passes undeviated at glass-air interface
(d) It passes along the normal at glass-air interface

Q. 5 **In an experiment to trace the path of a ray of light passing through a rectangular glass slab, the correct markings of angle of incidence (*i*), angle of refraction (*r*) and angle of emergence (*e*) is shown below in diagram**

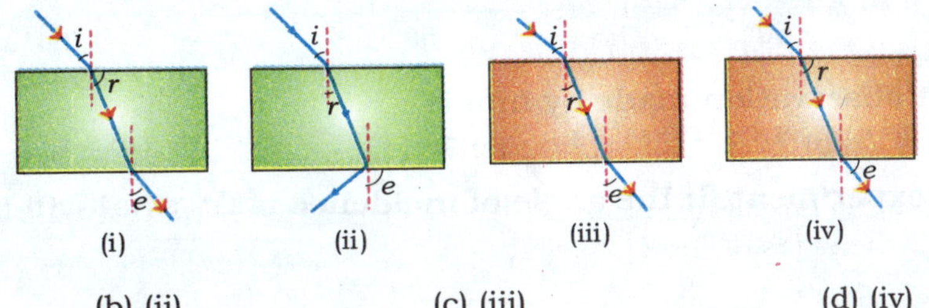

(a) (i) (b) (ii) (c) (iii) (d) (iv)

Q. 6 **When a ray of light is incident on a glass slab perpendicularly in glass slab experiment, then the ray of light**

(a) passes along the air-glass interface
(b) bends away from the normal
(c) passes undeviated
(d) retraces its path

Q. 7 **Ram while performing an experiment on tracing the path of a light ray passing through a rectangular glass slab, measured three angles marked as θ_1, θ_2 and θ_3 in the figure.**

He found that

(a) $\theta_1 < \theta_2$ but $\theta_1 = \theta_3$
(b) $\theta_1 < \theta_2 < \theta_3$
(c) $\theta_1 > \theta_2 > \theta_3$
(d) $\theta_1 > \theta_2$ but $\theta_2 = \theta_3$

Q. 8 **In a glass slab experiment, the angle of incidence for which the ray of light goes undeviated through the glass slab is**

(a) 30° (b) 90° (c) 60° (d) 45°

Q. 9 **If the refractive index of glass increases, what happens to the angle of refraction?**

(a) Increases
(b) Becomes 90°
(c) Decreases
(d) Remains unchanged

Q. 10 **The emergent ray is formed due to:**

(a) Absorption of light
(b) Total internal reflection
(c) Second refraction as light exits the slab
(d) Diffraction of light

Q.11 **Mohit performed the glass slab experiment using different angles of incidences. He measured the angles of refraction and emergence in each case and recorded them as given in the table.**

S.No.	Angle of incidence ($\angle i$)	Angle of refraction ($\angle r$)	Angle of emergence ($\angle e$)
1.	30°	25°	30°
2.	40°	45°	40°
3.	50°	52°	54°
4.	60°	58°	64°

The correct observation made by him is

(a) 1 (b) 2 (c) 3 (d) 4

Q.12 **During the experiment, if the angle of incidence is 0°, what will be the angle of refraction?**

(a) 90°
(b) Less than 90°
(c) 0°
(d) Cannot be determined

Answers

1. (c)	**2.** (b)	**3.** (b)	**4.** (a)	**5.** (c)	**6.** (c)
7. (a)	**8.** (b)	**9.** (c)	**10.** (c)	**11.** (a)	**12.** (c)

Experiment 12

AIM

To study (a) binary fission in *Amoeba* and (b) budding in yeast and *Hydra* with the help of prepared slides.

Materials Required

Slides showing binary fission in *Amoeba* and budding in yeast and *Hydra*, and budding, compound microscope, pencil, eraser, sharpener, notebook etc.

Theory/Principle

Reproduction

Reproduction is the ability of an individual to produce new generation of their own kind. This process involves the transmission of genetic material from parents to progeny which ensures that, the similarities up to an extent are inherited by offsprings.

Process of reproduction is of two types, as shown in Fig. 1.

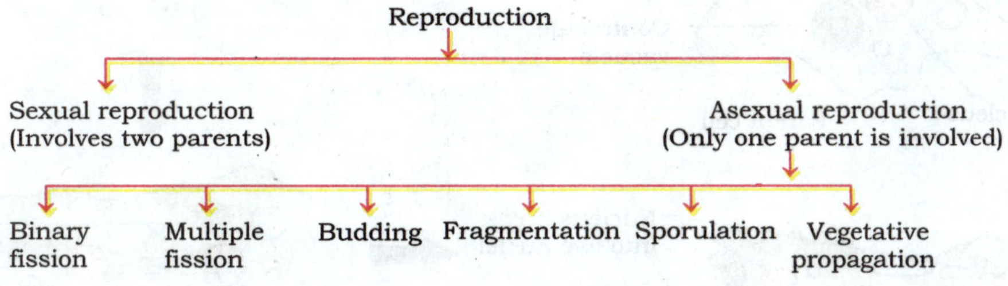

Fig. 1 Types of reproduction

Asexual reproduction is the method of reproduction involving only one parent and there is no gamete formation. The new organisms or offsprings produced are identical copies of the parent organism. These identical offsprings are thus also referred to as clones. Binary fission and budding are forms of asexual reproduction commonly occurs in lower organisms like bacteria, *Paramecium*, *Euglena*, yeast, *Hydra*, etc.

Binary Fission

The type of asexual reproduction, in which the parent cell divides itself into two identical daughter cells by amitosis. The division of nucleus is called amitosis due to the fact that the stages of a typical mitotic division are not observed in these cells. After division, the two daughter cells grow into adult cells, e.g. *Amoeba*.

Budding

The type of asexual reproduction where the parent cell produces daughter cell by developing a small bud-like outgrowth. On maturation, it breaks off from the parent body, often leaving behind a scar or connection point where it was attached like in *Hydra*. If detachment does not occur, it leads to the formation of a long chain of daughter cells, e.g. yeast.

Procedure

1. Take the permanent slides and mark them as slide 1 for *Amoeba,* slide 2 for yeast and slide 3 for *Hydra.*
2. Take slide 1 of *Amoeba* showing binary fission mode of asexual reproduction.
3. Focus the slide under low power of compound microscope.
4. Observe the slide carefully and record your observations.
5. Without removing the slide from the stage of compound microscope, the magnification or focus of the objective lens is changed from low to high.
6. Observe carefully and note the stages occurring during binary fission.
7. Similarly, repeat the above steps (3 to 6) for slide 2 and slide 3 and observe the stages occurring during asexual reproduction by budding in yeast and *Hydra.*
8. Draw a well labelled diagram of different stages of binary fission in *Amoeba* and budding in yeast and *Hydra.*
9. Comment on the features with established characteristics of fission in *Amoeba* and budding in yeast and *Hydra.*

Observations

A. Binary Fission in *Amoeba*

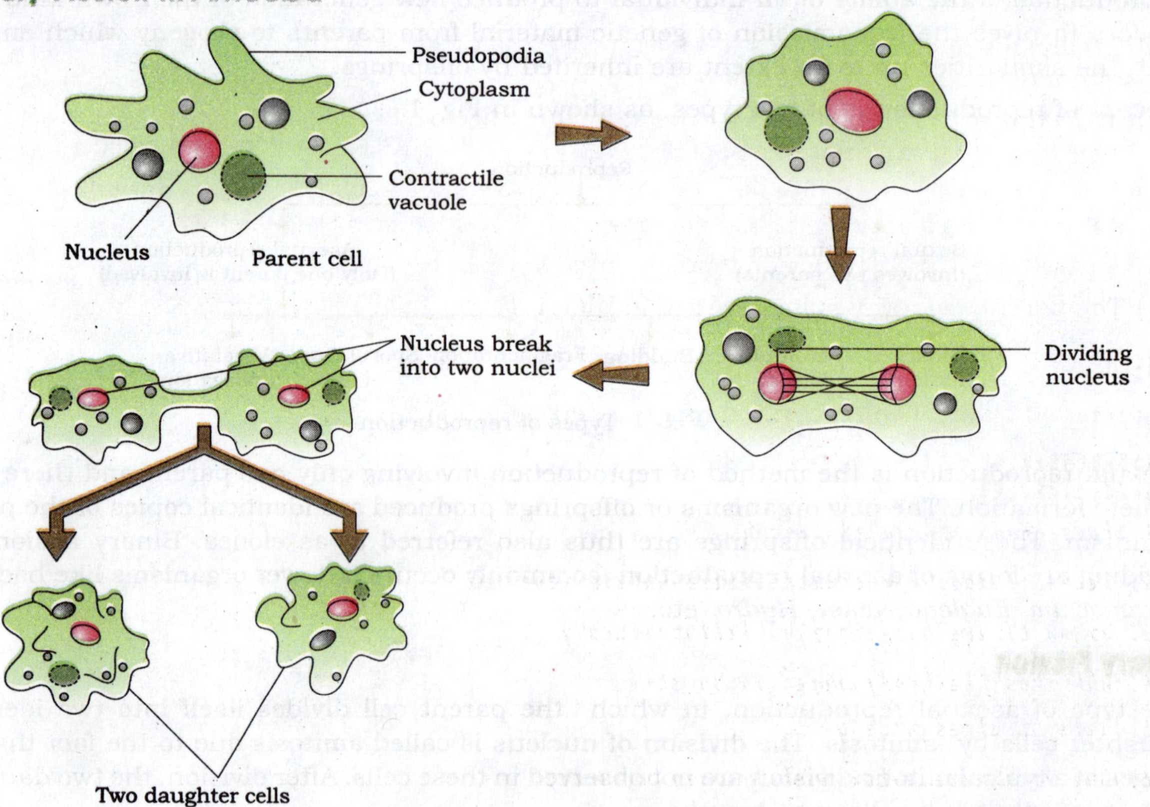

Fig. 2 Binary fission in *Amoeba*

(i) *Amoeba* reproduces by binary fission method where division of the parent cell and its components occur by dividing its body into two identical daughter cells.

(ii) The nucleus of parent cell grows and divides into two daughter nuclei (karyokinesis) by amitosis.

(iii) Division of nucleus is followed by cytoplasmic division (cytokinesis).

(iv) At the end of the process, a constriction appears, forming two identical daughter cells (see Fig. 2) and the identity of the parent organism is lost.

B. Budding in Yeast

(i) Yeast cells are spherical or oval in shape and reproduce by budding method of asexual reproduction.

(ii) Budding is the method, in which a bulb-like projection known as buds is formed on the parent body.

(iii) The parent nucleus divides by mitosis and forms two daughter nuclei.

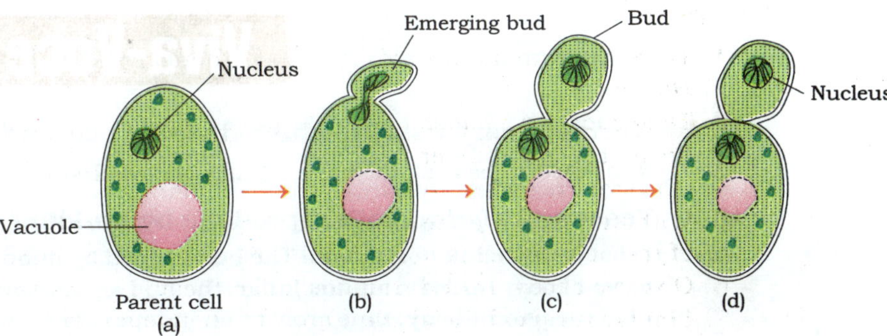

Fig. 3 Budding in yeast cells

(iv) One of the two daughter nuclei moves into the emerging bud forming a daughter cell (Fig. 3).

(v) The daughter cell enlarge and separate from parents body by developing a constriction at the base.

(vi) Budding can also continues by forming a chain of such buds.

C. Budding in *Hydra*

(i) Organisms such as *Hydra* use regenerative cells for reproduction in the process of budding.

(ii) In *Hydra*, a bud develops as an outgrowth due to repeated cell division at one specific site.

(iii) This bud develop into tiny individual and when fully mature, detach from the parent body.

(iv) Afterwards, it become new independent individual.

(v) The parent's identity is maintained in budding.

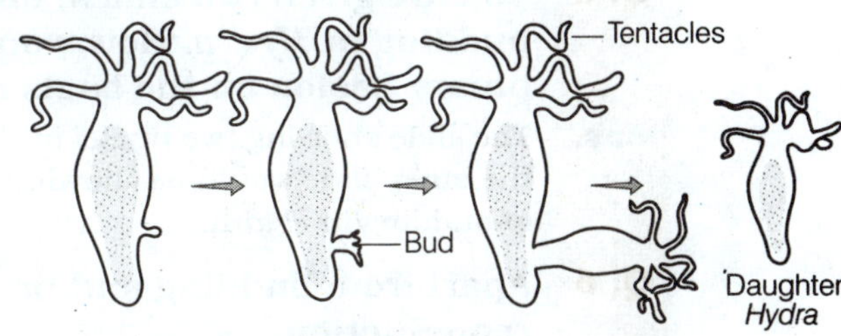

Fig. 4 Budding in *Hydra* cells

Result

The prepared slides display asexual mode of reproduction.

PRECAUTIONS

1. Slides should be handled carefully.
2. Clean the stage of microscope before and after the use.
3. Do not tilt the microscope and hold it vertically.
4. Slide should be firmly clipped on the stage.
5. Focus the slides properly.
6. Keep microscope in box carefully when not in use.

Suggested Experiments

1. Observe a prepared slide of other modes of asexual reproduction like fragmentation, sporulation and vegetative propagation.
   Make a report by compiling your observations under the following headings :
   (a) Name of the organism
   (b) Mechanism of reproduction
   (c) Characteristic features
2. Find out whether any eukaryotic organism undergoes reproduction by asexual method. If yes, then give reason.

Viva-Voce

Q. 1 During binary fission, which division occurs first—nucleus or cytoplasmic?

Ans. Nucleus divides first, i.e. karyokinesis occurs first followed by cytoplasmic division

Q. 2 Yeast and *Hydra*, both reproduce by budding yet there is a difference. What is it?

Ans. Yeast is unicellular organism. The bud formed by budding may or may not detach from the parent body. *Hydra* is multicellular, the bud appears as a branch and new organism separates from the parent body, thus grow as an independent individual.

Q. 3 List a few advantages of asexual reproduction.

Ans. (i) Faster mode of reproduction.

(ii) The offsprings produced are genetically identical to the parent.

Q. 4 How does the reproduction in yeast is different from the reproduction in *Amoeba*?

Ans. In yeast, the asexual reproduction takes place by budding while in *Amoeba* is takes place through binary fission.

Q. 5 You are given two slides, one with binary fission in *Amoeba* and one with budding in *Hydra*. How would you identify which of the given slide is showing binary fission on the basis of the number of nuclei present?

Ans. The slide showing two nuclei in the centrally constricted organism is of binary fission in *Amoeba*, the other slide would be showing one nuclei in the parent cell body and another one in the bud, is of budding in *Hydra*.

Q. 6 Apart from budding and binary fission, give two more methods of asexual reproduction.

Ans. Fragmentation and vegetative propagation.

Q. 7 *Amoeba* is immortal at the edge of knife. Is it true?

Ans. Yes, if we try to cut an *Amoeba* with a knife, the parts with nucleus will develop into a new organism but, the parts isolated without the nucleus will not survive. Thus, we can say that *Amoeba* is immortal at the edge of knife.

Q. 8 Organisms are produced asexually and sexually. Which of them will survive better?

Ans. Sexually reproducing organisms have better survival rate.

Q.9 To prepare a temporary slide for binary fission in *Amoeba*, where will you look for sampling?

Ans. Freshwater ponds, lakes, etc.

Q.10 What are the pseudopodia in *Amoeba*? What are the function of pseudopodia?

Ans. Pseudopodia (false feet) are the small, finger-like outgrowth that are present at one or more places on the body surface of *Amoeba*. The functions of pseudopodia include locomotion and the capturing of prey.

Q.11 Give example of a yeast used in food industry.

Ans. *Saccharomyces cerevisiae* is used in brewery industries.

Q.12 After observing slides of budding and fission, can you suggest which of the following organisms listed below would not reproduce by these methods?

(a) *Hydra* (b) *Rhizopus* (c) *Amoeba* (d) *Paramecium*

Ans. (b) *Rhizopus* would not reproduce by budding and fusion as it is a fungus and reproduces by formation of spores.

Questions From NCERT Lab Manual

Q. 1 Which type of cell division is involved in binary fission?

Ans. Amitosis.

Q. 2 How many daughter cells are formed in binary fission?

Ans. Each binary fission produces two daughter cells.

Q. 3 Why binary fission and budding are included under asexual reproduction?

Ans. In both of these processes, only one parent is involved in the reproduction process. There is no formation and fusion of male and female gametes.

Q. 4 Are binary fission and budding faster processes of reproduction when compared to sexual reproduction? Justify.

Ans. Yes, binary fission and budding are faster because there is no gamete formation, fusion, embryo development and pregnancy period like in sexual reproduction.

Practical Based MCQs

Q. 1 *Amoeba* reproduces asexually by the process of binary fission. Identify the option which correctly represents the sequence of events occurring during this process.

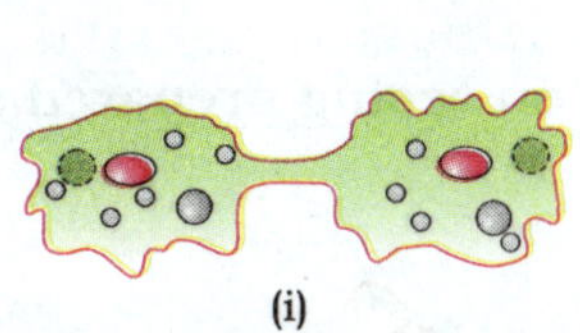
(i)

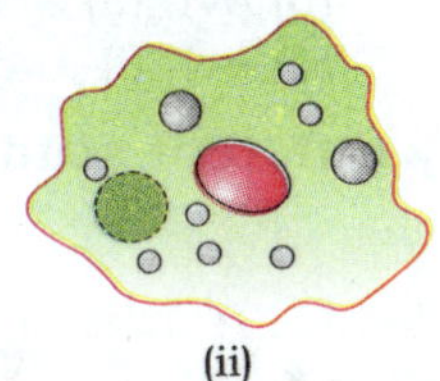
(ii)

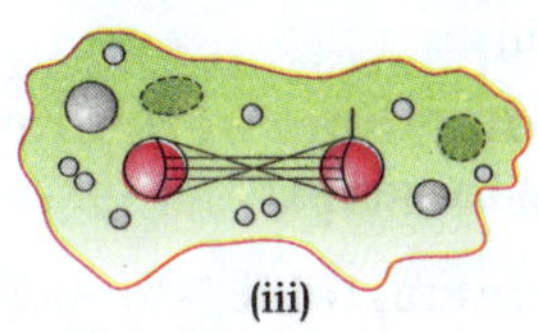
(iii)

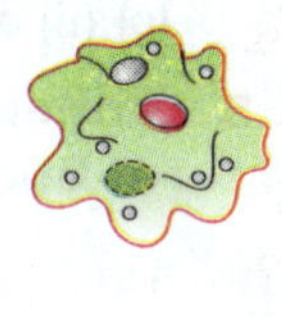
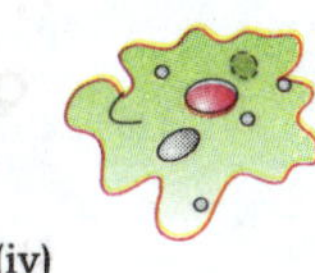
(iv)

(a) (i), (ii), (iii) and (iv)
(b) (iii), (i), (ii) and (iv)
(c) (ii), (iii), (i) and (iv)
(d) (iv), (iii), (ii) and(i)

Q. 2 Asexual reproduction by budding occurs in which of the organisms given below .

(a) Yeast
(b) *Amoeba*
(c) *Hydra*
(d) Both (a) and (c)

Q. 3 Select the option which correctly identifies the process occurring in figure given below.

(a) Budding in yeast
(b) Budding in *Hydra*
(c) Budding in *Amoeba*
(d) Reproduction in sponge

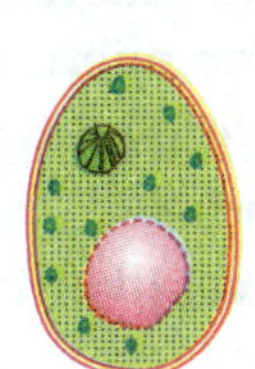
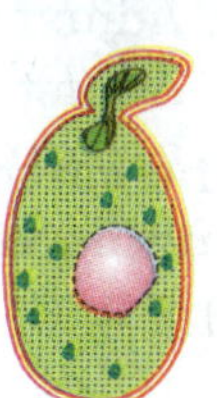
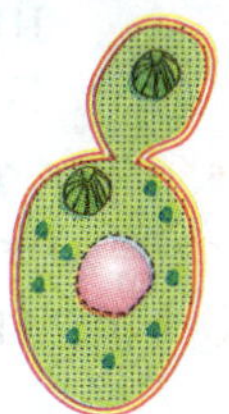
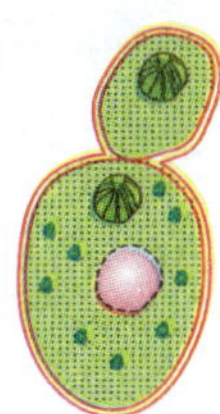

Q. 4 **The figure given demonstrates the process of ...... division in *Amoeba*.**

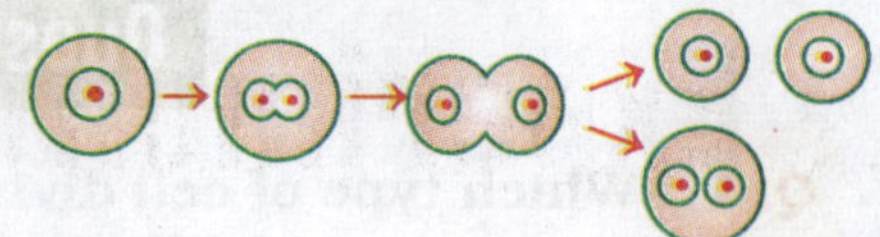

(a) budding
(b) fragmentation
(c) amitosis
(d) None of the above

Q. 5 **During the process of binary fission, the organism undergoes 3-4 stages of division. Identify the option which represents the first division of amoebic cell.**

(a) Division of nucleus
(b) Division of cytoplasm
(c) Duplication of cellular contents
(d) Either (a) or (b)

Q. 6 **The morphologically and genetically similar individuals produced in unicellular organisms are identified as**

(a) daughter (b) clone (c) bud (d) baby

Q. 7 **From the following diagrams, select the correct ones showing stages of binary fission in *Amoeba*:**

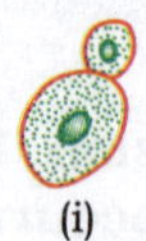
(i)
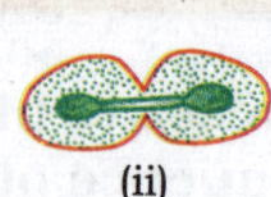
(ii)
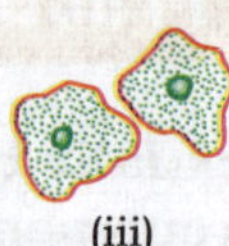
(iii)

(iv)

(a) (i), (ii) and (iii)
(b) (iv), (ii) and (iii)
(c) (ii) and (iii)
(d) (iv), (i) and (iii)

Q. 8 **Following diagrams were drawn by different students on seeing prepared slides of budding in yeast.**

(i)
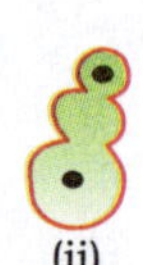
(ii)

(iii)
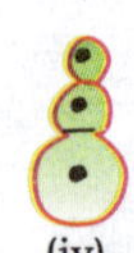
(iv)
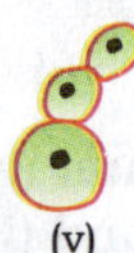
(v)

Correct diagrams are

(a) (i), (ii) and (iii) (b) (ii), (iii) and (iv) (c) (iii), (iv) and (v) (d) (i), (iv) and (v)

Q. 9 **A student has to focus his compound microscope to observe a prepared slide showing different stages of binary fission in *Amoeba*. The steps, he is likely to follow are listed below in a haphazard manner:**

I. Adjust the diaphragm and the mirror of the microscope so, that sufficient light may enter to illuminate the slide.
II. Fix the slide on the stage carefully.
III. Adjust the microscope to high power and focus.
IV. Adjust the microscope to low power and focus.

The correct sequence of the above steps to observe the slide under the microscope is

(a) I, II, IV and III (b) II, I, IV and III (c) II, IV, I and III (d) I, IV, II and III

Answers

1. (c)	**2.** (d)	**3.** (a)	**4.** (c)	**5.** (a)
6. (b)	**7.** (c)	**8.** (d)	**9.** (b)	

Experiment 13

AIM

To trace the path of the rays of light through a glass prism.

Materials Required

A glass prism, some drawing pins, white paper, a drawing board, adhesive tape, **a protractor,** a sharp pencil and a measuring scale.

Theory/Principle

Refraction of Light Through a Prism

Prism is a transparent refracting medium bounded by atleast two lateral surfaces, inclined to each other at certain angle. It has two triangular bases and three rectangular lateral surfaces. The angle between two lateral surfaces is called **angle of prism** ($\angle A$).

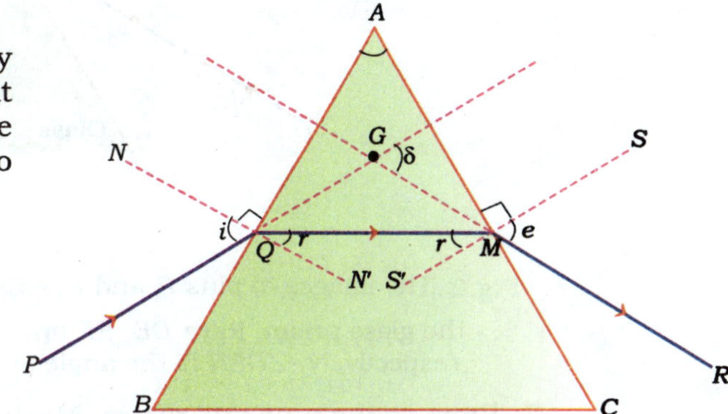

Fig. 1 Refraction of light through a prism

where,

PQ = incident ray,

QM = refracted ray,

MR = emergent ray,

$\angle A$ = angle of prism,

$\angle i$ = angle of incidence,

$\angle r$ = angle of refraction,

$\angle e$ = angle of emergence,

$\angle \delta$ = angle of deviation.

Note When a ray of light passes through a prism, it bends towards the thicker part of the prism.

Angle of Deviation ($\angle \delta$)

The angle of deviation is the angle between the emergent ray (produced backward) and the incident ray (produced forward).

It depends on the following factors:

Angle of prism ($\angle A$)

Angle of incidence ($\angle i$)

Angle of emergence ($\angle e$)

It is given by $\angle \delta = \angle i + \angle e - \angle A$

Procedure

1. Fix a white sheet of paper on a drawing board. Draw a thin line XY at the centre of the paper.
2. Draw a thin line NEN' perpendicular to the line XY at point of incidence E as shown in the figure. Also, draw a line DE making any angle, preferably between 30° and 60°.
3. Place the prism with one of its refracting surfaces AB along the line XY.
4. Mark the boundary ABC of the glass prism while holding it firmly with your hand.

5. Fix two pins P_1 and P_2 vertically by gently pressing their heads with your thumb, on line *DE* at a distance of about 5 cm from each other. View the images of pins P_1 and P_2 from the opposite face *AC* of the prism.
6. Fix two more pins P_3 and P_4 vertically such that thir feet of pins P_3 and P_4 appear to be on the same straight line as the feet of the images of the pins P_1 and P_2 as viewed through the face *AC* of the prism.

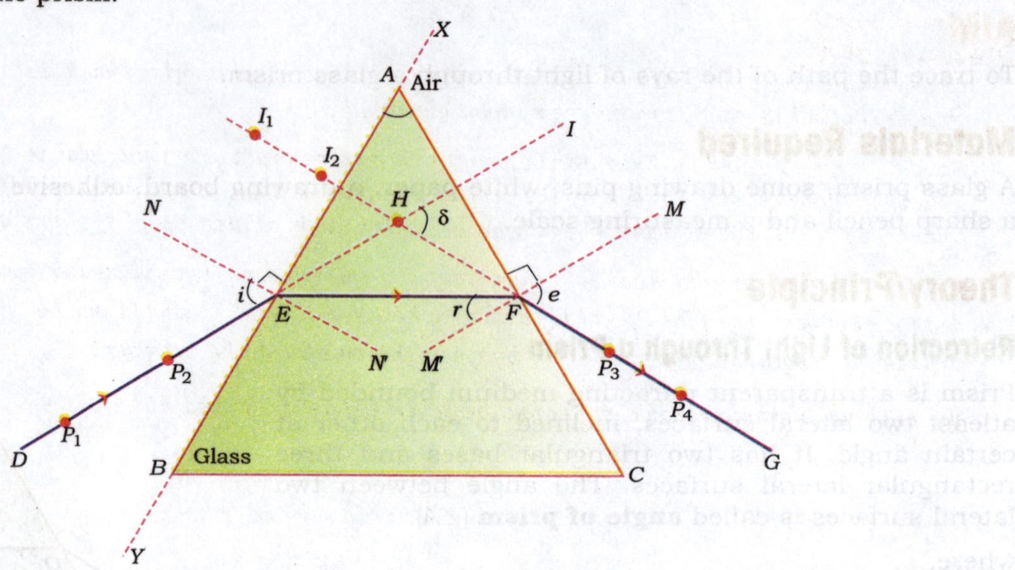

Fig.2 The images of pins P_1 and P_2 appear to be at I_1 and I_2 when viewed through the face *AC* of the glass prism. Rays *DE*, *EF* and *FG* represent the incident, refracted and emergent rays, respectively. $\angle DEN$ is the angle of incidence ($\angle i$) and $\angle FHI$ is the angle of deviation ($\angle\delta$).

7. Remove the pins and prism. Mark the positions of the feet of pins P_3 and P_4 on the sheet of paper.
8. Draw a straight line joining the mark the positions of pins P_3 and P_4. Extend this line until, it meets the face AC of the prism at point F. The line FG represents the path of the emergent ray.
9. Extend the direction of the incident ray *DE* until it meets the face *AC* at point *E*. Also, extend the ray *FG*. These two extended lines meet at point *H* (as shown in Figure).
10. Repeat this experiment for more angles of incidence.

Observations and Calculations

S.No.	Angle of incidence ($\angle i$)	Angle of deviation ($\angle\delta$)
1.		
2.		
3.		
4.		

Mean value of angle of incidence, $\angle i = \dfrac{\angle i_1 + \angle i_2 + \angle i_3 + \angle i_4}{4} \Rightarrow \angle i = \ldots\ldots\ldots$

Mean value of angle of deviation, $\angle\delta = \dfrac{\angle\delta_1 + \angle\delta_2 + \angle\delta_3 + \angle\delta_4}{4} \Rightarrow \angle\delta = \ldots\ldots\ldots$

Result

1. The path of a ray of light incident on one face of glass prism is shown by the ray *DEFG* in Fig.2.
2. Path of light ray varies as the angle of incidence changes.

PRECAUTIONS

1. *While viewing the collinearity of pins and images, the eye should be kept at a distance from the pins so that all of them can be seen simultaneously.*
2. *The pins P_1, P_2, P_3 and P_4 fixed on the paper may not be exactly perpendicular to the plane of paper. It is therefore desirable to look at the feet of the pins or their images while establishing their collinearity. Thus, the position of each pin is marked with pointed tip of the pins on the paper.*
3. *In order to locate the direction of incident ray and refracted ray with a greater accuracy, the distance between the pins P_1 and P_2 and that between P_3 and P_4 should not be too short or toolarge. A separation of nearly 5 cm between the pins would be sufficient.*
4. *The angle of incidence should preferably be taken between 30° and 60°.*

Sources of Error

1. Pins may not be exactly perpendicular to the paper.
2. The feet of the pins may not be in same straight line.
3. In observing images of P_1 and P_2, eye may be very close to the pins.
4. Prism may not be fixed properly.

Suggested Experiments

1. Perform a similar experiment for the light ray passing through prism and derive the relation between angle of prism, angle of incidence, angle of emergence and angle of deviation.
2. Perform an activity for the formation of an image in the case of right angled prism.

Viva-Voce

Q. 1 How can you define an angle of prism?

Ans. The angle between two lateral faces of prism is called an angle of prism.

Q. 2 What precaution must be taken for the refracting faces of glass prism while tracing the path of ray of light through it?

Ans. The refracting faces of the glass prism must be smooth and transparent without any air bubble or broken edge.

Q. 3 Name the process by which when a white light passes through a prism splits into its constituent seven colours.

Ans. Dispersion of light

Q. 4 Give the range of angle of incidence to complete this experiment accurately and successfully.

Ans. The range of angle of incidence is 30° to 60°.

Q. 5 What is the relation between angle of incidence ($\angle i$), angle of prism ($\angle A$), angle of deviation ($\angle\delta$) and angle of emergence ($\angle e$)?

Ans. The relation is $\angle i + \angle e = \angle A + \angle\delta$.

Q. 6 Does the angle of deviation of the emergent light change with the incident angle?

Ans. Yes, it decreases and then increases.

Q. 7 List the factors on which the angle of deviation through a prism depend.

Ans. Factors on which the angle of deviation depends are

1. Angle of prism
2. Angle of incidence

Questions From NCERT Lab Manual

Q. 1 Define angle of deviation.

Ans. The angle made by the incident ray and emergent ray is called angle of deviation.

Q. 2 Why does a ray of light bend towards the base when it passes through a glass prism?

Ans. A ray of light bends towards the base of a glass prism due to refraction. As the light enters the prism, it moves from a rarer medium (air) to a denser medium (glass), causing it to bend towards the normal. The triangular shape of the prism redirects this refracted light towards its base.

Q. 3 Why does white light split into different colours when passes through a glass prism?

Ans. White light splits because different colours (wavelengths) bend by different amounts when passing through the prism. This is called dispersion, and it happens because each colour has a different refractive index in glass.

Q. 4 Why does white light not split into different colours when it passes through a glass slab?

Ans. White light does not split in a glass slab because its parallel surfaces cause the dispersed rays to recombine, canceling the effect of dispersion.

Practical Based MCQs

Q. 1 In an experiment to trace the path of the rays of light through a glass prism, what happens to the ray of light striking on a face of prism?

(a) It gets reflected
(b) It gets refracted and bends towards the normal to the plane
(c) It gets refracted and bends away from the normal to the plane
(d) It passes through prism undeviated

Q. 2 In an experiment to trace the path of the rays of light through a glass prism, what happens to the ray of light emerging from a prism?

(a) It gets reflected
(b) It gets refracted and bends towards the normal
(c) It gets refracted and bends away from the normal
(d) It passes undeviated

Q. 3 A student traces the path of a light ray through a prism and finds that the emergent ray is bending towards the base of the prism. This bending is primarily due to:

(a) Light getting reflected inside the prism
(b) Light traveling faster in glass than in air
(c) Light traveling slower in glass than in air
(d) P The angle of incidence being 90°

Q. 4 **In an experiment to trace the path of a light through a glass prism, four students traced the path of ray of light refracted through prism as shown below.**

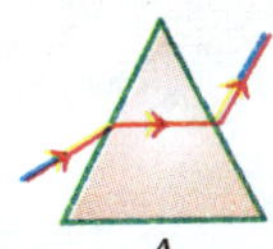

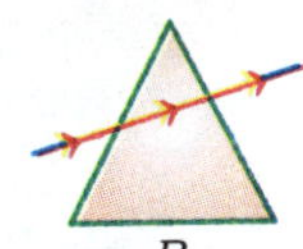

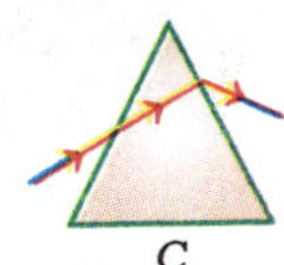

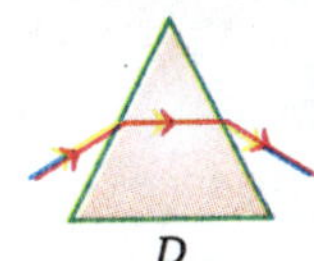

Which one of them traced the correct path?

(a) *A* (b) *B* (c) *C* (d) *D*

Q. 5 **A prism splits a beam of white light passing through it into seven colours because**

(a) velocity of light of different colours is different in the medium
(b) velocity of light of different colours is the same in the material of the prism
(c) all colours travel in the prism with same speed
(d) red colour travels faster than blue colour in the prism

Q. 6 **A ray of light passes through a prism of angle 60° in the minimum deviation position.The angle of incidence is**

(a) 60° (b) 30° (c) 45° (d) 15°

Q. 7 **In the formation of spectrum of white light by a prism, which of the colours are deviated the least and the most?**

(a) Violet and green
(b) Red and blue
(c) Red and violet
(d) Violet and orange

Q. 8 **In an experiment to trace the path of the ray of light through a glass prism, when a ray of light passes from water to a glass prism, it**

(a) bends away from the normal to the surface
(b) bends towards the normal to the surface
(c) gets reflected from the surface
(d) goes undeviated

Q. 9 **When a ray of light incident on a glass prism suffers minimum deviation, which one of the following options is incorrect?**

(a) $r = \frac{A}{2}$ (b) $i = e$ (c) $i = \frac{A + \delta_m}{2}$ (d) $i = A + \delta_m$

Q.10 **Which of the following is true about the emergent ray in a prism?**

(a) It is parallel to the incident ray but shifted
(b) It overlaps with the incident ray
(c) It is always perpendicular to the incident ray
(d) It is absorbed completely

Q.11 **When a ray of light is refracted through an equilateral prism, which one of the following statements is true?**

(a) The incident ray after first refraction bends towards the base of prism but the emergent ray bends away from the base of prism
(b) Both incident ray after first refraction and emergent ray bend away from the base
(c) The emergent ray bends towards the base but the incident ray after first refraction bends away from the base
(d) Both incident ray after first refraction and emergent ray, bend towards the base

Answers

1. (b)	**2.** (c)	**3.** (c)	**4.** (d)	**5.** (a)	**6.** (c)
7. (c)	**8.** (b)	**9.** (c)	**10.** (a)	**11.** (d)	

Experiment 14

AIM

To identify the different parts of an embryo of a dicot seed (pea, gram or red kidney bean).

Materials Required

Dicot seeds (gram, pea, rajma, etc), water, petri dish, forceps, needle, hand lens or dissecting microscope and cotton cloth/wool.

Theory/Principle

The Seed

In plants, the process of fertilisation leads to the formation of fruits, which is a ripened ovary. It contains seed (one or many), which is a mature ovule.

A seed is the final product of the sexual reproduction of a flowering plant, capable of developing into a new plant. It contains an embryo (a young plant), a supply of nutrients for the embryo, and is usually encased in a protective outer shell called the seed coat.

An embryo contains following parts:

(a) **A radicle** It forms the root system of the developing embryo.

(b) **A plumule** It constitutes the embryonic shoot system, i.e. new shoots arises from the plumule.

(c) **The cotyledons** The green, fleshy leaves of the embryo which forms the storehouse of nutrients especially proteins and starch for providing nutrients to the developing embryo.

On the basis of number of cotyledons present in a seed, the angiospermic plants are classified into two types :

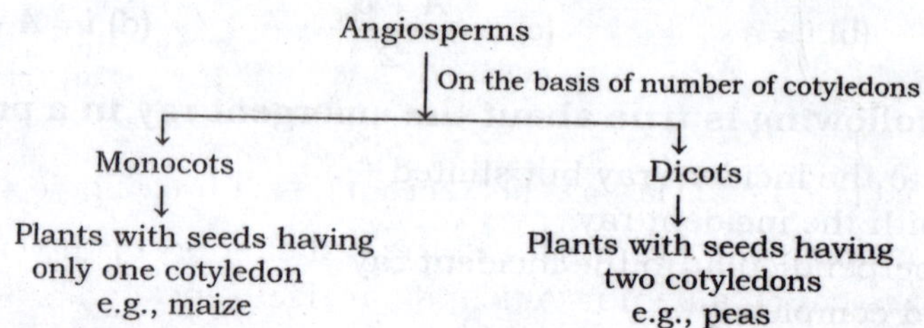

A dicot seed has a scar on its surface called hilum, which marks the point of attachment of seed to the fruit wall. A pore like structure, micropyle is present at one end of the hilum. Through this pore, the seeds take up the water and under favourable conditions (like air, temperature and light), the seedlings develop into a small, immature plant. This process is called as **germination**.

The process of germination involves:

(a) Swelling of seeds

(b) Roots start rising from the radicle of the seed.

(c) The plumule or embryonic shoot, grows upward, forming the stem and leaves.

In angiosperms, a tissue called endosperm is present which also contains nutrients for the growing embryo. On the basis of endospermic tissue, seeds are classified as:

(i) **Endospermic seeds** contain endosperm in their mature seeds. Monocots have these seeds, e.g. wheat and maize.

(ii) **Non-endospermic seeds** do not contain endosperm in their mature seeds (because endosperm has been used during seed development). Dicots have such kind of seeds, e.g. pea and gram.

Procedure

1. Take about 25-30 seeds of kidney bean.
2. Soak these seeds in water for overnight and then place them on a moist cotton cloth for 3-4 days for germination.
3. After 3-4 days, select a few well germinated seeds and place them in a petri dish.
4. Swiftly select one seed and remove the seed coat using a forcep and a needle.
5. Separate, very gently, the two parts of the seeds.
6. Study the different parts of seeds, using a hand lens. In case of dissecting microscope, take the embryo out, place it on a slide with few drops of water and study its structure.
7. Record your observations and make well labelled diagrams.

Observations

The germinating seeds when split open, showed following features:

1. A micropyle is present at the grooved sides of the seeds. It is a pore, through which water enters the seed coat, thus starting the process of germination.
2. Gently teased apart seeds will have an intact, small embryo, with a radicle and a plumule emerging from it.

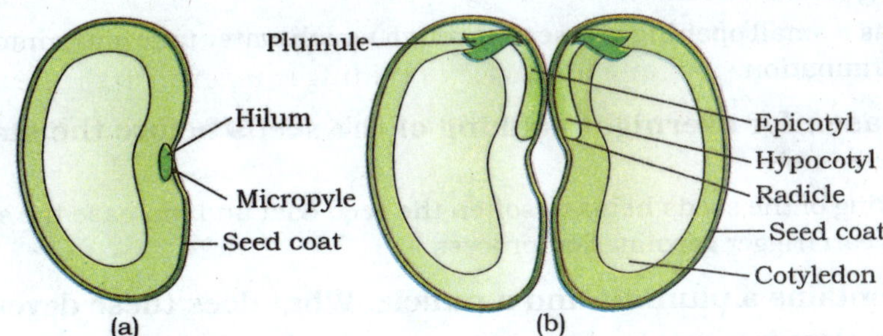

Fig. 2 Bean seed (a) Lateral view of whole seed (b) A mature embryo with its parts

3. The part present between the plumule and the radicle part of the embryo, i.e. the middle portion of the seed is called as embryonic axis or tigellum.
4. The embryonal axis consists of plumule above and radicle below.
5. The portion between plumule and the attachment point of cotyledons is known as epicotyl and the point between the radicle and the attachment point of cotyledons is called as hypocotyl. Thus, the embryonic axis bears both epicotyl and hypocotyl.
6. The cotyledons are broad, fleshy leaf-like structure of the seeds attached with embryonal axis, two in numbers. These are said to be the source of the reserve food material, necessary for the germination of seeds.

Result

Two cotyledons were observed, hence the kidney bean is a dicot seed.

1. *Choose healthy seeds for the experiment.*
2. *Before placing the seeds for germination, ensure appropriate availability of necessary conditions/requirements .*
3. *Cloth used should be clean and moist.*
4. *Use only properly germinated seeds.*
5. *While opening the seeds, be gentle otherwise the embryo can break.*

Suggested Experiment

Study and observe the seeds from a monocot plant like wheat, maize, rice, etc., and observe its different parts.

Viva-Voce

Q. 1 Clarify the meaning of a non-endospermic seed.

Ans. A non-endospermic seed is a type of seed where the endosperm is either absent or used up during the seed's development.

Q. 2 Name the opening present in a seed through which seed absorbs water at the time of seed germination.

Ans. The micropyle is a small opening of a seed through which water take entry into the seed at the time of seed germination.

Q. 3 Suggest a reason for overnight soaking of the seeds before the start of the experiment.

Ans. Overnight soaking of the seeds helps to soften the seed coat and increase the seed's moisture content, which can trigger germination process.

Q. 4 An embryo contains a plumule and a radicle. What does these develop into?

Ans. The plumule develops into the shoots and new roots develops from the radicle, initiating the formation of a new plant.

Q. 5 Describe tigellum.

Ans. Tigellum, also known as embryonal axis, is the central axis of the embryo that holds the cotyledons.

Q. 6 What are different parts of tigellum?

Ans. The tigellum consists of the plumule, epicotyl hypocotyl and radicle, forming the embryo axis between the shoot and root ends of the embryo.

Q. 7 How many layers are generally present in a seed coat?

Ans. Generally two layers are present in a seed coat, i.e. the outer one is testa and the inner one is tegmen.

Q. 8 Seed is a miniature plant. Comment.

Ans. Seed is a mature ovule, a unit containing an embryo in which the primordia of future structure are already established and is embedded with nutrients, all within a protective seed coat.

Q. 9 In a germinating seed, the radicle emerges before the plumule, why?

Ans. The radicle emerges before the plumule because it needs to penetrate into the soil to facilitate water and nutrient absorption for the growing embryo as radicle gives rise to the formation of root system.

Q.10 A seed is covered by a hard coat on its outer surface, what purpose is served by this seed coat?

Ans. (i) Protection of embryo present inside the seed .

(ii) Dehydration of embryo is prevented by the seed coat.

Q.11 Give examples of two common seeds and their uses.

Ans. Mustard seeds are used for making oil.

Cotton seeds are used as cattle feed and for production of fertilisers.

Q.12 Do you consider seed dead or alive? Explain.

Ans. A seed is considered alive as it has the potential to germinate and grow into a new plant under suitable conditions.

Q.13 Name few non-endospermic seeds.

Ans. Non-endospermic seeds are gram, rajma, pea, etc.

Q.14 What happens to the embryo in a gram seed when it is split open to make chana dal, and what part of the seed remains visible?

Ans. When a gram seed is split open to make chana dal, the embryo is removed along the seed coat and only the cotyledons remain visible.

Practical Based MCQs

Q. 1 Seed is

(a) an ovary
(b) a nutrient plant
(c) a triploid endosperm
(d) fertilised ovule

Q. 2 You are asked by your teachers to study the different parts of an embryo of a gram seed. Given below are the steps to be followed for the experiment.

I. Soak the gram seeds in plain water and keep them overnight.
II. Cut open a soaked seed and observe its different parts.
III. Take some dry gram seeds in a petridish.
IV. Drain the excess water.
V. Cover the soaked seeds with a wet cotton cloth and leave them for 3-4 days.

The correct sequence of these steps is

(a) III, I, V, IV and II
(b) III, I, II, IV and V
(c) III, IV, V, I and II
(d) III, I, IV, V and II

Q. 3 In the given figure which part of the dicot seed will develop into the shoot?

(a) A –Plumule
(b) D –Plumule
(c) C –Radicle
(d) B –Radicle

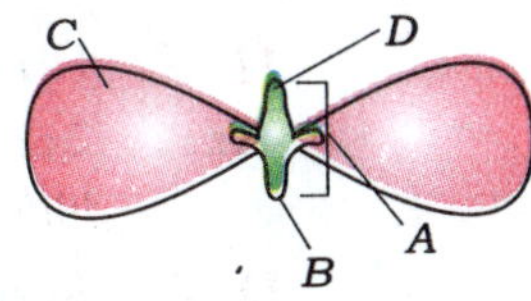

Q. 4 **The leafy part of an embryo is 'A' and 'B' is the embryonal axis holding A together. What are 'A' and 'B'.**

(a) A– Plumule, B – hypocotyl (b) A – Cotyledons, B – tigellum
(c) A – Radicle, B – tigellum (d) A – Epicotyl, B – hypocotyl

Q. 5 **The structures emerging out of the germinating seed can be identified as**

(a) epicotyl and cotyledons (b) tigellum and hypocotyl
(c) epicotyl and hypocotyl (d) None of the above

Q. 6 **Identify the opening present in a seed through which seed absorbs water at the time of seed germination.**

(a) Epicotyl (b) Micropyle (c) Hilum (d) Tigellum

Q. 7 **The part of a seed in which food material for germinating seed is stored.**

(a) Radicle (b) Plumule (c) Cotyledons (d) Embryo

Q. 8 **The scar marked on the seed present near the micropyle is known as**

(a) hilum (b) tigellum (c) micropyle (d) None of these

Q. 9 **Which of the following is not the exclusive function of the seed coat?**

(a) Absorption of water from surroundings
(b) Protection of embryo from physical damage
(c) Protection from microbial infections
(d) Protection of embryo from dehydration

Q.10 **After a seed is germinated, it will develop and grow into a young plant. Arrange the following to show the correct order of events taking place during germination.**

I. Root appears
II. Seed coat ruptures
III. Seedling
IV. Shoot appears

(a) I,II, III and IV (b) II, I , IV and III (c) II, IV, I and III (d) III, I, II and IV

Answers

1. (d)	**2.** (d)	**3.** (b)	**4.** (b)	**5.** (c)	**6.** (b)
7. (c)	**8.** (a)	**9.** (a)	**10.** (b)		

Experiment/Activity No.________ Date ________ Page No. ________

Teacher Signature ________________

Experiment/Activity No.________ Date ________ Page No. ________

Teacher Signature________________

Experiment/Activity No.________ Date ________ Page No. ________

Teacher Signature ________________

Experiment/Activity No.________ Date ________ Page No. ________

Teacher Signature ________

Experiment/Activity No.________ Date ________ Page No. ________

Teacher Signature ________

Experiment/Activity No.________ Date ________ Page No. ________

Teacher Signature ________________

Experiment/Activity No.________ Date ________ Page No. ________

Teacher Signature________________

Experiment/Activity No.________ Date ________ Page No. ________

Teacher Signature ________________

Experiment/Activity No.________ Date ________ Page No. ________

Teacher Signature ________________

Experiment/Activity No.________ Date ________ Page No. ________

Teacher Signature ________

Experiment/Activity No.________ Date ________ Page No. ________

Teacher Signature ________

Experiment/Activity No.________ Date ________ Page No. ________

Teacher Signature ________________

Experiment/Activity No.________ Date ________ Page No. ________

Teacher Signature ________________

Experiment/Activity No.________ Date ________ Page No. ________

Teacher Signature ________________

Experiment/Activity No.________ Date ________ Page No. ________

Teacher Signature________________

Experiment/Activity No.________ Date ________ Page No. ________

Teacher Signature________________

Experiment/Activity No.________ Date ________ Page No. ________

Teacher Signature ________

Experiment/Activity No.________ Date ________ Page No. ________

Teacher Signature ____________

Experiment/Activity No.________ Date ________ Page No. ________

Teacher Signature ________________

Experiment/Activity No.________ Date ________ Page No. ________

Teacher Signature ____________

Experiment/Activity No.________ Date ________ Page No. ________

Teacher Signature ________

Experiment/Activity No.________ Date ________ Page No. ________

Teacher Signature ________________

Experiment/Activity No.________ Date ________ Page No. ________

Teacher Signature ________

Experiment/Activity No.________ Date ________ Page No. ________

Teacher Signature ________________

Experiment/Activity No.________ Date ________ Page No. ________

Teacher Signature________________

Experiment/Activity No.________ Date ________ Page No. ________

Teacher Signature ____________

Experiment/Activity No.________ Date ________ Page No. ________

Teacher Signature________________

Experiment/Activity No.________ Date ________ Page No. ________

Teacher Signature ____________

Experiment/Activity No.________ Date ________ Page No. ________

Teacher Signature ____________

Experiment/Activity No.________ Date ________ Page No. ________

Teacher Signature ________________

Experiment/Activity No.________ Date ________ Page No. ________

Teacher Signature________________

Experiment/Activity No.________ Date ________ Page No. ________

Teacher Signature________________

Experiment/Activity No.________ Date ________ Page No. ________

Teacher Signature ________

Experiment/Activity No.________ Date ________ Page No. ________

Teacher Signature________________

Experiment/Activity No.________ Date ________ Page No. ________

Teacher Signature________________

Experiment/Activity No.________ Date ________ Page No. ________

Teacher Signature________________

Experiment/Activity No.________ Date ________ Page No. ________

Teacher Signature ________________

Experiment/Activity No.________ Date ________ Page No. ________

Teacher Signature ________________

Experiment/Activity No.________ Date ________ Page No. ________

Teacher Signature________________

Experiment/Activity No.________ Date ________ Page No. ________

Teacher Signature ________________

Experiment/Activity No.________ Date ________ Page No. ________

Teacher Signature________________

Experiment/Activity No.________ Date ________ Page No. ________

Teacher Signature________________

Experiment/Activity No.________ Date ________ Page No. ________

Teacher Signature ____________

Experiment/Activity No.________ Date ________ Page No. ________

Teacher Signature ________________

Experiment/Activity No.________ Date ________ Page No. ________

Teacher Signature ________________

Experiment/Activity No.________ Date ________ Page No. ________

Teacher Signature________________

Experiment/Activity No.________ Date ________ Page No. ________

Teacher Signature ________________

Experiment/Activity No.________ Date ________ Page No. ________

Teacher Signature ________________

Experiment/Activity No.________ Date ________ Page No. ________

Teacher Signature ________________

Experiment/Activity No.________ Date ________ Page No. ________

Teacher Signature ________________

Experiment/Activity No.________ Date ________ Page No. ________

Teacher Signature ________________

Experiment/Activity No.________ Date ________ Page No. ________

Teacher Signature ____________

Experiment/Activity No.________ Date ________ Page No. ________

Teacher Signature________________

Experiment/Activity No.________ Date ________ Page No. ________

Teacher Signature________________

Experiment/Activity No.________ Date ________ Page No. ________

Teacher Signature ________

Experiment/Activity No.________ Date ________ Page No. ________

Teacher Signature ________________

Experiment/Activity No.________ Date ________ Page No. ________

Teacher Signature ________________

Experiment/Activity No.________ Date ________ Page No. ________

Teacher Signature ________________

Experiment/Activity No.________ Date ________ Page No. ________

Teacher Signature ____________

Experiment/Activity No.________ Date ________ Page No. ________

Teacher Signature ________

Experiment/Activity No.________ Date ________ Page No. ________

Teacher Signature ________

Experiment/Activity No.________ Date ________ Page No. ________

Teacher Signature________________

Experiment/Activity No.________ Date ________ Page No. ________

Teacher Signature ________

Experiment/Activity No.________ Date ________ Page No. ________

Teacher Signature________________